NEW TECHNOLOGIES AND LANGUAGE LEARNING

CW00549513

LI LI

 macmillan education palgrave

First published 2017 by
PALGRAVE

Palgrave in the UK is an imprint of Macmillan Publishers Limited,
registered in England, company number 785998, of 4 Crinan Street,
London, N1 9XW.

Palgrave® and Macmillan® are registered trademarks in the United States,
the United Kingdom, Europe and other countries.

ISBN 978–1–137–51767–8 paperback

A catalogue record for this book is available from the British Library.

A catalog record for this book is available from the Library of Congress.

Contents

List of tables

List of figures

Abbreviations

ACMC: asynchronous CMC
AWE: automated writing evaluation
CAA: computer-aided assessment
CAI: computer-aided instruction
CALL: computer-assisted language learning
CELL: computer-enhanced language learning
CMC: computer-mediated communication
COBUILD: Collins Birmingham University International Language
            Database
DMs: discourse markers
DoE: Department of Education
EAP: English for academic purposes
EBP: English for business purposes
EOP: English for occupational purposes
ES/FL: English as a second/foreign language
ESP: English for specific purposes
IC: interactional competence
ICT: information and communications technologies
IELTS: International English Language Testing System
IGCs   intelligent grammar checkers
IM: instant messaging
ITSs: intelligent tutoring systems
LAD: Language Acquisition Device
L1:   first language
L2:   second language
MALL: mobile-assisted language learning
MILT: military language tutor
m-learning: mobile learning
MUVE: multi-user virtual environment
NBLT: network-based language teaching
OCL: online collaborative learning
PC: personal computer
PEG: project essay grade
SCMC: synchronous CMC

SFL:	systematic functional linguistics
SL:	second life
SLA:	second language acquisition
StCMC:	synchronous text-based computer-mediated communication
SVCMC:	synchronous voice/video-based computer-mediated communication
TELL:	technology-enhanced language learning
TPACK:	(teachers' integrated) technological, pedagogical and content knowledge
UAE:	United Arab Emirates
WELL:	web-enhanced language learning
ZPD:	zone of proximal development

Introduction

This research-led textbook takes new technologies (as opposed to traditional technologies) in language education as its primary focus. While there has been a plethora of research articles and paper collections on language and technologies across a range of contexts, and useful reference books on the topic, there have been considerably fewer research-led textbooks for in-service and pre-service teachers who would like to develop expertise in the area of new technologies in language education. Given the theoretical and conceptual importance of technology development in language learning, this book intends to map out the research-based application of technologies in language education, with a particular focus on linking theories to practice.

There are three major objectives: (1) to present a clear overview of the work which has been done in technologies in language education, (2) to provide examples of how technologies can be used in assisting language education by exploring how to link theoretical underpinnings of learning to technology application in classroom teaching, and (3) to address important but challenging issues faced by teachers around the world in integrating technology in teaching. The book is divided into three parts, which coincide with the following aims.

Part A Overview. This covers the existing body of research evidence and provides readers with a survey of the literature. The aim is to review and discuss seminal publications and cutting-edge research in the history, theories and development of technologies in language education. This overview aims to provide teachers with background knowledge of why technology is beneficial for language learning and of the role of technology in enhancing linguistic and affective aspects of learning.

Part B Technology, Language Skills and Knowledge, and ESP. In this part, the discussion is led more by data, presenting evidence and examples of particular technologies and their role in enhancing language learning. The particular topics under investigation consider the following questions:

- Why and how does technology enhance interactional competence?

- Why and how does technology enhance collaborative writing and online literacy?

- Why and how does technology enhance lexicogrammatical acquisition?

- Why and how does technology enhance ESP?

Part C Feedback, Materials and Teachers. In the third part of the book, the discussion looks at the more challenging issues which emerge from teaching for example, alternative assessment strategies when technologies are involved in learning, e-learning material evaluation and design. In addition, this part examines the role of the teacher in the process of integrating technology into teaching, with a focus on the issues that motivate or hinder teachers' using technology and how teachers approach these issues in practice.

In order to illustrate how technology can benefit language learning in various aspects, examples of technology application are included in the text. To help the readers bridge the gap between theory and practice, annotated readings are recommended at the end of each chapter. Some chapters also include completed student projects to shed some light on possible research ideas for postgraduate students and teachers who would like to conduct research in technology-enhanced language learning. There are also case studies, which report technology use in assisting language learning, and tasks, which can guide the reader to engage in critical reflection. These features are designed to engage readers and help them gain a closer understanding of the field and hands-on experience.

The chapters synthesise previous technology use (including CALL) theory and research, and they describe practical applications to both second and foreign language classrooms, including detailed examples of these applications and procedures for evaluating them. The implementation of technology in different learning environments (e.g. secondary classrooms, higher education institutions and online forums) are addressed, with attention to creating collaborative technology-based projects and to applying individual technologies in traditional classrooms. Although many chapters locate their descriptions of technology activities and projects within the English as a second/foreign language (ESL/EFL) setting, the principles and activities described are equally useful for other language settings. By integrating theoretical issues, research finding and practical guidelines on different aspects of technology use in language education, this book offers teachers multiple levels of resources for their own professional development, for the needs-based creation of specific technology-supported activities, for curriculum design and for implementation of institutional and inter-institutional projects.

The book will be appealing to researchers interested in using technologies in language education and teacher development, as well as to early researchers and students in postgraduate programmes.

Part A
Overview

1 An overview of new technologies in language education

Aims: This chapter reviews the development of technologies in language education by considering the connection between different learning theories and technology application in language classrooms. This review draws upon the literature and examples of technology use in classrooms to help the reader to make sense of theory and practice. The chapter has the three themes, as follows:

1. Overview of global technology policy in education

2. Learning theories

3. Technology use in language learning.

What does using technology in language learning mean?

Technology in language learning has been in constant evolution since its genesis in the 1950s, in part due to attempts to keep up with the ongoing developments in computer technology. The development of technology in language education is also the result of the development of learning theories and pedagogical considerations. Many terms and expressions have emerged, and different theoretical perspectives require different approaches to understand and define the concept.

Task 1.1: What does technology use in language learning mean?

Have you ever experienced using technology in language teaching or learning? When you talk about using technology in language learning, what do you mean? Could you explain your understanding to your colleagues?

The most widely used variant is perhaps CALL (computer-assisted language learning). The use of CALL was agreed at the 1983 TESOL (Teachers of English to speakers of other languages) convention in Toronto, Ontario, by people who attended the meeting where CALL issues were discussed. This term has been widely used to refer to the areas of technology and both second language teaching and learning despite frequent suggestions to revise the term (Chapelle, 2001, p. 3). Even though the term has been agreed and widely adopted, different scholars define the term differently. Levy (1997) defines CALL as 'the search for and study of applications of the computer in language teaching and learning' (Levy, 1997, p. 1). Beatty (2003) acknowledges the breadth of what may go on in CALL and proposes that a definition of CALL that accommodates its changing nature is the following: any process in which a learner uses a computer and, as a result, improves his or her language (Beatty, 2003, p. 7). Furthermore, he suggests that 'CALL has come to encompass issues of materials design, technologies, pedagogical theories and modes of instruction. Materials for CALL can include those which are purpose-made for language learning and those which adapt existing computer-based materials, video and other materials' (Beatty, 2003, pp. 7–8). So, broadly speaking, CALL is the study of computer applications or computer technologies in second or foreign language teaching and learning (Levy, 1997; Chapelle, 2001; Fotos and Brown, 2004; Egbert, 2005; Levy and Stockwell, 2006).

There are, of course, many other similar terms associated with technology use in language learning: for example, TELL (technology-enhanced language learning), CELL (computer-enhanced language learning), NBLT (network-based language teaching), WELL (web-enhanced language learning) and CMC (computer-mediated communication). In the literature, we can also see the use of ICT (information and communications technologies), e-learning and blended learning. In recent years, we have seen the popularity of mobile learning (m-learning), which brings 'mobility' into learning (see Pegrum, 2014). But do they really mean different things? Or are these just different terms referring to the same concept? In this chapter, I will consider some important aspects in understanding the meaning and scope of using technology in language learning. To do so, I will first outline the global growth of technology in education and then move on to technology use in language education, with a particular attention to English as a second/foreign language. Next, I will discuss learning theories, technology and pedagogy. Finally, I will provide a discussion on the issue of technology development in language learning.

Technology in education: the global picture

Perhaps it is fair to say that technology has changed our lives in every way, such as shopping, communicating, entertaining, teaching and learning, and even in the way we think. Most, if not all, teachers, educators and policymakers would support the use of technologies in enhancing learning. Computer technologies have for some time now played a significant role in improving education and reforming curricula across countries all over the world (Pelgrum, 2001; Kozma and Anderson, 2002). Governments, education authorities and schools have all made major investments into providing schools with computer equipment (Pelgrum, 2001; Macaro, Handley and Walter, 2012).

Globally, technology integration into education is an important feature of the education landscape. The U.S. Department of Education (DoE) has launched National Education Technology Plan 2010 to transform American education through 'learning powered by technology'. The Plan makes a specific statement to fully integrate technology in teaching, assessment, infrastructure and productivity. Similarly, the Australian government has poured money into technology infrastructure in education. It is estimated that the entire education sector had spent AUS$2.7 billion (£1.59 billion) on computer equipment in 2013, with nearly half going on actual hardware. Similar initiatives were observed in Europe. For example, in Spain, 'Escuela 2.0' (Pérez Sanz, 2011) aimed to equip over 14,000 classrooms in primary and secondary schools with interactive whiteboards (IWBs), wireless networks and PCs (personal computers) for both students and teachers. A similar plan was launched in Italy in 2009. In the Asian context, the Ministry of Education of Singapore developed the third Masterplan for ICT in Education (2009–2014) to enrich and transform the learning environments of students and equip them with the critical competencies and dispositions to succeed in a knowledge economy. In contrast, the Chinese government developed long-term goals to informationalise Chinese education by 2010 and made a considerable financial investment to establish a network for language teaching and language research at both provincial and institutional levels. In the Middle East, there is strong evidence that mobile devices play an important role in the development of education quality. For example, the Higher Colleges of Technology (HCT) in the UAE (United Arab Emirates) adopted cutting-edge technology at the earliest opportunity, such as the laptop initiative from 2003 to 2005 (all students were given laptops, and all campuses were fitted with Wi-Fi) and the iPad initiative (2012–2014), a world-first in equipping all new students with iPads (personal communication). We can see a huge investment has been made globally to embrace technology in education to create a twenty-first-century learning environment and style.

Apart from the policy and investment in technology use in education, it actually makes sense to use technology in teaching and learning, according to brain research experts (Tileston, 2000). For example, computers can promote visual, verbal and kinaesthetic learning and address different cognitive and psychological processes in learning by using multimodal materials.

Technology use in language education

Technology has been integrated into second language teaching and learning since the 1960s as a mechanical tutor to train repetitive language drills, the so-called drill-and-practice method. It is only since 2000 that computer technology has been largely used in reading, writing, literacy and cultural awareness (Chapelle, 2003). With the development of multimedia computing and the Internet, technology is becoming a vital feature of second language classrooms and an important issue confronting second/foreign language teachers and researchers. For example, Chapelle (2003), as an applied linguist, asserts that 'technology-based language teaching and research is not a departure from applied linguistics. It is a continuation – the 21st century version of what applied linguists do' (p. 31).

According to the British Council's research report published in 2014, there are approximately 750 million EFL (English as a foreign language) speakers and 375 million ESL (English as a second language) speakers. The British Council predicts that the number of people actively learning English around the world is set to exceed 1.9 billion by 2020. Of course there is no way to make an accurate estimate of potential English learners, but two messages to take away from these figures are that there are millions of English learners and that the development of technology is embracing these learners. There are over 3 billion Internet users, accounting for 40.4 per cent of the world's population. Approximately eight new Internet users add themselves to this growing percentage per second. The advantage of the Internet is that it allows language to come to the learner, rather than a learner having to go to a special place to learn the language. In institutional contexts, such as higher education sectors, secondary schools and primary schools, teachers face a generation which has grown up in an environment in which they are constantly exposed to computer-based technology; therefore, their methods of learning are different from those of previous generations. In a survey of first-year undergraduate students, Sandars and Morrison (2007) found that a large majority started university with experience of using online systems such as blogs and wikis; furthermore, their attitudes to the possible use of such tools in learning were positive. Clearly, determining how to teach the generation which has already integrated technology to their daily life is a challenge to the traditional teaching and learning philosophy. All these points suggest that language learning/teaching is embarking on a new trend, and it has become an urgent issue for teachers, applied linguists and learning theorists to think how new technologies should be integrated and utilised in language learning.

> **Task 1.2:** What does using technology in language learning/teaching mean?
> Now, think about what software, apps or technological tools you or people around you have used to learn English (or any language). Is it a good example for you? Why?

As one can imagine, there is a long list of various technological tools or apps to use in learning or teaching a language. The list might include websites, videos (e.g. YouTube), PowerPoint, images and sound files (e.g. podcasts), mobile phones, virtual learning environments and social networking sites. The list can be very long, but if we look at the research evidence, we can make an assumption that teachers are very creative, and various technological tools have been used in enhancing linguistic and communicative skills, but no doubt some tools are more popular than others. Various forms of technology have been reported in language classrooms, including both stand-alone computer tools and

....

The term 'Web 2.0' was officially coined in 2004 by Dale Dougherty, a vice-president of O'Reilly Media Inc. Web 2.0 refers to a group of technologies – such as blogs, wikis, podcasts, RSS feeds, etc. – which facilitate a more socially connected Internet where everyone is able to add to and edit the information space.

....

Web 2.0 technologies (see Liu, Moore, Graham and Lee 2002 for a pre-2000 review; see Macaro, Handley and Walter 2012 for a post-2000 review). Then in classrooms, how do teachers use technologies to facilitate teaching?

In the US, Meskill et al. (2006) surveyed 847 K-12 ESOL (English speakers of other languages) teachers regarding their uses of technology and found that the most frequently used software is word processing – a finding that resonates with the results of two national surveys, one by Becker (2000) and another by Doherty and Orlofsky (2001). Cuban (2001) also reported that word processing is the most frequently used technology for teachers in American classrooms. In Canada, Wozney et al. (2006) surveyed K-12 teachers' use of technology and concluded that teachers mainly used computer technologies for 'informative' (e.g. World Wide Web) and 'expressive' (e.g. word processing) purposes. In China, Li's (2008) survey of English teachers suggests that PowerPoint is regarded as the most popular and appropriate form of technology used in Chinese English language classrooms. Macaro et al. (2012) provide an in-depth review of 47 post-2000 studies investigating the efficacy of technology in the teaching of L2 (second language) English, asking what technology has been used and why. They pointed out that the most frequently studied technologies were multimedia (22 per cent), CMC technologies (22 per cent) and the Internet (15 per cent). Among CMC, email is the most popular. It is notable that no research has been done on chat or discussion forums before 2000, nor studies of Web 2.0 technologies before 2005. Technology has mostly been used to enhance every aspect of language learning, including (for example) lexical acquisition, speaking skills, intercultural awareness and so on. Furthermore, these studies revealed that most research studies focused mainly on vocabulary (24 per cent), writing (24 per cent) and reading (22 per cent) and, to a lesser extent, speaking (11 per cent), listening (10 per cent), grammar (7 per cent) and pronunciation (3 per cent). This review focused on only teaching English as a foreign or second language in primary or secondary levels; technology use in higher education might be different.

What is technology use in language learning then? In analysing technology use in language learning, the first thing to understand is its meaning and scope. The best way is to consider learning theories associated with technology use and the development of technology use in language learning, which are discussed in more depth below.

Learning theories

What are learning theories? A theory of learning aims to help people to understand how learning happens and informs practice. Major learning theories, such as behaviourist learning theory, cognitivist learning theory and constructivist learning theory, were all developed in the late nineteenth and twentieth centuries, and they have had strong influences on the nature of language, language learning pedagogy, technology use and the role of the teacher and learners. I will briefly discuss these three theories first and then move on to present online collaborative learning theory, which is frequently referred to when discussing computer-supported collaborative learning (CSCL).

Behaviourist learning theory

The behaviourist learning theory was a major breakthrough in the late nineteenth century. The nature of learning, what influences and supports learning and what is believed to be learning was developed mainly through experiments with animals, such as the well-known experiment by Pavlov on his dog. Pavlov found that if he rings the 'bell' (conditioned stimulus) with food (unconditional stimulus) to get the attention of his dog, his dog would have a conditioned response to the conditioned stimulus (bell) after a period of time. This experiment showed that learning associates an unconditioned stimulus that already brings about a particular response (i.e. a reflex) with a new (conditioned) stimulus such that the new stimulus brings about the same response.

Behaviourist learning theory views knowledge as something fixed and finite, and ultimately as truth. So from a behaviourist theoretical perspective, learning 'was reduced and simplified to simple conditioning: the stimulus and the response' (Harasim, 2012, p. 31). As the name suggests, the behaviourist learning theory focuses on an observable behaviour and pays little attention to what happens in the mind. Learning is therefore observable and measurable. The core of behaviourist learning theory is to change or elicit certain behaviours. In examining learning, in order to see whether X has an impact on Y, controlled methods, random assignments and the manipulation of variables are used to test hypotheses. As Harasim (2012) explains,

> In behaviorist theory, what is in the mind is not accessible for study, and hence irrelevant and should not be considered in research. The mind is viewed as a black box that is largely irrelevant, and, therefore, by extension educational practice based on behaviorist terms would not take the mind into account. The emphasis is on environmental stimulus and observed response. (p. 32)

Cognitivist learning theory

The cognitivist learning theory emerged as an extension of and a reaction to behaviourist theory, in particular to the 'stimulus-and-response' paradigm of behaviourism. The main argument behind the cognitivist learning theory is that it believes the direct link between stimulus and responses is insufficient to explain learning because the responses are also influenced by factors such as cognitive ability, motivation, age, aptitude and so on. Cognitivist theory does not reject the 'stimulus-and-response' theory completely, but rather, it shifts the focus to the cognitive (internal mental) process in learning to understand and improve the effectiveness of learning. Cognitivist theory concerns what goes on *between* stimulus and response. In the context of language learning, it concerns what happens between input and output in a learner's mind. In other words, a cognitive perspective is interested in how information is processed. So under the view of cognitivist theory, a learner is a processor of information. Cognitive information-processing theory is strongly associated with cognitivist learning theory, and its experimental design is closely linked to this view in understanding the impact of variables on learning.

Constructivist learning theory

As the name suggests, constructivist learning theory concerns learning as 'an active process of constructing rather than acquiring knowledge' (Duffy and Cunningham, 1996, p. 177). According to this theory, what individuals experience and their reflection on their experiences help them to construct knowledge of and an understanding of the world. Piaget and Vygotsky are the two most influential theorists in this tradition despite the differences they hold in understanding constructivism.

Piaget's theory takes the cognitive view of development and proposes two important elements in learning: age and stage. For Piaget, learning follows development: learning takes place differently at different stages of biological development. The depth and complexity of knowledge develops as humans move through the age-based stages. Therefore, humans cannot be 'given' information, and immediately understand and use such information. Instead, humans must 'construct' their own knowledge through experience. From a cognitive constructivism perspective, learning is an active process which needs to be authentic, meaningful and real to the learners.

Social constructivism maintains that human development is socially situated and that knowledge is constructed through interaction with others. Vygotsky (1978) is the major theorist among the social constructivists. One of the key messages we can infer from Vygotsky's seminal work is the important role of social interaction in learning and development. From Vygotsky's perspective, learning happens through the social encounters in which one uses the social and cultural artefacts in mediating their thinking. Sociocultural theory incorporates mediation as a core construct in its theorising about language learning. From the perspective of sociocultural theory, human forms of mental activity arise in the interactions we enter into with other members of our culture and with the specific experiences we have with the artefacts produced by our ancestors and by our contemporaries (Lantolf, 2000, p. 79). For Vygotsky, learning takes place first at the social level and then the internal level.

Vygotsky argued that cognitive development was a social, communicative process and described the social construction of knowledge within a 'zone of proximal development' (ZPD). **ZPD** is where learning and development come together and is 'the distance between the actual developmental level as determined by independent problem solving and the level of potential development as determined through problem solving under adult guidance or in collaboration with more capable peers' (Vygotsky, 1978, p. 86). According to Aljaafreh and Lantolf (1994), ZPD is 'the framework, par excellence, which brings all of the pieces of the learning setting together – the teacher, the learner,

ZPD (zone of proximal development) is the space where learning takes place with 'graduated', 'contingent' and 'dialogic' assistance/guidance. It is the distance between what learners know and what they will know with help.

Scaffolding is supportive behaviour from more able/knowledgeable to the less able/knowledgeable individuals.

their social and cultural history, their goals and motives, as well as the resources available to them, including those that are dialogically constructed together' (p. 468).

In short, learning takes place within the learners' ZPD, with the 'graduated', 'contingent', and 'dialogic' assistance/guidance (Aljaafreh and Lantolf, 1994, p. 495), which is usually offered by the more knowledgeable/able to the less knowledgeable/able individual. Such guidance has been metaphorically named **'scaffolding'** (Weissberg, 2006), although the concept of scaffolding was not originally discussed in Vygotsky's work.

Originally, Vygotsky's framework focused on child psychological development, expert–novice interactions and the co-construction of knowledge. However, in recent decades it has been argued that the idea and its two key constructs – ZPD and scaffolding – can also be extended to educational settings and to both asymmetrical (expert–novice) and symmetrical (equal ability) situations (Storch, 2002). One of its implications, for example, is for second language learning scenarios in which L2 learners need to be scaffolded in their ZPD in order to develop L2 competence (Lantolf, 2000, 2006). Ohta (1995) adapted the concept of the ZPD to L2 as 'the difference between the L2 learner's developmental level as determined by independent language use, and the higher level of potential development as determined by how language is used in collaboration with a more capable interlocutor' (p. 96). Accordingly, scaffolding in the L2 refers to those supportive behaviours employed by the more advanced partner in collaboration with the less competent learner that aims to foster an L2 learner's progress to a higher level of language proficiency. However, a number of researchers (e.g. de Guerrero and Villamil, 1994, 2000; Storch, 2002, 2005; Yong, 2010) have stressed not only that is scaffolding a unidirectional support from an expert to novice but also that it can occur between novices where both learners are acting as expert and supporting each other mutually and concurrently through dialogic interaction.

Online collaborative learning theory

In more recent times, a new school of thought on learning theories has been emerging. For example, Harasim (2012) argues that we need a new learning theory, one that focuses on collaborative learning, knowledge building and Internet use as means to reshape formal, nonformal and informal education for the Knowledge Age, and she proposed online collaborative learning (OCL). One main drive for OCL theory is that learners today are part of a collaboration generation because they spend time 'searching, reading, scrutinizing, authenticating, collaborating and organizing' (Tapscott and Williams,

2006, p. 47), and therefore a new mindset is needed. The Knowledge Age mindset seeks better or best solutions to problems, and knowledge is not static, fixed or universally true; rather it is dynamic, and context-specific. Harasim (2012) defines OCL theory as 'a model of learning in which students are encouraged and supported to work together to create knowledge: to invent, to explore ways to innovate and, by so doing, to seek the conceptual knowledge needed to solve problems rather than recite what they think is the right answer' (p. 90). She further explains that in the OCL theory, 'the teacher plays a key role not as a fellow-learner, but as the link to the knowledge community, or state of the art in that discipline. Learning is defined as conceptual change and is key to building knowledge' (ibid). Like online distance learning and online courseware, OCL can be asynchronous (not occurring at the same time), place-independent, text-based and based on Internet-mediated discourse. However, the unique characteristic of OCL is that the focus is placed on online discourse – the way learning happens, group learning and the development of group cognition – and it is led by instructor.

Task 1.3: Can you explain the following by using a learning theory?

When I was small, I lived in the countryside with my grandparents. They kept chickens in order to have eggs. My grandma used to chop some cabbage leaves for chickens in the afternoon, and I noticed that every time my grandma started to chop, the chickens would gather around her, waiting. I thought it was quite funny, so one day I decided to trick the chickens. I made some chopping noises, and all the chickens gathered around me. Of course, this time, they didn't get cabbage leaves. I was very pleased with my little experiment, and of course the chickens were very disappointed (and perhaps puzzled!). Can you explain this using a learning theory? Does cognitive theory account for this? Why or why not?

Technology and pedagogy

Technology embraces different pedagogical principles and practices, such as instruction and construction. The former is the approach followed by traditional classroom teaching, while the latter refers to an approach that facilitates full exploitation of the potential of technology but demands rethinking and a redefinition of the traditional approach as well as of the teacher–student relationship.

MacGilchrist et al. (1997), in their book *The Intelligent School*, discuss a 'traditional' model of learning, which views learning as 'the reception of knowledge, the learner as passive and the appropriate learning style as formal' (the behaviourist tradition) and a 'progressive' model, which sees learning as 'discovery, the learner as active and the learning style as informal (the cognitive, humanist and social interactionist traditions)' (p. 20). A teacher's traditional role is to present ready-made information and organise learning experiences. Learning with technology, however, is different in the sense that technology assume the roles of both presenter and organiser. Learning is seen to occur by making sense of knowledge that one is exposed to and with which one interacts by way of mental processes and/or interaction with other people. Rooted in general learning theories, such as behaviourism and constructivism, technology integration developed within education from the era of 'technology as a tutor' to 'technology as a tool' (Levy, 1997).

The following sections will discuss learning theories which influence technology use in second language learning practice and the development of technology in language education.

Technology development in language learning

There are a number of attempts to describe the development of CALL (e.g. Sanders, 1995; Warschauer and Healey, 1998; Delcloque, 2000; Levy, 2000; Warschauer, 2000a; Chapelle, 2001; Bax, 2003b). However, according to a recent historiography, Bax (2003b) claims that Warschauer and Healey's (1998) work is 'the only substantive, systematic attempt to analyse and understand the history of CALL in anything more than 'factual' terms' (p. 14). Basically, there are three main theoretical movements in the history of computer-assisted language teaching: behaviourism/structural perspective (Structural CALL: 1970s–1980s), cognitive/constructivist perspective (Communicative CALL: 1980s–1990s) and socio-cognitive perspective (Integrative CALL: late twentieth century or early twenty-first century) (Warschauer, 2004). Now in the Web 2.0 era, we are talking about more than these three CALL phases, and there are different voices suggesting that we need to move from CALL to TELL (e.g. Walker and White, 2013) or MALL (mobile-assisted language learning). In my view, this movement is making sense because we are relying less on computers now and more on various technologies, such as mobile phones, game consoles and other hand-held devices. Again, TELL perhaps is more appropriate in this context because we are at the stage of embracing all types of technological tools and apps, ranging from stand-alone computers to mobile devices and online environments. More importantly, technology is viewed as an integrated part of the learning process that enhances learners' experiences, rather than as an add-on. Table 1.1 summarises four views of technology in language education, which the following sections discuss briefly in turn.

	1970s–1980s: Structural CALL	1980s–1990s: Communicative CALL	1990s–2000s: Integrative CALL	Twenty-first century: Collaborative technology/TELL
Stage	1970s–1980s: Structural CALL	1980s–1990s: Communicative CALL	1990s–2000s: Integrative CALL	Twenty-first century: Collaborative technology/TELL
Technology	Mainframe	PCs	Multimedia and Internet	Web 2.0, virtual worlds, tablets, mobile devices and game consoles
English teaching paradigm	Grammar-translation and audiolingual method	Communicative language teaching	Content-based, ESP/EAP	Communication and interaction (English as a medium)
View of language	Structural (a formal structural system)	Cognitive (a mentally constructed system)	Socio-cognitive (developed in social interaction)	Sociocultural (interactional competence and intercultural competence)
Principal use of computers	Drill and practice	Communicative exercises	Authentic discourse	Communication and knowledge co-construction
Principal objective	Accuracy	Accuracy and fluency	Accuracy, fluency and agency	Accuracy, fluency, agency and autonomy within community
Principal role of computers	To provide drill, practice, tutorial explanation and corrective feedback	To provide language input and analytic and inferential tasks	To provide alternative contexts for social interaction; to facilitate access to existing discourse communities and the creation of new ones	To provide a space/environment for people to engage in communication and construct new knowledge

TABLE 1.1   FOUR STAGES OF TECHNOLOGY-ENHANCED LANGUAGE LEARNING

Structural (behaviouristic) CALL

Warschauer and Healey (1998) suggest that behaviouristic CALL was 'conceived in the 1950s and implemented in the 1960s and 1970s' (p. 57). According to Delcloque (2000), behaviouristic CALL dated back to the 1960s, when the Audiolingual Method was appealing. But Warschauer (2004) has presented a different time scale of behaviouristic CALL: from the 1970s to 1980s.

The underpinning theories of behaviourist CALL are based on a structural view of language and behaviourism learning theory. Theorists who hold a structural view of language, such as Charles Fries (1945) and Robert Lado (1957), consider language as a system with comparative stable structures and intrinsic regulations, and they focus on analysing the structure and drills of a certain language. Influenced by the behaviourists, the structural perspective regards language learning as a process of 'stimulus – reflection – consolidation' or well-known 'drill-and-practice' (or drill and kill) in which learners would learn the language and master the language rules by constant imitation and mechanical drills to form their own habits of using language. The basic premise behind this is that the more drill practice the learners encounter, the more and faster the learners can acquire the language. This earliest application of computer in learning was also termed CAI (computer-assisted instruction).

Technological applications in the behaviourist tradition tend to follow an instructional pattern (Kern and Warschauer, 2000). Learning is broken down into a sequential series of small steps, each covering a piece of the subject domain or a particular skill. The computer programme models the role of the tutor, offering some input or paradigm that the learner can 'drill and practice' followed by the provision of feedback. Essentially, the control of learning is in the hands of the programme designer and not the learner (although occasionally individualised customisations were implemented). This type of CALL was used as an add-on to the main language teaching. Warschauer (1996a) identifies the following rationales behind these programmes, which he considers to have value:

- Repeated exposure to the same material is beneficial or even essential to learning.

- A computer is ideal for carrying out repeated drills, since the machine does not get bored with presenting the same material and since it can provide non-judgemental feedback.

- A computer can present such material on an individualised basis, allowing students to proceed at their own pace and freeing up class time for other activities. (p. 4)

Bax (2003b) suggests that behaviouristic CALL is 'the most plausible' (p. 16) and that the 'drill and kill' is to some extent what learners need most (Nunan, 1987; Davies, 1989) because computers 'are excellent judges of what is demanded of them when they sit their exams' (Jung, 2005, p. 14). Crook (1994) notes that teachers might find this mode appealing because they consider such experiences to be important, and 'furnishing the necessary opportunities is not the easiest or most rewarding part of their responsibility' (p. 14). Although behaviourism is discredited in overall education because it does not explain all kinds of learning and ignores the activities of the brain, it still has a place in language learning, such as for the acquisition of vocabulary and grammatical morphemes (Lightbown and Spada, 2006). Research shows that at the beginning level, reproduction rather than construction of knowledge is necessary, as grammar-based activities allow learners to build or reinforce fundamental knowledge (e.g. Garrett, 1987). Hubbard and Siskin (2004) argue that behaviourist CALL (or computer as tutor) is still 'eminently justifiable' and have suggested some promising areas in which tutorial CALL can help with learning (p. 452). These explain why similar behaviouristic technological tools are still in use in many language classrooms today.

However, there are some particular problems with 'drill-and-practice' software, such as the potential to create 'a passive mentality which seeks only the 'right' answers, thus stifling children's motivation to seek out underlying reasons or to produce answers that are in any way divergent' (Bonnett, 1997, pp. 157–158). In terms of the technical aspects of learning a language, it is difficult to develop the 'individualization of problems and questions tailored to the (changing) needs of particular learners, and the delivery of constructive feedback' (Crook, 1994, p. 12). Basically, 'drill-and-practice' courseware is based on the model of computer as tutor (Taylor, 1980). Wolff (1999, p. 127), in his review of Levy's (1997) framework of the computer's role as either tutor or tool, remarks that behaviouristic CALL has no place, and so the only defensible role for the computer in language learning is that of tool. Some other research argues that this kind of practice does little to improve the learner's linguistic ability to produce the grammatically appropriate utterances (Armstrong and Yetter-Vassot, 1994).

Communicative CALL (cognitive/constructivist perspective)

Warschauer and Healey (1998) propose that communicative CALL 'emerged in the late 1970s and early 1980s', but then it was said to date to the 1980s and 1990s (Warschauer, 2004). Although it is difficult to set a clear boundary between behaviouristic CALL and communicative CALL, it is widely accepted that behaviouristic CALL was largely swept away by the tides of 'communicative competence' (Hymes, 1972) privileged in the late 1970s and early 1980s. Communicative CALL is mainly based on two learning theories: cognitive learning theory and cognitive constructivism. The cognitive learning perspective sees the learner not as a passive recipient but as a mentally active participant in the learning process. Information processing and cognitive constructivism are two distinguished schools of thought. Information processing derived from cognitive theory explains how human behaviour is formed in terms of how the brain works with information intake, storage and processing, while the constructivism paradigm is concerned with how human beings construct knowledge and facts or develop skills. Cognitive constructivism emphasises personal experience, and 'constructivists postulate that there is no reality independent of the human being. Reality is always constructed by the human being and exists, therefore, only subjectively in his or her brain' (Wolff, 1997, p. 18). As discussed earlier, Jean Piaget proposed the stages of cognitive development for human beings, claiming that cognition develops from the use of basic senses to more sophisticated ones, in particular abstract reasoning.

Noam Chomsky (1957) and Stephen Krashen (1981) are representatives of the cognitive perspective, who consider that imitation and language habit formation cannot be the basis of language acquisition because language is constructed upon cognitive knowledge in interaction with comprehensible, meaningful language during learning (Chomsky, 1986). They emphasise that learning a language is an individual psycholinguistic act. Only after analysis, judgement, inference and deduction of the language input can learners form a set of personal language systems in order to achieve communication. In language learning, providing a large amount of comprehensible input is vitally important because it is the foundation of cognition and language construction.

The PC is suited to facilitating language learning and allows learners the maximum number of opportunities to be exposed to language in a meaningful context and to construct their own individual knowledge. Learners can control the programme, the learning process, learning pace and content to meet their individual needs. The learners are in a simulated micro-language world where they can analyse the material, solve problems, authenticate hypotheses and renew understanding. Multimedia simulation software allows learners to enter into computerised learning environments with exposure to language and culture in a meaningful audiovisual context, helping to achieve communicative competence. Associated with cognitive learning theory is intelligent CALL. Intelligent CALL provides opportunities for learners to be involved in language instruction: for example, intelligent grammar checkers (IGCs) that perform an analysis of students' written work to point out errors; and intelligent tutoring systems (ITSs) which 'combine the problem-solving experience and motivation of "discovery" learning with the effective guidance of tutorial interaction' (Sleeman and Brown, 1982, p. 1). Compared to CAI, ITSs require specific knowledge domains to be taught to the individual students by the computerised tutor. So the key characteristic for designing ITSs is that four types of knowledge are required: subject knowledge, learner knowledge, technology knowledge and pedagogical knowledge. Although there are authoring tools which allow instructors to create their own courseware, it is still challenging for instructors to design and create their own courseware to meet their students' needs. Of course, in CALL under such a perspective, grammar is taught implicitly and language is manipulated rather than replicated.

'Microworlds' were originally proposed by Papert as environments which supply 'simple, concrete models of important things, ideas and their relationships' to help children work creatively to acquire 'powerful authentic knowledge' (Lawler and Yazdani, 1987, p. x). Microworlds for language instruction provide a meaningful context for language learners to experiment using the language as a tool to solve a problem. This enables implicit language learning while the student carries out a purposeful experiment in some subject areas by using the 'foreign' language to give instructions, conduct investigations, record observations and discuss results (see Schoelles and Hamburger (1996) for some of the benefits of microworlds). According to Chapelle (1989), '[I]ntelligent microworlds provide a partner to converse with students about a given topic. These programmes use knowledge representation techniques and natural language processing to transform computers so that communicating with them "can be a natural process … like learning French by living in France"' (60). Three principles need to be considered in designing a microworld activity:

- implicit feedback, which is believed to be more effective than explicit feedback in assisting individualised learning;

- overlearning through intrinsic reward, which enables repeated practice by motivating learners intrinsically;

- adaptive sequencing, which provides the individualisation of instruction to accommodate particular learners' problems.

It is worth noting that 'communicative CALL' (Warschauer and Healey, 1998; Warschauer, 2000a) is not the same term as the 'communicative' being used in language teaching methodologies, even if the criterion of being 'communicative' has a general communicative 'flavour' (Underwood, 1984) but without the central characteristics of the communicative approach that enables learners to learn how to communicate best through the process of

---

Case study 1.1:

Military Language Tutor (MILT), first developed for a military audience but intended generally for adults learning language, is an example of using microworlds in language learning. In the MILT microworld, learners are immersed in a task-relevant environment that they can explore by speaking or typing commands to an animated agent who understands only the target language. The agent solves problems such as searching a series of rooms for hidden documents (books, letters, maps, etc.) and reading and extracting the information contained.

Holland et al. (1999) described a version of MILT that pairs discrete ASR (automated speech recognition) with animated graphics to give job-relevant communicative practice in selected languages.

Read more about this project here: https://calico.org/html/article_624.pdf

How does a microworld provide the learners with a supportive environment to learn the language?

---

communication itself (Littlewood, 1981). Bax (2003b) questions if communicative CALL is ever actually communicative at all 'in any significant way' because it lacks the 'central features of human communication and interaction' (p. 18). Bax then describes and critiques the three main 'models' of computer use, arguing that the *computer as tutor* model provides very limited computer–student communication; that the *computer as stimulus* is not considered as a distinctive feature of communicative CALL in spite of its function of promoting some valuable communications which can be achieved by other means as well; and that *computer as workhorse/tool* again has no clear features of CLT because the computer is used mainly to analyse and manipulate language rather than to communicate ideas. By examining the 'actual practice' of CALL between 1980 and 1990 in the two fundamental prerequisites of communication – speaking and listening – Jung (2005) argues that Bax's claim 'that communicative CALL in the 1980s was never communicative at all' is right (Bax, 2003b, p. 18). Jung (2005) further suggests that this period should be called 'post-behaviouristic' because 'it is an experimental phase with teachers trying to distil an essence of speaking out of software that was essentially deaf and dumb' (p. 9).

Integrative CALL

Likewise, there is a timescale difference in integrative CALL from Warschauer and Healey (1998) to Warschauer (2004). The underpinning theory of integrative CALL is the socio-cognitive perspective of learning or social constructivism. Language learning is developed through the negotiation of meaning in dialogues with the target language in the real world. It adds the importance of the context of human learning within a sociocultural environment to the idea of learners constructing their own knowledge and understanding.

As explained earlier, the best-known proponent of this learning paradigm is the Russian psychologist Lev Semeonovich Vygotsky (1978), who pioneered such a sociocultural approach in which the experiences at the social level – communicating and sharing ideas with a community – are seen as crucial in internalising knowledge. Vygotsky maintains that human beings make use of symbolic tools, such as language, 'to mediate and regulate our relationships with others and with ourselves and thus change the nature of these relationships' (Lantolf, 2000, p. 1). Under a Vygotskyan view, the role of psychology is to understand how human social and mental activity is organised through symbolic tools, and the prime symbolic tool available for the mediation is language. It means people formulate a plan, design a task or articulate the steps to solve a problem through language. Vygotsky affords great importance to the role of language in the interaction of learners with one another. From his point of view, learning occurs through collaborative talk and engagement with contextualised and situationalised sociocultural environments, as well as from inter-mental activity to intra-mental activity. Vygotsky (1978) stresses its 'transactional' nature: learning occurs in the first instance though interaction with others and then through internalisation. During this part of the process, language is used to clarify and make sense of new knowledge through discussions. Vygotsky (1978) has argued powerfully that the social process by which learning occurs creates a bridge that spans the learners' ZPD. Under a Vygotskyan perspective, the presence of an 'expert knower', such as a parent or a teacher, is vital to helping the learner develop his or her ZPD. One cannot be capable of independent functioning but can achieve the desired outcome given the relevant 'scaffolded help' offered by other people.

In language learning, both the stimulus from outside and inner cognitive ability is equally important. Halliday (1993) and Hymes (1971) point out that language is a socio-cognitive phenomenon, but not a system existing in humans' brains. Learning a language is viewed as a process of apprenticeship or socialisation into particular discourse communities (Schieffelin and Ochs, 1986; Gee, 1996). The goal of learning language is to communicate, and therefore, the process of communicating is as equally important as the linguistic products. Students need to be given a maximum number of opportunities to engage in authentic social interactions; they need to be provided with not only grammatical structures and comprehensible input but also practice in the kinds of 'real' communication they will later engage in within the society. In the learning process, learners must finish authentic tasks and projects collaboratively with the others while simultaneously learning both content and language.

From a social constructivist perspective, the computer is not only an ency-clopaedia and a patient adviser but also a medium of communication and a site for publishing works. The organisation of technology-enhanced teaching and learning style in this period is mostly free from limitations of time and place. The idea is that learners can learn anywhere, anytime. The Internet can be seen as the best example of the socio-cognitive approach to language learning and teaching, which largely accounts for the new enthusiasm for using technology in language classrooms. Technology can also be seen to have mediatory poten-tial in the Vygotskian sense, scaffolding the learners in the process of learning through cooperation in a certain situation. 'In integrative CALL, task-based, project-based, and content-based approaches all sought to integrate learners in authentic environments, and also to integrate the various skills of language learning and use' and 'students learn to use a variety of technological tools as an ongoing process of language learning and use, rather than visiting the computer lab on a once a week basis for isolated exercises (whether the exercises be behav-iouristic or communicative)' (Warschauer and Healey, 1998, p. 59). WebQuest is another good example of integrative CALL (see www.webquest.org for more information), which provides inquiry-oriented simulation tasks, which involve problem solving by using online resources and working col-laboratively. Because of the 'integrative' features of computers in the language learning process, integrative CALL largely develops learners' autonomy because they are responsible for their own learning during the evaluation and selection of technological media. Furthermore, the availability and authenticity of elec-tronic resources greatly increase the potential for meaningful knowledge con-struction. However, it is considered to be vital for teachers to be aware of how the use of technology affects teacher–student and student–student interactions.

CMC has been focusing on this line of inquiry in particular. CMC has several key features, and the predominant ones include allowing learners to control their own learning and taking an active role (Bikowski and Kessler, 2002). Earlier work on CMC focused on meaning negotiation (taking up the interactionist perspective on the acquisi-tion of a second language) in communi-cation to encourage students to pay less attention to the language form (Blake, 2000; Toyoda and Harrison, 2002). In recent developments in CMC, it has has switched its focus to allow second language teachers to offer Internet-based collaborative learning.

CMC is understood to include both synchronous (at the same time) and asynchronous (at different times) communication.

Both synchronous CMC (SCMC) and asynchronous CMC (ACMC) are effective in the instruction of communication skills. Compared to ACMC (e.g. online forums), SCMC (e.g. text chat) is believed to have more affor-dances in offering participants greater social presence because it offers an environment similar to face-to-face communication. In this environment, learners are able to use similar communication devices (Blake, 2000; Lee, 2002) to accommodate each other by modifying some aspects of their communication behaviour, such as speed of response and use of easily understandable words, accordingly. Initially, most CMC projects took place within a single class and used synchronous forms (such as MOOs and chat), and the research focused on learners' attitudes and motivations (e.g. Warschauer, 1996b; Meunier, 1998), comparisons of interaction in online versus face-to-face environments (e.g. Kern, 1995; Warschauer, 1996c) and linguistic descriptions of online discourse (Chun, 1994; Herring, 1996). Because CMC research was broadly situated in an interactionist perspective of SLA, many research studies adopted quasi-experimental designs and discourse analysis inventories to document learner use and acquisition of particular language forms. However, recently, more and more research has been exploring the social aspects of CMC (e.g. Jenks, 2014).

Task 1.4: Can you explain my pedagogical considerations and the theories underpinning my design?

When I was a teacher in a secondary school, I found my students were not doing well with their grammar. So I designed an online learning platform where students could read the grammar explanations on a particular topic and then choose to do some follow-up exercises. If they got all the items right, they could move on. But if they got some items wrong, they would be 'diagnosed' by the computer to read the explanations for the items they did wrong, and it would suggest further readings. After that, they would be directed to a new section where they could take further exercises until they completely understood the grammar. What are my pedagogical considerations in the design? Which theory is underpinning my design?

Collaborative TELL (social constructivism)

The twenty-first century underwent the rapid development of technology and a growth in the number of technology users. Learners in the twenty-first century are digital natives, who have grown up with digital technology and who inevitably see this technology as part of their life rather than as an add-on. Indeed, they are the 'mobile generation' who spend more time on their mobile devices and have mobile learning experience rather than with textbooks and learning in a classroom. This in turn requires a new mindset for learning, as people spend time searching, reading, scrutinising, authenticating, collaborating and organising information. In terms of a learning paradigm, we see a clear movement from a cognitive orientation to a social orientation, from classroom contexts to naturalistic settings, from an acquisition metaphor to a participation metaphor, from L2 learning to L2 use (Block, 2003; Firth and Wagner, 1997, 2007) and from individual learning towards collaborative learning (e.g. project-based learning, inquiry-based learning and task-based learning). According to such a view, language learning is not a stand-alone activity, but instead, it is integrated in a process of knowledge co-construction. In this sense, language is used as a medium to engage in knowledge creation, exploration and problem solving.

Telecollaboration is a good example of collaborative TELL. Telecollaboration involves establishing online educational exchanges between language learners. Although telecollaboration still focuses on learning the target language through communication, it is social in nature. Traditionally, telecollaboration projects have been established between schools and universities, but in recent years they have come to transcend institutional boundaries, as in the case of massively multiplayer online games (Thorne et al., 2009; Rama et al., 2012). A number of books and review articles have surveyed research on telecollaboration (e.g. Belz and Thorne, 2006; O'Dowd, 2007; Dooly and O'Dowd, 2012; Blake, 2013). Apart from focusing on linguistic gains, much attention has been placed on intercultural learning and increasing intercultural awareness. There are contradictory findings about the use of telecollaboration, with some claiming that it provides motivating language practice and opportunities for developing intercultural awareness (e.g.

Case study 1.2:

One of the best known and the most longstanding telecollaborative projects is Cultura, developed at MIT in 1997 by Gilberte Furstenberg, Sabine Levet and Shoggy Waryn. Cultura is an online intercultural project – based in a language class – that connects American students with others from different countries, with the aim of helping them develop an in-depth understanding of each other's culture.

Originally developed for student cohorts in the US and France, Cultura has also been used with students from Germany, Italy, Mexico, Russia and Spain as well.

Cultura is not the only online intercultural project of its kind, but it is particularly well known for its pedagogically sound design, approach and methodology. Sharing a common website, students compare a similar set of materials from their different cultures and exchange viewpoints and perspectives via online discussion forums and videoconferences, gradually constructing together a deeper understanding of each other's cultural attitudes, beliefs and values.

See more information about this project here: https://cultura.mit.edu/

What makes this project a successful example of using technology in promoting learning?

Kinginger, 2000; Meskill and Ranglova, 2000; von der Emde and Schneider, 2003) and others showing that intercultural contact does not necessarily lead to cultural understanding (Thorne, 2003; Ware, 2003, 2005; O'Dowd, 2006a, b). Many other factors influence learners' experiences and achieve cultural understanding, such as language ability and the medium of interaction.

The use of Web 2.0 tools and applications is another good example of fostering collaboration. Web 2.0 technologies are rooted in social constructivism, which are predominantly used as social tools because the fundamental attributes of Web 2.0 are affordances of participation, information sharing, communication and collaboration. Compared to Web 1.0, which is information-oriented, Web 2.0 focuses on communicative networking because Web 2.0 sites are 'fundamentally about community' (New Media Consortiu, 2007, p. 12). Examples of Web 2.0 tools include blog, micro-blog, wiki, Twitter, Facebook, social networking, Second Life, virtual world; the most commonly investigated Web 2.0 technologies are blogs and wikis.

Task 1.5: Explore the following popular tools for collaborative learning

1. Google Apps for Education include tools like Google Docs and a calendar. Have you tried to use Google Docs? It is a tool to help student and teachers collaborate.
2. Twitter: See how an English teacher turned his ordinary class discussion into addictive debate. www.theatlantic.com/education/archive/2014/09/the-case-for-having-class-discussions-on-twitter/379777/
3. YouTube can be used either as a motivator, in the lead-in activity or as a channel where students can collaboratively make and share videos.
4. WordPress (and other blogging software) can be used to create a class blog that all students can contribute to. Group blog turns out to be a really useful collaborative activity in learning because it encourages all members to participate, critically think, engage and share ideas.
5. Wikispaces Classroom is a social writing platform for education. It is incredibly easy to create a classroom workspace where the teacher and students can communicate and work on writing projects alone or in teams. Rich assessment tools are available too to assist the teacher to measure student contribution and engagement in real time. www.wikispaces.com/content/classroom
6. Facebook is a great collaboration tool where students can participate in activities and share ideas / documents. A Facebook group can be set up to enable students to collaborate when they conduct projects. See a successful story here: www.emergingedtech.com/2011/05/facebook-summit-2011-an-excellent-academic-use-of-the-popular-Internet-app/

Explore these tools and choose one or two of them to design activities to enhance language learning in your context.

The impact of Web 2.0 technologies on language learning and teaching is indeed great, from changing pedagogy to transforming curriculum design and even the conception of language learning (Sykes et al., 2008; Warschauer and Grimes, 2008; Sturm et al., 2009). The key characteristics of collaborative TELL are as follows:

- Students are encouraged and supported to work together to create knowledge, learning therefore is collaboration-oriented and community-based.

- Knowledge is multifarious, and therefore there is no single form of knowledge.

- Learners are encouraged to push the boundary and challenge thinking.

- Group cognition rather than individual cognitive development is valued.

- Learning is not restricted by place and time.

- Learners are not left alone in learning – the teacher plays a key role.

- Online discourse is the form of communication.

- There is a rich blend of cultures, languages and dynamic use of media.

Case study 1.3:

Sun (2009) explored how voice blogs can be used as a platform for an extensive study of language learners' speaking skills in a university in Taiwan. She concluded that blogs can constitute a dynamic forum that fosters extensive practice, learning, motivation, authorship and the development of learning strategies. More information about this study can be found here: llt.msu.edu/vol13num2/sun.pdf

What are the advantages of voice blogs in your opinion?

M-learning perhaps merits further discussion here. In recent years, TELL also embraces m-learning, which brings 'mobility' to the central place of learning. Here mobility can refer to 'devices' being mobile, and this view is widely discussed and adopted. With the advancement of technology and Web 2.0, mobility also refers to 'learners' (Woodill, 2011) and learning itself (Traxler, 2007). In particular, the latter ones are linked to situated learning (Comas-Quinn et al., 2009) and embodied learning (Klopfer, 2008). When aided by mobile devices, learners can change real-world contexts into learning contexts via their actions. As such, they create *learner-generated contexts* (Luckin, 2010), which subsequently changes the nature of learning and the learning process.

Summary

Technology is generally defined as a tool for learning, creating, communicating, thinking, representing and researching (Bell, 2001). As indicated in the previous sections, uses of technology in the language classroom have advanced from the structural CALL to the communicative CALL, the integrative CALL and finally the collaborative TELL. Technology use in language learning varies in many forms, ranging from the drill and practice of certain language skills, such as reading or writing, to reconstruction through using a word processor, even to electronic conferencing to raise cultural awareness, and using Web 2.0 to co-construct knowledge. However, in both research and teaching, the above-mentioned forms of technology do not fall into neatly contained timelines. As each new stage has emerged, the previous stage continues. Current uses of computers/technology in the language classroom correspond to all forms mentioned above, and teachers use various types of technologies to facilitate learning without restricting themselves to a singular form of CALL. In the next chapter, we will look at the specific relationship between second language learning and the affordances of technology, in particular in relation to enhancing student motivation.

Annotated further reading

1. Kern, R. & Warschauer, M. (2000) Introduction: Theory and practice of network-based language teaching, in M. Warschauer and R. Kern (eds), *Network-based Language Teaching: Concepts and Practice* (pp. 1–19). Cambridge: Cambridge University Press.

   This book chapter provides an overview of perspectives of CALL, linking to the paradigm shifts of language learning.
2. Wang, S. & Vásquez, C. (2012) Web 2.0 and Second Language Learning: What does the research tell us? *CALICO Journal*, 29(3), 412–430.

   This article reviews current research on the use of Web 2.0 technologies in second language (L2) learning. Its purposes are to investigate the theoretical perspectives framing Web 2.0, to identify some of the benefits of using Web 2.0 technologies in L2 learning and to discuss some of the limitations.
3. Macaro, E., Handley, Z. & Walter, C. (2012) A systematic review of CALL in English as a second language: Focus on primary and secondary education. *Language Teaching*, 45(1), 1–43.

   This article provides a comprehensive review of the use of technology in second language teaching in the primary and secondary sectors since 1990. In it, 47 post-2000 studies were reviewed in depth in the aspects of what technology had been used, along with why, what evidence there was that technology facilitated language learning, and what other insights can be drawn in the field.

4. Harasim, L. (2012) *Learning Theory and Online Technologies*. New York: Routledge. This book explains and discusses various learning theories and their underpinnings of current technology use in education. It is worth reading Chapters 3–6 in details in order to understand behaviourist learning theory, cognitivist learning theory, constructivist learning theory and OCL theory, as well as technology use in learning associated with each theory.

2 The role of technology, motivation and SLA

Aims: This chapter considers the role of technologies in language education by reviewing learning theories discussed in the literature. In particular, this chapter looks at factors contributing to successful second language learning (SLL) and the potential of technology for enhancing SLL. One of the important benefits of technology in SLL is to enhance learner motivation and engagement. Empirical studies will be used to illustrate how technologies enhance the development of autonomous language learners. This chapter has three sections, as follows:

1. Key factors contributing to effective second language learning

2. Affordances and roles of technology

3. Focus on motivation.

Introduction

A vast amount of research has been carried out over the last several decades to gain insights into effective language learning. As a result, new methodological approaches have been proposed, abundant print and digital materials have been developed and various learning strategies have been put forward. In the review of the development of TESOL methodology and the underpinning theories of language and language learning, different factors may account for effective L2 learning, including *authentic input, conscious noticing on form, opportunity for interaction, in-time and individualised feedback, low affective filter* and *an environment where language can be used*. In this chapter, I will examine these influential factors and discuss *affordances* and *roles of technology* in addressing these key elements of second language learning. Of course, caution has to be advised regarding the possibility that other factors, especially on a personal level, might contribute to effective learning, and this is not an exhaustive list of elements on which any teacher or learner needs to work. We also need to acknowledge that learning is not simply linear and that many factors influence each other in the process of learning.

In this chapter, I will first examine these key elements for second language learning, and then I will discuss the benefits and roles of CALL and evidence of its 'value and usability' (Chapelle, 2003, p. 67). I will pay particular attention to its *affective role* in promoting motivation and autonomy.

Key factors contributing to effective second language learning

When we talk about effective language learning, various theorists have proposed different factors that contribute to it. Despite different theoretical positions on what learning is and what language is, there are factors which theorists, teachers and learners all agree are important. These are elaborated below.

Authentic input and focus on meaning

Input, in particular authentic input that focuses on meaning, is of utmost importance in second language learning. Second language acquisition (SLA) theorist Rod Ellis (2005) remarks, 'language learning, whether it occurs in a naturalistic or an instructed context, is a slow and labour-intensive process. If learners do not receive exposure to the target language they cannot acquire it. In general, the more exposure they receive, the more and the faster they will learn' (p. 45). Simply put, input is the most influential factor contributing to the speed and success of language learning. In this regard, SLA pioneer Stephen Krashen established the **Monitor Model**, which highlights the importance of input in SLA.

Krashen (1982) postulated that in SLA, the primary determinant is comprehensible input, which triggers automatic processes that are ultimately responsible for successful language learning. The input hypothesis explains how SLA actually happens. According to this hypothesis, learners improve and progress along the 'natural order' when they receive second language input at the level which is a little beyond their current level of (acquired) competence. For example, if a learner's stage is 'i', then acquisition occurs when he/she

Because Krashen is one of the most influential theorists of SLA, his Monitor Model is probably the most renowned among linguists and language practitioners and also the one which has attracted an onslaught of criticism. The Monitor Model consists of five hypotheses, namely the acquisition-learning hypothesis, the monitor hypothesis, the natural order hypothesis, the input hypothesis and the affective filter hypothesis, and it is an example of the 'nativist theory'. According to this model, to acquire an L2, the learner needs to focus on messages and meanings.

is exposed to *comprehensible input* that belongs to the level 'i+1'. This 'i+1' comprehensible input can be achieved by reading and hearing, and therefore, based on this assumption, the input hypothesis claims that listening and reading comprehension are more important than writing and speaking, which will come on in their own time. The hypothesis further points out that speaking is not 'taught' but instead '"emerges" after the acquirer has built up competence through comprehending input' (Krashen and Terrell, 1983, p. 32). Since not all of the learners can be at the same level of 'i', Krashen suggests '*natural communicative input*' as the key to designing a syllabus so that every learner will receive some appropriate 'i+1' input to their current linguistic competence. He also offers the idea of the input being finely – and roughly – tuned. The finely tuned input targets the current level of the learner's acquisition, learning one structure at a time. The roughly tuned input itself includes learners' 'i+1', like a net spreading around the learner's current acquisition level. In such situations, the goal is to make oneself understood. Krashen explains it as 'when communication is successful, when the input is understood and there is enough of it, 'i+1' will be provided automatically' (Krashen, 1982, p. 22). Good roughly tuned input is caretaker speech, foreigner talk and teacher talk. Krashen and Terrell (1983) argued that roughly tuned input has several real advantages over finely tuned exercises:

> With rough tuning, we are always assured that i+1 will be covered, while with finely tuned exercises, we are taking a guess as to where the student is. With roughly tuned input, we are assured of constant recycling and review; this is not the case with 'lock-step' exercises. Third, roughly tuned input will be good for more than one acquirer at a time, even when they are at slightly different levels. Finally, roughly tuned caretaker-like speech in the form of teacher talk or foreigner talk, will nearly always be more interesting than an exercise that focuses just on one grammatical point. (p. 35)

Task 2.1: Does 'i+1' make sense to you?

Think about your own learning experience or your teaching context. Are there any problems you can observe about 'i+1'?

Although Krashen's 'i+1' attempts to explain how language is acquired and provides a theoretical environment for language development, the theory has raised some questions; for instance, Ellis (1992) points out that Krashen fails to provide a single study that has demonstrated the input hypothesis. Several theorists have also proposed that SLA can take place without two-way communication or interactional modifications (Larsen-Freeman, 1983; Ellis, 1985). This means input is not entirely necessary for language learning.

Developed by Merrill Swain, the comprehensible output (CO) hypothesis states that learning takes place when a learner encounters a gap in his or her linguistic knowledge of the second language (L2). By noticing this gap, the learner becomes aware of it and may be able to modify his output so that he learns something new about the language.

Further, Hadley (1993) proposes that this comprehensive input happens only when the learners use the language in context and when they communicate or interact with the environment. Moreover, Swain (1983) has argued that the input hypothesis fails to recognise the importance of **comprehensible output** (this is discussed later on). Lee and VanPatten (1995) have made the point that while input is critical, it is far from the only factor that determines SLA. Krashen (1982) acknowledged that comprehensible input *alone* is an insufficient condition for SLA; SLA happens only when *input* becomes *intake*. It is still not entirely known how the learner selects input and what is assimilated and fed into their internal system (e.g. Language Acquisition Device (LAD). In addition, it is difficult to define what 'i' level the learner is at, and how to cover the learners' different 'i' levels in actual classrooms. Mitchell and Myles (1998) argue 'the concepts of "understanding" and "noticing gap" are not clearly operationalised or consistently proposed; it is not clear how the learner's present state of knowledge ("i") is to be characterised or indeed whether the "i+1" formulation is intended to apply to all aspects of language, from lexis to phonology and syntax' (p. 126). In reviewing comprehensible input, Krashen (2011) further argued that in order for learning to happen, the input must be compelling, meaning that the input is so interesting that the learners forget that it is in another language. When input is compelling, learners are in a state of 'flow' (Csikszentmihalyi, 1990). Compelling goes beyond 'interesting' because it requires learners to take an active role in the learning process, such as when learners select their own reading materials.

Despite the debates and controversial views regarding Krashen's 'i+1' input, very few would dispute the role of authentic input in second language learning. Omaggio (1986) suggests 'a proficiency-oriented methodology that emphasizes the use of authentic language in instructional materials wherever and whenever possible' (p. 41). The underpinning theory is that through using authentic sources in instruction, learners will be able to acquire 'usable skills' in real-life situations (Nunan, 1989, p. 54). Ellis (2005), in his review of the literature of SLA, suggests that learners need to develop 'both a rich repertoire of formulaic expressions and a rule-based competence' (p. 39). It is the rich repertoire of formulaic expressions that caters to fluency, and it is the rule-based competence that consists of the knowledge of specific grammatical rules that caters to complexity and accuracy (Skehan, 1998). Ellis (2005) further proposes that learners need to focus predominantly on meaning in learning activities: not only semantic meaning (i.e. the meanings of lexical items or of specific grammatical structures) but also meaning relating to pragmatic meaning (i.e. the highly contextualised meanings that arise in acts of communication). Therefore, it is clear that any input needs to be authentic in these ways if it is to enable learners to acquire the language that exists in real-life situations.

Focus on form and conscious noticing

Long (1988, 1991) proposed that grammar instruction may be of one of two types: 'focus on form' and 'focus on forms'. Focus on form refers to drawing students' 'attention to linguistic elements as they arise incidentally in lessons whose overriding focus is on meaning or communication' (Long, 1991, pp. 45–46). The latter refers to the traditional teaching of discrete points of grammar in separate lessons.

Focusing on meaning does not necessarily mean that students do not need to worry about form or accuracy. Some theorists (e.g. Schmidt, 1990, 1995) have argued that there is no learning without conscious attention to form. This is in line with **focus on form** (Long, 1988, 1991). In particular, Schmidt (2001) is of the opinion that learners need to attend to specific forms as they occur in the input to which learners are exposed, not to an awareness of grammatical rules. Research has shown that linguistic input increases when the learners notice linguistic features, using techniques such as marking salience, modification or elaboration (Schmidt, 1990; Sharwood Smith, 1993; Robinson, 1995, 2001; Skehan, 1998) (see Table 2.1 for explanations and examples).

Technique	Explanation	Example
Marking salience	Marking up the structure or particular feature of the input, or repeating the input	Underline the grammatical structure of a sentence
Modification	Modifying the input so that it is understandable using various methods, such as images and L1 translation	Provide L1 translation for new vocabulary
Elaboration	Increasing understanding by adding grammatical phrases and clauses	Provide an elaborated version of the sentence by adding the grammatical parts

TABLE 2.1   EXPLANATIONS AND EXAMPLES OF SOME TECHNIQUES TO ENHANCE INPUT

Interaction

Interaction has been a mainstay in SLA research, and Ellis (1999) describes the benefits of interaction to successful L2 learning through different theoretical perspectives: interaction hypothesis, sociocultural theory and depth of processing theory. No matter what perspectives they take, cognitive (Gass, 2003) or sociocultural (Lantolf, 2001), the researchers in SLA agree that interaction can prompt L2 development.

Long (1996), has combined Swain and Krashen's positions to formulate the Interaction Hypothesis, which proposes that language acquisition arises from the *negotiation for meaning* that occurs during the use of the target language in interaction, thus expressing the need for both language input and output. Negotiation can come in the form of repetitions (when a speaker repeats his/her own utterance), confirmation checks (when the listener repeats the speaker's utterance to ensure that it was understood correctly), comprehension checks (where the speaker attempts to determine whether or not the listener understood correctly) and clarification requests (when the listener asks for assistance in understanding an utterance). According to the Interaction Hypothesis (Long, 1996), interaction fosters acquisition when a communication problem arises and learners then need to negotiate for meaning. This has been 'perceived as an important factor for successful L2 acquisition' (Ellis, 1990, p. 16) and facilitates L2 development (Long, 1996). Communicative efforts that learners make during the negotiation of meaning provide them with opportunities for achieving fluency and therefore the acquisition of L2 knowledge (Ellis, 1990). In this view, a learning environment which can provide students with opportunities to engage in interactions for negotiation of meaning is crucial (Doughty and Pica, 1986; Willis, 1996). In particular, tasks for language learning are important, and they should be specifically designed to meet the needs of language development rather than spontaneous conversations to achieve communicative goals (Long, 1996) and to increase output comprehensibility (Nunan, 1993; see e.g. Pica, 1995; Gass et al., 1998; Mackey and Philp, 1998). As a result, task authenticity is required for meaningful and authentic communication, and hence students should be provided with 'actual tasks which a person may undertake when communicating through the target language' (Breen, 1987, p. 162).

Noticing, according to Gass and Selinker (2001), is 'at the heart of the interaction hypothesis' (p. 298). From the learners' point of view, there is a long period when they struggle to communicate in the target language via their own interlanguage (Gass and Selinker, 1994, p. 11). During this communication, learners typically encounter different difficulties: lexical, grammatical or phonological. To clarify the confusion, learners need to negotiate meaning. In Gass's words, (1997) negotiation of meaning refers to 'communication in which participants' attention is focused on resolving a communication problem as opposed to communication in which there is a free-flowing exchange of information' (p. 107). Through meaning negotiation, the learners receive *negative evidence*. *Negative evidence* is 'direct or indirect information about what is ungrammatical' (Long, 1996, p. 413), and therefore, meaning negotiation increases input comprehensibility, which results in continued language development. This kind of negotiation of meaning is also described as 'focus on form': 'focus on form … overtly draws students' attention to linguistic elements as they arise incidentally in lessons whose overriding focus is on meaning or communication' (Long, 1991, pp. 45–46). Thus, learners benefit from form-focused instruction so that they reach a high level of awareness of the correct forms (Dekeyser, 2000). Here, it is important to mention that corrective feedback enhances linguistic forms and raises the awareness of noticing, which facilitates bringing about correct output.

Apart from the important role that input plays in L2 acquisition, research has shown that the output during the interaction process (Pica et al., 1989; Swain and Lapkin, 1995) and 'negotiation of meaning' are essential in order for learners to reach their language learning potential (Ellis, 1999; Gass, 1997; Lyster, 1998a, b). Some studies have suggested that interaction facilitates comprehension better than conditions without the interactive component (Gass and Varonis, 1994; Loschky, 1994; Polio and Gass, 1998), and other studies have also pointed out a positive effect of negotiating for meaning on the quality of immediate production (Holliday, 1995).

On the other hand, the sociocultural theory of mind offers a different view of interaction in learning. According to this theory, interaction enables learners to construct new meanings collaboratively (see Lantolf, 2000). The sociocultural perspective highlights the interrelationship between language, interaction, learning and community to offer a holistic perspective of language learning (Ellis and Barkhuizen, 2005). Vygotsky (1978) posits that human beings make use of symbolic tools to both interpret and regulate the world and relationships with people around them. The relationship with the world and people is therefore a mediated one, which is established through the use of a symbolic tool: language (Vygotsky, 1978; Lantolf, 2000). Sociocultural theory also views language as a psychological tool, a 'tool for thought'. Language is 'a means for engaging in social and cognitive activity' (Ahmed, 1994, p. 158). While thought and speech are separate, they are 'tightly interrelated in a dialectic unity in which publicly derived speech completes privately initiated thought' (Lantolf, 2000, p. 7). It is therefore critical of 'transmission' theories of communication, which assume that ready-made messages are passed from speaker to hearer (e.g. Donato,

1994, pp. 33–36; Platt and Brooks, 1994, p. 498). Vygotsky (1978) suggested that there is a close link between the use of these two functions of language, and therefore, learning is seen as first social, then individual and as first inter-mental, then intra-mental, with thinking embedded in the ways in which language is used. In a language classroom, it very quickly becomes apparent that learners access and acquire new knowledge and skills through the talk, interaction and collaboration which take place. Language is learned, problems are solved, new understandings are accomplished and breakdowns are repaired through the ensuing talk and according to the ways in which interaction is managed. Crucially, not only is language central to absolutely everything which takes place; it is also very often the goal of the interaction, the target of the talk; as Long (1983, p. 9) points out, language is ' the vehicle and object of instruction'.

Clearly, there is a strong link between language and learning, and language plays a mediational role in the learning which takes place (Vygotsky, 1978); in other words, all learning requires language, the basic 'tool' which underpins or 'mediates' the learning process. Furthermore, interaction is central to learning: it is 'the most important element in the curriculum' (van Lier, 1996, p. 5). This is a position echoed by Ellis, who tells us that 'learning arises not *through* interaction, but *in* interaction' (2000, p. 209, original emphasis). As such, the relationship between talk, interaction and learning is central to classroom practice.

Task 2.2: Comparing the views of interaction

While comparing the views of interaction discussed above, could you elaborate why interaction is important for learners? How do you understand the role of interaction in your teaching context?

Motivation

When learners are motivated, they learn better. If learners are autonomous and self-regulated, they take more control over their learning and become more active. Both motivation and autonomy fit with the model of the **affective filter** hypothesis, which argues that a number of 'affective variables' act in a facilitative role in SLA. These variables include motivation, self-confidence and anxiety. Krashen claims that the 'filter' is 'down' with highly motivated,

According to Krashen (1985), the affective filter refers to 'a mental block that prevents acquirers from fully utilizing the comprehensible input they receive for language acquisition' (p. 3).

self-confident and relaxed learners and 'up' with poorly motivated, bored, stressed and anxious learners. Therefore, 'when the filter is "down" and appropriate comprehensible input is presented (and comprehended), acquisition is inevitable' (Krashen, 1985, p. 4). This effect is of great importance to the acquirer in a classroom setting, so Krashen and Terrell (1983) suggest that 'our pedagogical goals should include not only supplying optimal input, but also creating a situation that promotes a low filter' to ensure learners' success in obtaining acquired competence (p. 38). For example, the Natural Approach is a pedagogy that aims to provide good comprehensible input and lower the affective filter.

What is motivation? In general, motivation is defined as 'a psychological construct that refers to the desire and incentive that an individual has to engage in a specific activity' (Loewen and Reinders, 2011, p. 119). In reviewing the literature, many definitions have been proposed, and it is hard to come up with a commonly agreed definition, because of the complexity of the concept. However, very few would dispute the importance of motivation in accomplishing a particular activity. For example, in a language learning context, Hall (2011) suggests, '[I]t is difficult to imagine anyone learning a language without some degree of motivation' (p. 134). In teaching, we often hear from teachers who comment that some students have high motivation while others do not, and they ascribe achievement or disappointment mostly to the absence or presence of motivation (ibid.).

In the SLA literature, Dörnyei (2005, p. 65) argues that motivation provides 'the primary impetus to initiate L2 learning and later the driving force to sustain the long and often tedious learning process'. It is clear that motivation refers to a process that starts with a need and leads to a behaviour that moves an individual towards achieving a goal (Melendy, 2008).

L2 motivation research has gone through different stages, and researchers have conceptualised various L2 motivation models in the field, from the psychological cognitive model to Gardner's socio-educational model (1985, 2001, 2005) and Dörnyei's L2 Motivational Self System (2005, 2009; see also Dörnyei and Ushioda, 2011). Motivation can be classified according to different perspectives. From a cognitive viewpoint, they are recognised as extrinsic and intrinsic. Whereas extrinsic motivation is applied by others and involves systems of rewards and punishments, intrinsic motivation is self-applied, lying in the affective domain of feelings and emotional responses (Slavin, 2003). In other words, extrinsic motivation is related to doing/accomplishing a task, in order to receive a reward or to avoid punishment, while intrinsic motivation is about getting involved in order to achieve inner satisfaction (Dörnyei, 2001). From a socio-educational perspective, motivation can be viewed as integrative or instrumental (Gardner, 1985). Integrative motivation refers to an individual's openness to taking on characteristics of another cultural/linguistic group (Gardner, 2005, p. 7), which has frequently been cited to be related to second language learning achievement (Hedge, 2000; Lightbown and Spada, 2006; Loewen and Reinders, 2011) and cited as an indicator of a learner's desire to identify with the culture of the second language community (Ellis, 2008). Instrumental motivation refers to a drive or need from a perception of the real benefits that learning the second language might bring about, such as passing exams, gaining positions in overseas universities and job promotion (Loewen and Reinders, 2011). Therefore, integrative motivation can be viewed as socially or culturally oriented, and instrumental motivation can be viewed as academically or career oriented (Brown, 2007). It is widely acknowledged that in second language learning, both types of motivation play a key role, and the lack of either would cause problems (Cook, 2001, p. 118).

In recent years, Dörnyei (2005) has proposed a new model of motivation based on the empirical findings and theoretical considerations to reconceptualise L2 motivation as part of the learner's self system (see more about the self-approach in Dörnyei, 2009; Dörnyei and Ushioda, 2009). In the self-approach, Dörnyei (2005) proposes that the 'L2 Motivational Self System' is made up of three key elements:

- The *Ideal L2 Self* is the L2-specific facet of one's 'ideal self'. If the person we would like to become speaks an L2, the '*ideal L2 self*' is a powerful motivator to learn the L2.

- The *Ought-to L2 Self* concerns the attributes that one believes one *ought to* possess to meet expectations and to *avoid* possible negative outcomes.

- The *L2 Learning Experience* concerns situated motives related to the immediate learning environment and experience (e.g. the impact of the teacher, the curriculum, the peer group, the experience of success).

Task 2.3: Your motivation

Think about your experience of learning a foreign language, and jot down a list of motivating factors that got you started and prompted you to continue learning it for a period of time.

Use different theories to analyse the motivating factors and explain how they contributed to your learning of the language.

Affordances and roles of technology

Learning a foreign language 'requires more formal instruction and other measures compensating for the lack of environmental support' (Stern, 1983, p. 16), and computer-mediated learning is viewed as providing an ideal condition for successful L2 acquisition when natural learning takes place.

> **Task 2.4:** Analysis of the role of technology
>
> What roles do you think technology can play in second language learning? Consider the context in which you (will) teach. What are the potential benefits of technology for the learners? Could you think of an example of using technology to illustrate this and explain the rationale behind your thinking?

As early as the 1990s, Dunkel (1991) and Crookall et al. (1990) describe in detail many advantages of using simulations for language learning. Since 2000, research has flourished in the use of technology in second and foreign language learning (Chapelle, 2001; Lim and Shen, 2006). There are a number of benefits to integrating technologies into language teaching and learning (for a review, see Liu, et al., 2002; Zhao, 2003; Macaro et al., 2012). According to Egbert et al. (1999), technology seems to encompass

> all the elements that SLA theory points to in order for the conditions for optimal language learning to be created i.e. create opportunities for learners to interact and negotiate meaning (using the internet and email services), learners interact in the target language with an authentic audience (they can use email, video conferencing, blogs to develop their target language and interact with their peers in another country), they are involved in authentic tasks (which contain cognitive challenges and resemble real-world tasks) set by the teacher, learners are also encouraged to produce varied and creative language where Web-based resources serve as language input, learners receive immediate feedback (the correct version can be returned to a pupil or placed in the school network). (p. 3)

Li (2015) conducted a systematic literature review and suggested six benefits that technology can offer in language teaching and learning. These six benefits are closely related to the second language learning key elements addressed above.

- First, technology (e.g. the Internet and multimedia resources) provides students with high quality and authentic linguistic and cultural materials.

- Second, technology can act as a cognitive tool to facilitate the acquisition of linguistic knowledge and the development of language skills, such as by increasing the noticing of linguistic forms.

- Third, technology is a tool that mediates learning and through which learners acquire new understandings.

- Fourth, technology provides students with more opportunities to interact, a key construct of sociocultural perspectives on learning, which attach huge importance to the role of interaction in learning.

■ Fifth, computers can also be used as a 'tutor', offering immediate and individualised feedback.

■ Finally, perhaps the most widely acknowledged benefit is that technology increases student motivation and enhances engagement.

Authentic input

Technology is widely used as a language resource for authentic input, as well as to provide a context for the study of language use. In language learning, many teachers and researchers believe comprehensible input is the primary determinant in SLA. Omaggio (1986, p. 41) suggests 'a proficiency-oriented methodology' that emphasises the use of authentic language in instructional materials wherever and whenever possible. The underpinning theory is that through using authentic sources in instruction, learners will be able to acquire 'usable skills' for real-life situations (Nunan, 1989, p. 54). An electronic medium is believed to serve well the authenticity of the text and the authorship of the language user – the two key elements of communicative language learning (Kramsch, et al., 2000). According to Jung (2005), 61 examples in the bibliometric analysis are about retrieving authentic materials, and interestingly, 98 per cent of them are from after 1992. The Impact2 Study claims that technology can make the attractiveness, currency and variety of resources available to students (Harrison et al., 2003). The literature also suggests that computers provide students with the necessary resources to accomplish a task and to regulate it online. The issue about how technology assists teachers to explore authentic materials and enhance authentic input will be explored in the following chapters.

Conscious noticing

Computers are believed not only to provide authentic resources for language learning but also to increase learners' linguistic knowledge. Multimedia presentations, including graphics and video clips, have a positive effect on vocabulary acquisition (e.g. O'Hara and Pritchard, 2008; Silverman and Hines, 2009) and in writing (e.g. Mak and Coniam, 2008), but there is insufficient research concerning technology in enhancing grammar acquisition or reading. Of course, facilitating knowledge acquisition is not limited to linguistic information: studies show the value of technology for the development of intercultural awareness (Müeller-Hartmann, 2000; O'Dowd, 2006a, b), especially with CMC and network-based learning.

   For some researchers, 'noticing' is a necessary condition in successful SLA (Schmidt, 1990, 2001), and it is something that technology can be used to promote (Chapelle, 1998; Hegelheimer and Chapelle, 2000). Research has shown that linguistic input increases when learners notice linguistic features, using techniques such as marking salience, modification or elaboration (Schmidt, 1990; Skehan, 1998). Modification, making the input understandable to the learner through any means that 'gets at the meaning' – for example, images, second language (L2) dictionaries and first language (L1) translation – enhances linguistic acquisition. Salaberry (2000) states that, 'arguably, the specific characteristics of the medium of communication represented in CMC may increase the chances that learners will focus their attention on both function and form, thereby increasing the likelihood that morphological development will occur in such an environment rather than in face-to-face settings' (p. 19). Lai and Zhao (2006) have reported that text-based online chat promotes noticing (including their own mistakes). Further, they argue in their study that noticing plays a significant role in negotiating meaning. These studies share the feature that text-based online chat helps learners 'notice both their own problematic L2 utterances and the feedback on problematic linguistic forms provided by their interlocutors' (Lai and Zhao, 2006, p. 104). The ways in which technology can raise learners' noticing will be illustrated further in Chapter 4.

Interaction

Long (1985) proposed that interaction is important for ideal target language episodes for SLA and that it has been an important research area. Interaction can be classified in the CALL context as 'interaction between people', 'interaction between a person and the computer' and 'interaction within a person's mind' (Chapelle, 2003). Interaction between people can benefit L2 learning because it provides opportunities for negotiating meaning, participation and collaboration. The negotiation of meaning is 'an important factor for successful L2 acquisition' (Ellis, 1990, p. 16), and CMC enhances opportunities for meaning negotiation (Blake, 2000; Warner, 2004; see also Shekary and Tahririan, 2006; Yanguas, 2010).

It is suggested that computers not only provide students with the same opportunities as face-to-face interactions do but also produce more complex and accurate instances of language because the learners are allowed more time to reflect on and monitor their language as well as more access to the references (e.g. González-Bueno, 1998). This translates into their better *noticing* their utterances as well as their better capability to monitor their output. There is also evidence that CMC provides an ideal medium for students to benefit from interaction because the written nature of discussion fosters a focus on form as well as communicative interaction (Lamy and Goodfellow,

1999; Kern and Warschauer, 2000). Along the same lines, Peterson (1997) claims that CMC provides a non-threatening and less restrictive language environment such that learners have a 'free space' where they take control over the learning process (Cooper and Selfe, 1990, p. 857). Interaction between a learner and the machine actually promotes enhanced input while offering help for using language (for example, online dictionaries, glossaries, transcripts, grammar aids, etc.). Intrapersonal interaction provides learners with an opportunity to focus on linguistic forms as well as *deep thinking*, to enhance the process of input. A more social constructivist model of 'blended environments' is a recent trend, given its unique feature of combining both e-learning and face-to-face learning based on the same pedagogical approach (Wolff, 2003). Felix (2005) confirmed the Web as a viable environment for language learning, especially as an add-on to face-to-face teaching.

Students are engaged in more social aspects of the language when they work on an authentic task, and research suggests that computer-mediated tasks facilitate natural language use (Blake, 2000; Smith, 2004). In such learning environments, computer technologies also provide students with a context in which they can collaborate. This is especially true with Web 2.0 technologies (e.g. blogs, wikis and other social networking websites) and knowledge co-construction tools (e.g. computer-supported collaborative learning). The role of technology here is to create a social context where learners are able to use the language in social interactions. Technology becomes an environment where students use the language, the 'symbolic tool', to clarify and make sense of new knowledge, with their relying heavily on discussions with the 'expert knower'.

Output

If 'comprehensible input' and 'interaction' are the main criteria for language learning potential, linguistic output is almost as crucial as they are. Swain (1985) suggests that only when learners produce 'comprehensible output' can they realise what lexicogrammatical forms they do not yet master. Nagata (1998, p. 29) states that 'given the same grammatical instruction, output-focused practice is more effective than input-focused practice for the development of skills in producing Japanese honorifics and is equally effective for the comprehension of these structure'. The results support Swain's argument that 'there are roles for output in SLA that are independent of comprehensible input' (Swain, 1985, p. 34).

Jamieson et al. (2005) have pointed out that from the cognitive view, 'the benefits of producing language may be enhanced when learners have the opportunity to plan before speaking or writing and to correct linguistic output, which can be promoted by feedback from others or from self-evalua-tion' (p. 406). Computer-mediated communication provides such a planning opportunity for learners to notice their utterances. Swain (1995) identifies three functions of output – to notice the gap, to test learner hypotheses and 'to internalize linguistic knowledge' (p. 126). Leahy's study (2004) suggests that CALL serves well the first and the third of these functions.

Feedback

Feedback is an important element in second language learning. Ellis et al. (2002, p. 430) conclude 'there are strong theoretical reasons for claiming that the teacher's role in a communicative task should not be limited to that of a communicative partner. The teacher also needs to pay attention to form'. However, there are some problems with face-to-face feedback: for example, (1) feedback from the teacher can be inconsistent and unpredictable; (2) the teacher might find it difficult to realise the full range of feedback types; and (3) the teacher may sometimes be unwilling to encourage learner output during feedback due to time constraints or student embarrassment (Van den Branden, 1997).

Empirical research suggests that computers provide more consistent and individualised feedback (Tsutsui, 2004). Studies also suggest that natural language processors generate linguistic feedback (Coniam, 2004; Nagata, 2002), such as immediate individualised grammatical feedback (Nagata, 1993, 1997). The comprehensible meta-linguistic feedback is more effective than traditional feedback, and the students who receive the former perform much better on a post-test than those receiving no feedback (Nagata, 1993, 1997; see also Yang and Akahori, 1999). Pellettieri (2000) examined task-based, real-time computer interaction between adult learners of Spanish, finding that computer-mediated interaction helps learners achieve higher levels of meta-linguistic awareness with corrective feedback during meaning negotiation. This will be discussed further in Chapter 7.

An affective tool

The 'affective filter', posited by Dulay and Burt (1977), has a claim to being a very influential variable outside the language acquisition device. The 'filter' acts to facilitate or impede the delivery of input to the language acquisition device. Motivation, self-confidence and anxiety are all key affective variables which decide the degree and rate of second language learning.

Technologies in general are widely reported to engage and motivate learn-ers (Braine, 2004; Warschauer, 2000a). As Stockwell (2013) has pointed out in his comprehensive discussion of motivation and technology, there are two ways that technology can motivate or engage learners. First, there are learners who are motivated because they possess a genuine interest in technology, which promotes language learning through the use of computers and other electronic devices. Second, learners who are interested in language learning will take advantage of technology to enhance the learning process.

It is widely recognised in the CMC literature that electronic devices offer non-threatening and less restrictive language environments, which provide learners with spaces where they can take control. Research also suggests CALL feedback reduces embarrassment and psychological anxiety (Torlakovic and Deugo, 2004). The use of CMC also provides learners with opportunities to 'operate their agency'. For example, Warschauer (2000a) claims that 'agency is really what makes students so excited about using computers in the classroom: the computer provides them a powerful means to make their stamp on the world' (p. 65).

A mediational tool

In facilitating linguistic acquisition, technology is also used as a mediational tool. Mediation can be defined as the way in which people use 'culturally constructed artefacts, concepts and activities to regulate the material world or their own and each other's social and mental activity' (Lantolf and Thorne, 2006, p. 79). Language is considered the primary mediational tool relevant to thinking, learning and other cognitive development. Haas (1996) extends Vygotsky's idea of language as a psychological tool and proposes that the use of technologies is a new psychological tool which can mediate interaction between a user and the environment around him/her. The use of shared screens, images, music and other artefacts can enhance shared understandings and facilitate linguistic acquisition (Li, 2015).

Focus on motivation

The positive effects of CALL on students' motivation was one of the very early research foci of CALL. There is ample evidence that technology-enhanced language learning has a positive effect on students' confidence, motivation, learning opportunities and language output. Chun (1994), Kern (1995), Warschauer (1996a) and Brinton, (2001) for example, have highlighted the positive effects of computer-assisted classroom discussion (CACD), compared to face-to-face class discussion on university-level L2 students in the areas of opportunities to participate in discussion, their motivation and anxiety, turn-taking patterns and so on. These studies clearly report that CACD motivates student-initiated discussion more than teacher-initiated discussion while increasing the number of opportunities for students to produce more output regardless of their individual personality differences. Similarly, Beauvois (1994, 1998) and Beauvois and Eledge (1996) report extremely positive attitudes by intermediate French learners who perceived linguistic, affective and interpersonal benefits from their experiences of using CACD.

The positive effects of technology on affective factors in language learning is evidenced in different areas. In technology-mediated L2 writing classes, Warschauer (1996b) identified empowerment as one of the factors that motivated students, believing that CMC increases students' motivation by bringing a sense of achievement and enhancement of learning opportunities. In a similar vein, Jogan et al. (2001) reported positive evidence of an email exchange project between college students of advanced Spanish in the United States and college students of English in Chile. The email exchange motivated students to write about and learn about each other's cultures and, more importantly, to enjoy language learning.

Web-based assignments are reported to have positive effects on students' attitudes and their motivation to learn about the target language and culture, and much research has been conducted in this area, such as that by Osuna and Meskill (1998). Virtual learning environments are similar. Gruber-Miller and Benton (2001) used a MOO environment 'Vroma' to create a programme for students to gain virtual Rome experience and to be immersed in Latin language and culture simultaneously. The programme was found to be a satisfying, useful and motivating resource for learning Latin language and culture.

In all, studies of the effect of technology-enhanced learning have identified a broad range of benefits for students and teachers, including increased motivation, improvement of language skills, a better self-concept and reduced workload. The previous research showed the following:

1. Computers heighten pupil interest and enjoyment and are also regarded as one of the most important factors which have a positive effect upon the status of subjects.

2. Computers assist pupils in concentrating on their work and increase commitment to the learning tasks; therefore, the standard of work produced is assumed to have a higher quality than it would be otherwise.

3. Learning with computers provides pupils with opportunities to work in an open-ended way which enables them to become actively involved in the learning process rather than being a passive receiver.

4. Computers enhance the sense of achievement in learning.

5. Computer-assisted learning enhances self-esteem, which very likely leads to greater expectations of achieving long term goals.

Computer simulations that incorporate synchronous chat functions can also motivate language learners who would otherwise be intimidated by face-to-face interactions to participate more actively (Freiermuth, 2002; Ranalli, 2008). Furthermore, computer-assisted language learning can promote collaborative learning between learners in knowledge sharing and construction and can offer a more comfortable and less threatening environment than that provided by traditional classroom instruction and discussion (Dickson et al., 2008).

Summary

This chapter discusses the general benefits of technology in second language learning, in particularly in its role in promoting motivation. However, what this chapter presents is not an exhaustive list of the affordances of technology. There are specific roles in which technological tools can be explored in relation to teaching different linguistic skills and knowledge. This will be further discussed and illustrated in the following chapters, and we will focus on the development of interactional skills in Chapter 3.

Student project

Li (2004) investigated the impact of using web-based learning and the Internet on second language motivation in a Chinese social and cultural context. This study utilises mixed-methodology (a combination of qualitative and quantitative approaches) to investigate perceptions of 16/17-year-old learners and their English teachers. A questionnaire with 24 closed questions and nine ranking items investigated 174 participants' attitudes towards the English language and Western culture, to language learning and to the language learning environment, which comprises three levels of the motivation framework developed for this study. Then two four-student semi-open focus-group interviews and four individual interviews were conducted to probe their opinions on using ICT to assist their learning in depth and to find out which aspects motivated them. It was found that students from the computer group had more positive attitudes towards the English language and Western culture, to language learning and to the language learning environment than those from the non-computer group. Students from different groups have different ideas about the role that computer knowledge plays in affecting their motivation. Over 13 motivating aspects were proposed by both students and teachers, some of which were testified in the previous research. She suggests that use of computers also improves linguistic competence. Teachers' beliefs heavily influenced their decision making in classrooms, and testing system played crucial role as well.

Annotated further reading

1. Stepp-Greany, J. (2002) Student perceptions on language learning in a technological environment: Implications for the new millennium. *Language Learning & Technology*, 6(1), 165–180.

   This article presents survey data from beginner Spanish classes using a combination of technologies: Internet activities, CD-ROMs, electronic pen pals and threaded discussions. It focuses on exploring students' perceptions of (a) the role and importance of the instructor in technology-enhanced language learning (TELL), (b) the accessibility and relevance of the lab and the individual technological components in student learning and (c) the effects of the technology on the foreign language learning experiences. Students attributed an important role to instructors and perceived that cultural knowledge, listening and reading skills, and independent learning skills were enhanced, but they were divided in their perceptions about the learning or interest values of the individual components.

2. Li, L. (2015) What's the use of technology? Insights from EFL classrooms in Chinese secondary schools, in C. Jenks and P. Seedhouse (eds), *International Perspectives on Classroom Interaction* (pp. 168–187). Basingstoke: Palgrave Macmillan.

   This chapter provides an overview of the role of technology in second language learning and episodes where technological tools are used in facilitating language learning in five Chinese classrooms. It links theory to classroom practice.

3. Reinders, H. & Hubbard, P. (2013) CALL and Learner Autonomy: Affordances and Constraints, in M. Thomas, H. Reinders and M. Warschauer (eds), *Contemporary Computer-Assisted Language Learning*. New York: Continuum.

   This chapter reviews the role of learner autonomy in language learning and teaching and outlines the potential affordances offered by technology in its development. It highlights ways in which technology poses constraints on this development and suggests ways in which these can be overcome. The authors argue for a potentially symbiotic relationship between the fields of autonomy and CALL, which has important practical benefits for learning and teaching.

Part B

Technology, Language Skills and Knowledge, and ESP

3   Technology and developing interactional skills

Aims: This chapter considers the use of technology in facilitating teaching and developing interactional skills. In particular, it examines how to teach speaking, listening and interactional competence (IC) and considers various technological tools to enhance fluency, accuracy and interactional competence. Examples and case studies are offered to link language and technology, especially the use of podcasts, web-based programmes and CMC. This chapter has two main sections, as follows:

1. Developing speaking and listening

2. Focus on developing interactional competence.

Introduction

Interactional skills, involving speaking and listening, are probably the most important language skills for a learner. Why is that? First of all, language is a tool for communication, and people learn a language in order to communicate. One conveys and responds ideas through interaction. That is, in a conversation, the interpretations of other's utterances and comprehension of ideas and the negotiation of meanings are carried out through interaction. Second, there is a strong link between interaction and learning, and language plays a mediational role in learning (Vygotsky, 1978); in other words, all learning requires language, the basic 'tool' which underpins or 'mediates' the learning process. To this end, interaction is central to learning. When learning a language, interaction can be viewed as a channel for learning, a space in which to learn and also the learning outcome. Drawing on the theoretical underpinnings of interactional competence, this chapter provides readers with hands-on examples of how technology can (should) be used in promoting communicative skills. First, this chapter discusses relevant theories and principles of developing interactional skills, focusing specifically on speaking, listening and IC. In the following sections, I will present how technology can enhance the development of these skills.

Developing speaking and listening skills

Traditionally, speaking and listening have been considered as two separate skills. However, in real-life interactions, we know that speaking and listening are closely related. Speaking skills should be viewed as incorporating listening skills, a view proposed by Hodges et al. (2012, p. 502), who refer to 'languaging' as 'the actual speaking and listening to others'. So it makes sense to consider teaching these two skills together, but perhaps with a particular emphasis on each in an activity. Here, I will discuss ideas focusing on speaking and listening separately.

Focus on speaking

> **Task 3.1:** Issues in developing speaking skills
>
> Developing speaking skills is probably the goal of most EFL language classrooms. Can you see any difficulties (problems) that EFL learners have? Why do some learners speak more than others in speaking-practice activities?

In general, many language learners find that **speaking and listening skills** are difficult to develop. Difficulties lie in the following areas:

- Students are not confident with their speaking and listening skills, because teaching and learning in their contexts usually focus on grammar, vocabulary, reading and writing. In these cases, accuracy is more important. Students therefore feel worried about speaking in public because they might make mistakes.

- Learners sometimes have difficulty in finding something to say. Even if they are able to say something, they may have nothing to say in response to a particular question or topic.

- Learners might find it difficult to express their opinions due to language barriers, and they might struggle to understand each other.

- Learners might rely on their L1 in interaction.

Speaking and writing are productive skills because learners need to produce language to do them. They can be contrasted with the receptive or passive skills of listening and reading.

- Speaking requires performance, and learners may feel exposed.

- Some learners are more dominant in class, while others are reticent.

- In a large class, it may not be possible for all learners to take part.

- Tasks do not provoke discussion.

Some difficulties that learners face are to do with vocabulary size and grammar knowledge, but more often, when we consider teaching speaking, we examine the difficulties that students might have in achieving fluency and accuracy.

Fluency

Speaking occurs spontaneously and requires immediate responses in real time, so producing spoken language can be time constraining (Wang and Acero, 2006). Speaking can be influenced by cognitive, linguistic and affective factors, and using language forms correctly is critical for L2 oral proficiency (Saunders and O'Brien, 2006). The literature on fluency is, unsurprisingly, extensive yet 'replete with vacuous definitions' (Hieke, 1985, p. 135). There seems to be no common view on what fluency is, but drawing together the relevant literature, McCarthy (2010) has proposed four themes in researching and teaching fluency.

The first theme is speech rate and delivery. Research suggests that a fluent learner can deliver more words than a less fluent learner in a given time frame (e.g. Kormos and Dénes, 2004; Rossiter, 2009). However, using delivery rate alone to measure fluency does not tell the whole story, because the delivery rate depends largely on context, speech genre topic and also the interlocutor's responses. What is worth mentioning here is the existence of pauses. Pauses occur frequently in natural interaction and can be viewed as a space for thinking, rehearsal and understanding. The second theme is automaticity, which addresses the automatic retrieval of words and fixed expressions. This contributes to smooth performance and normally paced delivery. Being able to use language chunks can greatly reduce retrieval and processing time (Conklin and Schmitt, 2008). Learners who are able to use language chunks appropriately demonstrate more communicative efficiency and oral proficiency in the L2 context (Boers et al., 2006). Both speech rate and automaticity are connected to the view that language fluency is a mono-logic affair, which can be achieved and managed by the speaker on their own. However, in real-life contexts, fluency is not just one speaker's demonstration but an outcome of a collaborative effort between interlocutors. Fluency is also measured by turn management (e.g. turning-taking, -holding, -giving). Therefore, other aspects of fluency research emphasise the social nature of it. The third theme relates to professional perceptions of fluency and implications for professional practitioners such as teachers, curriculum designers and examiners (Derwing et al., 2004; Kormos and Dénes, 2004). The fourth theme addresses perceptions of fluency by non-professionals and their real-world implications, such as the general public, employers (actual and potential) and social peer groups. In the third and fourth thematic areas, fluency is viewed in the social contexts in relation to other interlocutors.

In examining fluency in teaching, we probably need to look at the broad meaning of fluency as an ability 'to express oneself intelligibly, reasonably accurately and without too much hesitation' (Byrne, 1986, p. 9). This includes such features as

- learners' initiating a topic/discussion and taking part in this freely;
- learners' demonstrating responsibility in topic change and turn management;
- learners' imitating less and initiating more;
- learners' using interactional strategies to negotiate meaning, seek clarification and engage in collaboration;
- learners' listening skills needing to be integrated into developing speaking skills;
- learners' using language chunks.

Then how can technology be used to enhance fluency? We will explore a few tools next to discuss some affordances of technology in developing fluency.

CMC

Like a face-to-face conversation, computer-mediated communication (CMC) takes place in real-time interactions in which users negotiate meaning through either verbal or written language. When talking about CMC, many would think about synchronous text-based computer-mediated communication (StCMC), such as text-based chat rooms (Jenks, 2009). As argued by other researchers, multi-participant StCMC is linguistically and interactionally unique because participation and contribution become quite complex to investigate (Abrams, 2003; Lotherington and Xu, 2004; Simpson, 2005; Jenks, 2009) and possibly difficult to use to teach interactional strategies. However, text-based chat rooms do offer learners a space to communicate in real-life and can raise learner motivation in learning a language. Consequently, language teachers and learners rely on CMC to increase participation and enhance learning (e.g. Kung, 2004; Yamada and Akahori, 2007). With the development of technology, it has become possible for teachers and learners to use voice-based or even video-based CMC. In the written format, interlocutors communicate online by typing a message to each other. In the voice/video format, interlocutors communicate the same way as face-to-face interaction through software such as Skype, with audio and video enabled. During online communication, learners are expected to input, feedback and interact in a way similar to what they would experience in face-to-face interaction. Because of the similarity of voice/video-based communication with face-to-face interaction, the turn-taking is less disrupted and messy. Research has been done in this area to show how participants manage their turns and how they learn using voice-based communication (e.g. Jenks, 2009, 2014). It is believed the similarity of **SVCMC** to face-to-face communication may prepare students better for the challenge of real-life oral communication.

....

SVCMC is also called audiographic conferencing (see e.g. Hampel, 2003; Hampel and Hauck, 2004).

....

A growing body of research has explored the benefits of SVCMC on language learning. There are at least five areas in which learners might benefit. First, the use of synchronous discussion enhances language skills and improves oral proficiency (Hampel, 2003; Satar and Özdener, 2008; Yang and Chang, 2008). Second, SVCMC reduces students' anxiety levels (Satar and Özdener, 2008) and motivates learners (Pellettieri, 2000; Hampel, 2003). Third, students are more willing to participate and make an effort because the tasks are more challenging than those in traditional learning environments (Rosell-Aguilar, 2005). Fourth, SVCMC provides enhanced input. Because the input is relevant to individual learners and around their competence level, the likelihood of input uptake is higher. For example, an interlocutor might notice how other participants use particular vocabulary and construct sentences (St. John and Cash, 1995; Sauro and Smith, 2010; Smith, 2012). Finally, because students are engaged in real-life communication, they use significantly more repair moves, especially pronunciation-related repair moves (Jepson, 2005; Alastuey, 2010) and initiate more self-repair (Yamada, 2009), thus improving their pronunciation.

Going back to the factors accounting for the difficulty in developing speaking skills, I will further examine how CMC can contribute to developing these skills. Some of the pedagogical purposes that teachers might have for using SVCMC are as follows:

- SVCMC can be used to promote oral proficiency in distance learning.

- It can be used to conduct cross-culture, project-based learning where students from different cultures work on a project together. This might be similar to some work of telecollaboration. Project-based learning can be set up between learners of similar age in two different learning environments, such as Spain and China.

- It can be used with learners from the same class as a complementary after-school oral practice – the teacher helps to set up topics. This could be considered a virtual 'English corner'.

In the literature, various factors have been reported to be influential in using SVCMC. After having reviewed the research evidence, I now outline six conditions for success.

Condition 1: Teachers need to know how the technological tools, software and applications work. When there is a problem on the technical side, such as an interruption of audio transmission or Internet disconnection, the teacher should be able to help solve the problem. Remember that 'the technology requires a certain degree of technical expertise' (Hampel and Hauck, 2004: 69), therefore it might be a good idea to provide students with adequate support and training. If necessary, technical support should be available during the chat.

Condition 2: Everyone involved must have a good Internet connection. Research suggests that bandwidth can be a serious issue in implementing SVCMC (Wang, 2004).

Condition 3: Developing communication must be the pedagogical purpose. If the focus is on fluency, then it might generate sufficient interest among students to participate in using SVCMC.

Condition 4: Students must have a certain level of proficiency that is required for the task.

Condition 5: The task itself must be collaborative and appropriate to students' interests and cognitive level.

Condition 6: Ground rules must be established, including the role of L1. It should be used to assist in, but not complete, the task.

Skype, one form of SVCMC, has been used in classes at various levels, providing many possibilities for teaching and learning (Blankenship, 2011). In particular, Skype facilitates language tandem exchange in which 'two people of different mother tongues collaborate in the learning of each other's language' (Elia, 2006, p. 271). It allows language learners to start language exchanges wherever they can connect to the Internet. Apart from talking to each other, participants can also share files or screen shots.

Task 3.2: Using Skype

Amy has 45 students in her class, and she divides her students into nine groups of five. She suggests that students meet twice a week to discuss selected topics from her list. Amy drafts her discussion list every week, including topics such as sports, politics, health and entertainment. Here is how she set up the virtual English corner:

1. All students download and install Skype.
2. Each group sets up a group account complying with the following instructions:
    i.   In Skype, click the + New icon under your profile picture.
    ii. Type the name of a contact you would like to add.
    iii. When you find a contact you want to add, click on them and click Add.
3. Each group meets and discusses topics from Amy's list.
4. The group finishes by the end of term 1, and new groups are set up in term 2 so that everyone can have a chance to speak to other people.

Now, consider this example of using Skype video chat. What pedagogical thinking is behind Amy's design of the virtual English corner? And what methods can you use to help students to actively take part in this activity?

The appearance of *Skype in the classroom*, a website for learners worldwide to share information, has expanded the potential of using Skype for language teaching and learning. Mystery Skype is a fun global guessing game that gets students learning about geography, culture and the similarities and differences of how children live all over the world. It is a fun activity where two classrooms can be connected through technology. It is simple to join and start:

1. Register at https://education.microsoft.com/connectwithothers/play mysteryskype.

2. Find a classroom to play with (you can narrow down your selection by age group, country, subject and language).

3. Connect and start the guessing game.

The pedagogical thinking behind using Mystery Skype is to provide children with opportunities to use language in real-life situations. It also gives them an opportunity to work as a team to win the game. It is a challenge which motivates learners to use their knowledge about culture, geography and history to solve a mystery when they use English to communicate. The questions that students pose to each other can vary: for example, they could ask direct questions like 'Are you in the United States?' to narrow down based on country. Then they can design a set of questions to figure out where exactly their partner is, by asking questions like 'Do you have dry weather?' This encourages creativity and openness. Students can learn beyond four walls and use language to communicate and solve a problem. They can share information about their school life once they work out each other's location. Language fluency can be naturally developed in such an activity.

Accuracy

Focusing on developing fluency does not mean that accuracy is not important. Compared with native speakers, it is harder for EFL learners to use accurate pronunciation, grammar and vocabulary (Bygate, 2005). Therefore, for many language learners, fostering accuracy in fluency-oriented activities is very important in developing speaking competence. In a meaning-oriented activity, students are able to focus on form in a real-life activity.

The fluency-oriented task can be used to raise awareness of the accurate use of language. This principle is extremely relevant to young learners due to their limited linguistic knowledge. For young learners whose spoken English perhaps is not advanced enough to participate in a free discussion on a topic, creating a speaking avatar is a useful way to help them practise the language. Voki is a website (www.voki.com) that allows students to create speaking avatars (see Figure 3.1). A task can be designed to focus on fluency or accuracy, or even both.

There are four steps to making a speaking avatar:

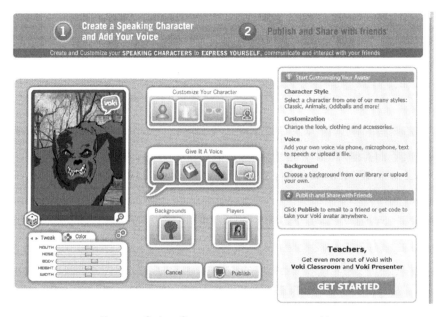

FIGURE 3.1   CREATING AN AVATAR USING VOKI

1. Register an account on www.voki.com

2. Choose a character and customise it by changing the look, clothing and accessories.

3. Add your own voice via phone, microphone or text to speech or by uploading a file.

4. Publish it by emailing it to a friend or getting a code to take your Voki avatar anywhere.

Task 3.3: An example of using Voki

In my class, I showed a group of learners how to make Voki and asked them to play a game of who's who? as a follow-up speaking activity. Each student chose a famous historical figure/celebrity to research. Then they created a Voki and turned it into the person they had selected, but without stating the name of the character that they were portraying. The student then presented their Voki, asking the class to guess who the character was.

   Invite your colleagues to participate in this game, and you can follow the steps and create a Voki. What potential advantages does Voki have in fostering accuracy in this meaning-oriented activity?

The design of the above task is based on the assumption that a meaning-oriented activity provides students with more opportunities to speak, and a repeated similar task gives students a space to notice the form, which fosters accuracy. First of all, because this task is designed for a consolidation purpose and carried out after class, students will have sufficient time to plan the speaking content and its related vocabulary. Second, this task helps learners improve both fluency and accuracy. Voki also gives students the opportunity to play back their speech and notice any language errors. Finally, the repeated task motivates students and may ease their anxiety of speaking in public without preparation.

An integrated approach

Although fluency and accuracy is discussed separately above, it make sense that both are developed in a speaking lesson. Goh (2007) proposes a four-stage model extending fluency tasks to focus on accuracy: (1) pre-speaking support in vocabulary and knowledge; (2) mainly developing learners' fluency; (3) language-focused activity – learners' awareness of the accurate use of the language is enhanced; and (4) further practice – by means of task repetition, learners can develop fluent and accurate speech. When a speaking lesson is designed, an integrated approach should consist of four stages, with each stage focusing on either fluency or accuracy (see Figure 3.2).

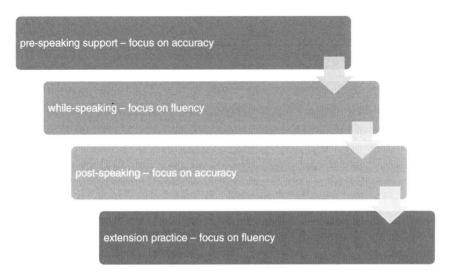

FIGURE 3.2   A FLOW MAP OF AN INTEGRATED APPROACH
TO FOCUS ON FLUENCY AND ACCURACY

Pre-speaking support (with a focus on accuracy)

Pre-speaking support gives learners enough time to plan, offers them some support in language as well as knowledge (Skehan, 1996) and can let learners achieve greater accuracy (Skehan and Foster, 1999) and increased fluency (Yuan and Ellis, 2003). Pre-speaking support can be offered through (1) pre-task planning, (2) pre-speaking support and (3) authentic input.

Without any preparation before speaking, learners find it very challenging to handle all the speaking processes of conceptualisation, formulation and articulation simultaneously. Therefore, learners should be given enough time to plan what to say and how to say it. In addition, pre-speaking support is vital to ease anxiety. Some related vocabulary and background information enables learners to generate more ideas, and certain speaking strategies help to deal with possible breakdowns in conversation with such a 'supportive and constructive classroom environment' (Horwitz, 2001, p. 119). Finally, authentic input (e.g. film) motivates learners as they are exposed to sufficient 'authentic resources'. In this authentic exposure, learners can easily transfer 'from comprehension (input) to expression (output)' (Tschirner, 2001, p. 312).

In providing pre-speaking support, efforts can be made to give opportunities to students to explore vocabulary associated with a topic. Here are some ideas that use technology to support speaking activities:

- Exploring vocabulary: students can be advised to use an online application to collect vocabulary associated with a topic. One such application is Visuwords, a web-based visual dictionary and thesaurus tool. Students can

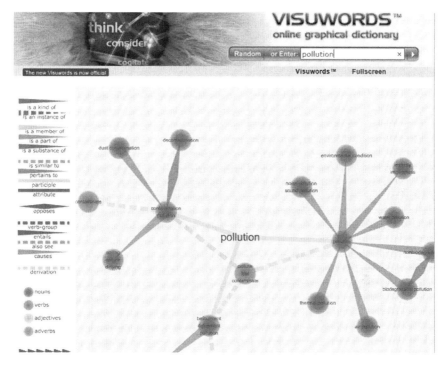

FIGURE 3.3   DEVELOPING VOCABULARY USING VISUWORDS

search for words and look up their meanings and associations with other words in a visual interface. Figure 3.3 displays what Visuwords renders when 'pollution' is searched for: words and phrases associated with it are revealed.

- Developing a mind map or structure for the speaking activity: when students are given a topic to speak about, they can work collaboratively to develop a mind map about the topic. This can be done using technological tools, such as bubbl.us (Figure 3.4). There are some advantages to using online software to develop a mind map: (1) it can be selected and included in different documents that students are working on; (2) it can be exported, or a different mind map can be imported to the one that students are working on; (3) the mind map can be shared in other social networks or referred to during the speaking activity.

While-speaking activity

Due to limited attentional capacity, it might be difficult to focus on both fluency and accuracy equally at the same time. Therefore, fluency should be the focus of while-speaking activities whereas accuracy (language form) can be emphasised afterwards (Willis, 2005).

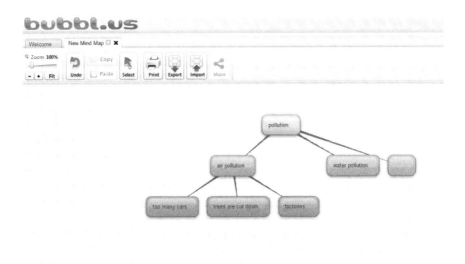

FIGURE 3.4   DEVELOPING A MIND MAP FOR A SPEAKING ACTIVITY

Goh (2007) proposes three types of speaking tasks to develop fluency:

1. information-gap tasks: learners exchange information/ideas to bridge the gap;

2. problem-solving tasks: learners solve problems collaboratively;

3. social monologues: learners are offered many opportunities to talk on a given topic.

While-speaking tasks should be built on pre-speaking activities. In this way, learners reduce the time pressure and cognitive load (McLaughlin and Heredia, 1996) and thus increase their speaking fluency (Wood, 2001, 2004; Zhou and Wang, 2007). Task 3.4 below describes an example of how a while-speaking activity is developed from pre-speaking activities.

Task 3.4: Mind maps

After students have collected sufficient materials and developed their own mind map on the given topic, such as *pollution and its solutions*, I ask students to bring their mind map to class to talk in a small group and make a pitch to each other. Then students are required to work together to produce a different mind map collaboratively on the topic based on their discussion. Then each group makes a presentation to the whole class.

Repeat the activity above with your colleagues. Record your discussion and analyse how the use of mind maps help learners develop fluency and accuracy.

Post-speaking activities

Both fluency and accuracy can be focused on in post-speaking activities, such as offering language-focused activities and providing corrective feedback. Self-repair also helps learners to focus on the correct use of the language form (Lyster and Ranta, 1997; Gilabert, 2007). It is not sufficient for learners to use the language alone; instead, they need to analyse and evaluate their output (Lazaraton, 2001) and correct their own mistakes in the language use in order to become independent learners (Bygate and Samuda, 2005). However, if the feedback or self-repair opportunities are given *after* speaking activities, some errors may go unnoticed. To overcome this, recordings can be used to facilitate self-correction, peer feedback and corrective feedback from instructors.

- Students can transcribe their own speech so that they notice incorrect use of language (Burns et al., 1997); thus 'higher rates of accuracy' in terms of pronunciation, grammar and vocabulary can be achieved (Lynch, 2007, p. 311).

- Students obtain corrective feedback from their instructor (Larsen-Freeman, 2001, p. 37). The teacher then listens to the tapes one by one and gives responses individually, which is more specific and detailed than commenting generally to the whole class.

- Learners can provide each other with feedback.

Extension practice

In developing proficiency in speaking, extension practice needs to be implemented through **task repetition**. Task repetition can be talking on the same topic to different persons, asking different people about a similar question or using the same materials to communicate more than once (Bygate and Samuda, 2005). Task repetition might be considered dull in some cases, but for EFL learners, it provides an opportunity to consolidate what has been learnt and to perform with less cognitive load (Bygate, 2005). Repeating tasks can also help learners make 'fewer errors' (Bygate, 1996, p. 138) and achieve 'greater fluency' (Ellis, 2005, p. 18). So task repetition can be useful and should be incorporated in EFL teaching when both fluency and accuracy are trying to be achieved (Bygate, 2001; Lynch and Maclean, 2001). The extension practice should encourage students to produce extended responses, which means that an explanatory and argumentative task is desired. For example, the above task

> Task repetition is "the repetition of the same or slightly altered tasks whether whole tasks, or parts of a task" (Bygate and Samuda, 2005, p. 43).

Mailvu: mailvu.com/index.htm
Recording and emailing 10 minute
videos from webcam is as easy as
Click, Record, Send. You only need a
webcam, and Adobe Flash version 10
or higher in your browser.

during while-speaking activity can be further repeated after class. Consider the following two options:

1. The same group of students work together to discuss another similar topic and to come up with a group mind map and presentation. Because it is not necessarily easy for students to meet after class, the discussion and plan can happen online, such as by using Skype to discuss their topic and using bubbl.us to develop the mind map. The final presentation can be recorded as a podcast and submitted to the teacher, who can put all the presentations on their class blog for students to comment on.

2. Based on what students have done in class, individuals now work on their own to give a three-to-five-minute speech about the topic. The speech should be addressed to their peers using the online software **Mailvu**, which is also available for mobile phones. Then after recording the speech, the student needs to send it to another student and the teacher for feedback.

Task 3.5: Pedagogical thinking

Consider the two tasks I have described above for extension practice. What pedagogical thinking is behind the design of the two tasks? Which one would you prefer to use in your own context, and why?

Focus on listening

Listening is a process of receiving what a speaker actually says (receptive orientation); constructing and representing meaning (constructive orientation); negotiating meaning with the speaker and responding (collaborative orientation); and creating meaning through involvement, imagination and empathy (transformative orientation) (Rost, 2002). Therefore, listening is a complex, active process of interpretation in which listeners match what they hear with what they already know. Listeners must discriminate between sounds, understand vocabulary and grammatical structures, interpret stress and intention, and retain and interpret this within the immediate as well as the larger sociocultural context of the utterance (Wipf, 1984).

Listening and reading are receptive
skills because learners do not need to
produce language; people receive and
understand it. Because learners are
taking a passive role when listening
and reading, these skills are also
known as passive skills.

Listening is important but challenging because 'it internalizes the rules of language and facilitates the emergence of other language skills' (Vandergrift, 2011, p. 455). Listening is also considered the most difficult language skill to learn because of its temporal nature and the special features of spoken language (Lynch, 2009; Vandergrift, 2011). In recent years, many efforts have been made to research how to teach this important skill well (Field, 2008; Vandergrift, 2011).

Task 3.6: Listening is difficult

When I started at university in the early 1990s, we had a mock TOEFL exam. The only thing I remember about that test is that a lot of students finished the listening comprehension section before the actual recording was finished. It was not because they were very good; it was because they had no clue what was being said and because they had problems keeping up with the recording. In fact, for many of the students, it was a pretty difficult listening activity despite having learnt English for six years.

Now think about why is listening difficult for a EFL learner? And what kind of skills are required for adequate comprehension?

You might have worked out a few difficulties that every learner might face, but broadly speaking, problems occur in three main areas:

1. The content: listeners might have difficulty in understanding and following the content. First of all, listeners cannot predict what is to be said and might have no contextual or content knowledge about the topic. Second, the content is usually not as well organised as a piece of written text. Third, irrelevant information might be included in the materials. And finally, the speed of delivery might cause problems. Some listening materials are difficult to follow by listeners because they cannot be slowed down to the speed that is appropriate for learners' preference.

2. Linguistic features: listeners might find it difficult to distinguish individual words and therefore miss the key focus of the message. First, some elision and linking words are present to enable the smooth flow of the speech, but listeners might have difficulties in recognising these linguistic features because they are used to recognising each word when they read in a foreign language. Second, colloquial expressions and slang are frequently used in less formal listening materials. Third, spoken materials might be considered ungrammatical.

3. The physical environment: background noise or lack of extralinguistic knowledge could impede understanding. First, the recording might

contain background noise: for example, if the recording is about daily life, it might contain relevant noise from the actual environment. Second, the lack of facial expressions and gestures might cause misunderstanding of the message. Without the help of these extralinguistic features, listeners might have difficulty deciphering what the speaker really means.

Of course, there are also factors around the listener, such as his or her own life experience, vocabulary and personal confidence.

Listening activities are traditionally classified as bottom-up and top-down activities. In real-life listening, students have to use a combination of these two processes, but in many language classrooms, teachers like their students to practise these two processes separately as the skills involved are quite different. The bottom-up process starts with identifying sounds or lexical items according to their linguistic function. The activities focus on phonological, lexical and grammatical knowledge, and the key idea here is decoding. The top-down process focuses on the listener as active and assumes that he or she will bring contextual, content and co-text knowledge to the process of listening. The focus is placed on understanding the general idea of the discourse and the speaker's purpose for communicating. A listener is supposed to use schemata to infer the contextual information from the heard speech or conversation. The activities are designed to help learners develop their pragmatic and discourse knowledge, with a focus on meaning rather than form.

Despite the differences in the two processes, it is important to understand the purposes of a listening text. Richards (1990) differentiates between an interactional and a transactional purpose for communication. Interactional use of language is two-way communication and involves interaction between people, whereas transactional use of language is more message oriented and is used to convey information from one speaker to another, such as announcements and broadcasting.

Then what about skills? What kind of skills are involved in a listening activity? Willis (1981, p. 134) lists a series of micro-skills, which she calls enabling skills:

- predicting what people are going to talk about;

- guessing the meaning of unknown words or phrases without panicking;

- using one's own knowledge of the subject to help one understand more clearly;

- identifying relevant points; rejecting irrelevant information;

- retaining relevant points (notetaking, summarising);

- recognising discourse markers – *well*; *oh, another thing is*; *now, finally* and so on;

- recognising cohesive devices, such as *which*, linking words, pronouns, references and so on;

- understanding different intonation patterns and uses of stress and so on, which give clues to meaning and the social setting;

- understanding inferred information, such as the speakers' attitudes or intentions.

Having understood the potential difficulties that a learner might face in a listening activity, we will examine how technology can be used to facilitate the development of listening skills.

Podcasts and vodcasts

Podcasts are audio clips on the Internet in MP3 format. They can be downloaded, and links to resources can be sent in emails. Podcasts can be made and used on a wide range of devices, including computers, tablets, MP3 players, mobile phones and some games consoles. They can be played using a variety of software applications on these devices when they are produced using standard formats. For technical aspects of podcasting, see Borja (2005) and Campbell (2005).

Research proves that technology promotes the development of listening skills (Merler, 2000). Since 2005, there have been rapid advances in **podcasts**, digital audio programmes on the Internet. Indeed, many researchers have pointed out the benefits that podcasting can offer language education, especially with regard to developing learners' listening and speaking skills (Stanley, 2006). Constantine (2007) explained the importance of using podcasts in the L2 classroom:

Even at the beginning levels, learners can benefit from global listening even if they only listen from three to five minutes a day. Beginning students will be exposed to the new language. … The intermediate learner has a need for authentic texts and to be exposed to a variety of voices. By the time learners reach the advanced stage, they must be able to learn from listening. (pp. 1–2)

What makes podcasting unique is its capacity for 'subscription': through an RSS (really simple syndication) feed, which means listeners can 'subscribe' to their favourite podcasts. Once new episodes have been posted, they will receive 'alerts'.

Podcasts can generally be classified as 'radio podcasts' and 'independent podcasts'. Radio podcasts are existing radio programmes turned into podcasts, such as those produced by the BBC (British Broadcasting Corporation) while 'independent podcasts' are web-based podcasts produced by individuals and organisations. Both types have huge potential for teaching listening. The second type can be made by teachers and learners to tailor to the needs of learners (Stephens, 2007; Harris and Park, 2008). In ELT, there are teacher podcasts and student podcasts. The former are designed for teachers to reach out and provide students materials for more practice after class. These podcasts are also designed to motivate and engage learners. The student podcasts are those created by learners, which give students opportunities to develop materials for real-life audiences and also work collaboratively.

Podcasts have many benefits for enhancing listening:

1. Authentic materials are used to engage learners.

2. A wide range of possibilities exist for extra listening, both inside and outside of the classroom: 'Supplementing the (often) scripted and stilted textbook listenings with the real life authentic conversations you can find on many podcasts is an attractive option for language teachers. … Chosen carefully, extracts can … bring a range of different voices and varieties of English into the classroom' (Stanley, 2006, para. 1 under 'Authentic listening extracts').

3. They can be tailored to individual learning needs and styles. Students can work at their own pace. This can also address issues in a mixed ability class.

4. They motivate students to become more engaged with learning.

5. They promote collaborative work between students when those students produce podcasts together.

6. They provide students with a space to work with language.

7. A large amount of practice is enabled.

8. They address the issue of large class size.

9. They encourage more inter-school projects.

10. The use of podcasts challenges the traditional approach to teaching listening, known as the comprehensive approach (CA), as CA mainly focuses on testing comprehension rather than teaching listening skills (Vandergrift, 2011; Field, 2008; Flowerdew and Miller, 2005).

How do you make a podcast?

What do you need to create a podcast? There are three steps you need to follow:

1. Think of a *topic* to podcast.

2. *Make a recording* using a digital voice recorder (or possibly a good mobile phone) or a microphone that plugs into your laptop or computer (USB mics or mics on headsets are probably the best) and software to record with.

3. *Edit* the recording using software, or change the format if needed (some devices will record to MP3 and others to WAV or WMV). If desired, sound can be included as 'sound effects'. Audacity is good and free software for editing recordings.

You can also record to PowerPoint slides, though strictly speaking, this is less podcasting and more multimedia webcasting – but still very effective. Other materials like transcripts and visual images can also be provided in podcasts. Video podcasts are also known as vodcasts or podclips. Vodcasts can help expand topics that require displaying images (Corl et al., 2008, p. 26).

The length of the podcast needs to be taken into consideration, as students may find it difficult to be focused for a long period without any visual support. Usually, the length of the podcast should be about *three to five minutes*, roughly the length of a typical song. It is always a good idea to get students involved in making podcasts. Student podcasts can be created after registering an account for the whole class with a free podcasting site (e.g. podomatic.com/). The class can share the same username and password and upload their podcasts to the site on their own. However, the teacher needs to think clearly about the tasks for the podcasts.

Task 3.7: Traditions and festivals

Traditions and festivals carry cultural values and norms. Choose a topic on traditions and festivals to create a podcast. Together, create two activities for enhancing listening skills. Bear in mind the level of your learners.

Alternatively, you can ask students to work in groups to make podcasts and then create a blog for the class to host podcasts (e.g. wordpress.com). Also, design some listening tasks for each podcast.

Zanón (2006) classifies subtitles under three categories: (1) bimodal: from English dialogues to English subtitles; (2) standard: from English dialogues to subtitles in the learners' mother tongue, and (3) reversed subtitling: from dialogues in the learners' mother tongue to English subtitles. However, there is ongoing debate on which type is more beneficial for second language learners and more research needs to be done in this area.

Captioned video

L2 listeners must learn to cope with genuine speech and authentic listening situations. Multimedia materials are more useful than traditional paper-based instruction because videos provide visual, contextual and nonverbal input. Captions have also proved to be the most useful and efficient auxiliary for watching videos (Hsu, 1994), and authentic videos are considered to be good listening resources.

Research suggests audiovisual materials with **subtitles** are powerful pedagogical tools that are believed to help improve L2 listening and reading comprehension skills (Park, 2004; Stewart and Pertusa, 2004; Winke et al., 2010). Markham (1999) found 'positive evidence concerning the influence of second language captions directly on second-language listening' (p. 326). This is especially true when the input is slightly beyond their linguistic ability (Bird and Williams, 2002; Danan, 2004). In this regard, Danan (2004) makes an explicit observation:

> Audiovisual material enhanced with captions or interlingual subtitles is a particularly powerful pedagogical tool which can help improve the listening comprehension skills of second-language learners. Captioning facilitates language learning by helping students visualize what they hear, especially if the input is not too far beyond their linguistic ability. Subtitling can also increase language comprehension and leads to additional cognitive benefits, such as greater depth of processing. (p. 67)

Movies with subtitles are one of the effective tools in English language teaching and learning. Subtitles help to increase learners' attention, reduce anxiety and increase motivation. For example, Danan (2004) and Markham (2001) suggested more successful language learners seemed better able to process information through reading subtitles. Moreover, videos with subtitles, as opposed to those without, aid novel vocabulary recognition (Winke et al., 2010).

Videos (e.g. YouTube) which, if they don't already contain subtitles, can easily have subtitles added by teachers and curriculum developers using software such as Adobe Premier, iMovie or ViewPoint. The videos with subtitles can be used in online foreign language courses or blended learning (e.g. Sanders, 2005; Chenoweth et al., 2006; Scida and Saury, 2006). For example, Gunderson, et al. (2011) show how same language subtitling has been a success in promoting literacy and reading through this simple and effective method.

Tschirner (2001) argued that DVDs provide learners with multimodal representations that may give them access to oral communication both visually and aurally, and they make the classroom conditions similar to specific cultural environments. Zanón (2006) tested the efficiency of the use of the TV series Stargate for learning pragmatics in the EFL context to find that the use of TV series may enhance pragmatic skills when accompanied by explicit instruction. Equally, Perez Basanta and Rodriguez Martin (2006) argue there is a value for using film discourse because it mimics face-to-face communication and thus provides the contextual features of everyday conversation. So when students are presented with multimodal materials, they are able to use more than one semiotic modality – for example, language, gestures, movement, visual images, sound and so on – in order to produce text-specific meaning in the meaning making process (Tschirner, 2001, p. 311). However, Sert (2009) cautions that there are many variables in selecting appropriate DVDs in language classrooms, like the proficiency level of students, the age of students, the target interactional skills to be taught, curricular considerations, the genre and the sociocultural backgrounds of the learners. Therefore, for teachers, assessing the suitability of multimodal materials has become a challenging task. We will discuss more about evaluating materials in Chapter 8.

Case study 3.1: *The impact of subtitles*

Case study 1: Hayati and Mohmedi (2011) examined the efficacy of subtitled movies on the listening comprehension of 90 intermediate English learners. They used six episodes (approximately five minutes each) of a DVD entitled *Wild Weather*. Participants were divided into three groups with one of these three procedures: English subtitles, Persian subtitles or no subtitles. The results of six sets of multiple-choice tests revealed that the English subtitles group performed better than the Persian subtitles group, which in turn performed at a substantially higher level than the no subtitles group.

Case study 2: Yuksel and Tanriverdi (2009) examined the effectiveness of captions on listening comprehension with a group of 120 intermediate-level language learners. Students were randomly divided into groups who would have subtitles and those who would not. The findings show a significant gain for both groups, but the group who had subtitles outperformed the group without.

Have you ever used subtitles in watching a foreign film? To what extent did it help you understand the film?

Interactional competence

Based on the earlier work of Kramsch (1986), He and Young (1998) introduced a concept of interactional competence in order to study learners' discursive practices by focusing on turn-taking strategies, topic management and a host of interactional strategies used in various learning contexts. Young (2008, p. 71) built on this work, proposing a number of linguistic and interactional resources used by learners, listed below:

Identity resources

1. Participation framework: The identities of all participants in an interaction – present or not, official or unofficial, ratified or unratified – and their footing or identities in the interaction.

Linguistic resources

2. Register: the features of pronunciation, vocabulary and grammar that typify a practice.

3. Modes of meaning: the ways in which participants construct interpersonal, experiential and textual meanings in a practice.

Interactional resources

4. Speech acts: the selection of acts in a practice and their sequential organisation.

5. Turn-taking: how participants select the next speaker and how participants know when to end one turn and when to begin the next.

6. Repair: the ways in which participants respond to interactional trouble in a given practice.

7. Boundaries: the opening and closing acts of a practice that serve to distinguish a given practice from adjacent talk.

Kasper (2006) extended the construct of IC to include repairing problems while speaking, hearing and understanding. In Kasper's (2006) view, semiotic resources, such as nonverbal and non-vocal conduct, are important for successful communication. She also highlights the ability to recognise that boundaries include 'transitions from states of contact to absence of contact' (opening and closing acts) and the transition between activities during continued conduct (Markee, 2004). In other words, it is important to recognise topic opening, topic closing, changes in a conversation and the interactional strategies and resources that one can use in doing so. Similarly, Markee (2008) also acknowledges paralinguistic features and gaze as part of IC constructs. IC can therefore be defined as learners' ability to

1. understand and produce social actions by jointly managing their roles and reflecting on other participants' contributions to the interaction;

2. employ interactional, linguistic and paralinguistic resources appropriate to the goal of interaction by managing co-construction of talk with other participants in the turn-taking system, sequential organisation and repair practice. These skills or strategies enable a learner to be able to use the language to achieve communicative purposes.

The development of L2 IC could enhance linguistic competence because interaction requires appropriate use of grammar, vocabulary and intonation.

Kasper and Rose (2002) described pragmatic competence as the ability to (1) understand and produce a communicative action, which implies speech acts; (2) engage in various discourse types and speech events; (3) be able to attain social goals; and (4) relate appropriately in interpersonal situations, which involves the use and comprehension of politeness strategies in an appropriate context.

At the same time, interaction requires considerable **pragmatic understanding** of interlocutors' 'social action' and the local context. In interactional exchanges, participants co-construct meanings and demonstrate an understanding of each other's contributions, through active listening, claims of understanding, collaborative completion, various interactional strategies and embodied actions. In a way, L2 interactional competence incorporates intercultural competence, which shows interlocutors' grasp of sociocultural norms of interaction.

In order to develop learners' interactional competence, teachers need to address all these aspects, not just listening or speaking skills. EFL instruction needs to attend to all of its components: organisation of a conversation, pragmatic awareness, strategic and communicative resources, and paralinguistic resources. According to Brown (2000, p. 29), communicative goals are best achieved by giving attention to language use in specific contexts rather than correct language usage; to fluency and not just accuracy; to authentic language and contexts; and to the students' eventual need to apply classroom learning to unrehearsed contexts in the real world. Despite the importance of interactional skills, they are often given less attention compared to reading and writing due to time constraints in the classroom, but they remain the most difficult language skills to grasp for many language learners. Developing learners' interactional competence requires their active participation in class (see also a perspective shared by other scholars such as Hall et al., 2011; Young, 2013). This active participation requires teachers to give learners interactional space/opportunities in class (Walsh and Li, 2013).

In developing students' interactional competence, there are various areas to consider: for example how discourse markers are used in making the flow of a conversation smooth and how the intended meaning is displayed in interaction. Here, I will consider how we can use technological tools to help develop students' knowledge and awareness of interactional resources such as speech acts and turn-taking. First, I will explain what they are and why they are important, and then I will present some technological tools that can be used to develop them.

Speech acts

A speech act is an utterance that serves a function in communication, such as an apology, greeting, request, complaint, invitation, compliment or refusal. Learners sometimes have difficulty understanding the intended meaning of a speech act or producing a speech act using appropriate language. That is because speech acts include real-life interactions and require not only knowledge of the language but also appropriate *use* of that language within a given culture. Speech acts have been taught in some second language classrooms, yet most materials have been written based on the intuition of the textbook writers or what should be said grammatically rather than what might be said in real-life situations.

Task 3.8: What's the problem?

I have a friend who is Chinese and married to a British man, Sam. Her mum, Judith, came to visit her one summer and stayed with them. Soon after Judith arrived, she rang me and complained that Sam was very rude, so she might go back to China earlier. Apparently, when Judith asked Sam, 'how are you?' he said, 'all right'. However, when she learnt English in China, the correct conversation should be like this:

A: How are you?

B: I am fine, thank you. And you?

A: I am fine too.

Sam didn't follow the correct rule, so she thought he was not interested in talking to her. Have you ever experienced something similar? Clearly, Judith has misunderstood Sam. Could you explain what the problems might be?

AntConc is a freeware, multiplatform tool for carrying out corpus linguistics research and data-driven learning. It runs on any computer running Microsoft Windows, Macintosh OS X and Linux. AnoConc can be download here: www.laurenceanthony.net/ software/antconc/

The program is downloaded as a single .exe file (with an additional PDF 'ReadMe' guide available). It can also be run from a USB memory stick.

The problem above is that the dialogue is grammatical, but in real-life situations, people very rarely follow these rules. Textbooks sometimes do not reflect the accurate use of language when people actually interact, so there is a need to expose students to authentic speech acts.

There are many technological tools which can be used in developing learners' IC, and I will illustrate this point by referring to the use of videos and TV series, as well as a corpus analytical tool: **AntConc** (Anthony, 2011). The idea of using authentic corpora is to see how a particular speech act is displayed in real-life conversations (e.g. movies and TV series).

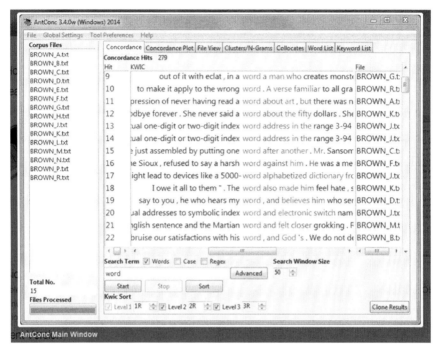

FIGURE 3.5   ANTCONC MAIN WINDOW
(Reproduced with kind permission from Laurence Anthony, 2017)

AntConc has a user-friendly interface (see Figure 3.5). The key features include the following:

- It provides explanations on the screen for each feature that the user clicks on.

- No Internet connection is needed once AntConc is downloaded and installed on a computer.

- AntConc allows users to look for word clusters of different sizes and types.

- It is possible to change font colour and size and background colour in AntConc.

- AntConc can display the distribution of preselected words or word clusters along the text. This feature can provide researchers with insights about the structure of the text. (Diniz, 2005)

AntConc helps one perform a wide variety of tasks, ranging from creating concordances, concordance plots, word clusters and word lists to keyword lists. AntConc's strength is hidden in its sophisticated text analysis that is more than creating simple concordances; its functionality is paired with useful statistical measurements and its support of various character encodings and formats in both input and output (Wiechmann and Fuhs, 2006).

Next we will examine how corpus analysis can be used to facilitate teaching and learning speech acts, and we will take 'making an apology' as an example. For a second language learner, assessing the degree of seriousness of an offence and offering an acceptable apology is not always straightforward, because the elements involved in an apology often vary from culture to culture. When learning to 'make an apology', a learner will have to learn to recognise situations that require an apology, to apologise appropriately and to politely respond when somebody offers an apology. Here I will explain how the use of TV series can help learners develop IC. Subtitles are selected from dyadic and multiparty interactions in TV series *How I Met Your Mother*. All interactions reflect real-life situations and ordinary conversations; couples and friends interacting in different settings like pubs, shops, houses or workplaces. Therefore, it can be claimed that the conversations are well contextualised and may be considered authentic materials in language classrooms. Using this collection of subtitles and AntConc, a task is designed to teach apology as a speech act.

Step 1: Students search for episodes following these steps:

- Open and run AntConc.

- Load the file of subtitles for *How I Met Your Mother*.

- Search for phrases and sets of key words, such as 'sorry' and 'apology'.

The outcome list will now identify all the episodes that contains making an apology.

Step 2: Each student chooses a particular episode to analyse how 'serious' the offence is and reflect how to deal with this kind of situation in their own culture. They can share their thoughts with their classmates.

Step 3: Students then work as a group to discuss 'when to make an apology', 'how to make an apology' (e.g. do they need to express regret before doing so) and 'how social relationships affect apologising'.

In communication, apart from developing pragmatic awareness around using appropriate language, it is also important to know how to use interactional resources and strategies to communicate, such as the use of discourse markers (DMs). DMs are highly context specific and indexed to attitudes, participants and text, and they bear the characteristics of being oral and multifunctional (Lenk, 1998; Müller, 2004). Examples of DMs include words like *right, yeah, well, you know, OK*. Fung and Carter (2007) have categorised a core functional paradigm of DMs, listed below:

- Interpersonal DMs are about making shared knowledge (e.g. *you see, you know*), indicating attitude (e.g. *well, really, sort of, I think*) and showing a response (e.g. *OK, yeah, I see, great*).

- Referential DMs serve as sentence connectives, including cause (e.g. *because*), contrast (e.g. *but, yet*), consequence (e.g. *so*), digression (e.g. *anyway*) and comparison (e.g. *similarly*).

- Structural DMs signal topic shifting and turn-taking, including opening and closing a topic (e.g. *now, right, let's say*), sequence (e.g. *first, second*), topic shifts (e.g. *so now, how about*), summarising opinions (e.g. *so*) and continuation of topic (e.g. *so, yeah, and*).

- Cognitive DMs denote the thinking process (e.g. *well, I think, I see, and*), reformulation/self-correction (e.g. *I mean*), elaboration (e.g. *I mean, like*), hesitation (*well, sort of*) and an assessment of the listener's knowledge of the utterances (e.g. *you know*).

DMs play an important role in understanding discourse and information progression (Schiffrin, 1987). Therefore, it is critical to learn how to use them in conversation. Again, it is a good idea to ask students to explore the functions of DMs by using corpus analysis.

Task 3.9: Using a TV series and corpus tool to learn discourse markers
In my class, nine seasons of *How I Met Your Mother* are used as the corpora, with a total number of 1,119,965 words. The discourse markers to teach in the videos are *hmmm, oh, you know, what I mean*, and *well*.

Students are divided into groups, with each group searching for one discourse marker and making a small presentation about its function with illustrations from the video (see Figure 3.6 for an example of using *mmm-hmm*). In this activity, students need to work together to search through the corpora, identify the right episodes, discuss the function of their chosen discourse marker and prepare a presentation for the whole class.

What are the benefits of using TV series and corpus tools in my lesson? Choose a TV series you are familiar with and then use it as a corpus to search 'what about' to see in what situations the phrase is used.

Turn-taking

Turn-taking is an important aspect of interactional competence. When people engage in a conversation, it requires a large amount of coordination between participants because they need to know when it is their turn to talk and how to give the turn. Conversation mechanisms facilitate the

FIGURE 3.6   Mmm-hmm

coordination of conversations by helping people know how and when to start and stop speaking.

Sacks et al. (1974) developed a model that explains how people manage turn-taking during conversations and why turn-taking is so important:

> The organisation of taking turns to talk is fundamental to conversation, as well as to other speech-exchange systems. A model for the turn-taking organisation for conversation is proposed, and it is examined for its compatibility with a list of grossly observable facts about conversation. (Sacks et al., 1974, p. 696)

This framework can be applied across cultures and contexts to explain conversational structure and dynamics. Sacks, et al. (1974) summarised the following rules about turn-taking in any conversation (pp. 700–701):

1. Speaker change recurs, or at least occurs.

2. Overwhelmingly, one party talks at a time.

3. Occurrences of more than one speaker at a time are common, but brief.

4. Transitions (from one turn to a next) with no gap and no overlap are common. Together with transitions characterised by slight gap or slight overlap, they make up the vast majority of transitions.

5. Turn order is not fixed but varies.

6. Turn size is not fixed but varies.

7. Length of conversation is not specified in advance.

8. What parties say is not specified in advance.

9. Relative distribution of turns is not specified in advance.

10. Number of parties can vary.

11. Talk can be continuous or discontinuous.

12. Turn-allocation techniques are obviously used. The current speaker may select a next speaker (as when he or she addresses a question to another party); or parties may self-select in starting a talk.

13. Various 'turn-constructional units' are employed: for example, turns can be 'one word long' or sentential.

14. Repair mechanisms exist for dealing with turn-taking errors and violations; for example, if two parties find themselves talking at the same time, one of them will stop prematurely, thus repairing the trouble.

In a conversation, knowing how to take, give and hold turns is important, especially in a multiparty conversation. Interactional strategies and resources can be taught to students in order for them to better manage a conversation.

When teaching turn-taking, video, film, corpus and CMC are useful tools for teachers to explore. First of all, videos, films and existing corpora can be used as examples of how turns are managed in natural conversation and in institutional talk (e.g. in a courtroom or in a classroom). Students should be involved in identifying strategies in opening conversation, closing conversation, turn shifting and topic changing in various situations. Again, this can be done through collaborative group work. Second, students should be offered opportunities to engage in the discourse community. Other aspects of interactional competence can be developed and taught using the same approach, such as repairs, the use of extralinguistic resources and humour.

Case study 3.2:

Sert (2009) has analysed the conversations in supplementary audiovisual materials to be implemented in language teaching classrooms in order to enhance the IC of learners. Based on a corpus of 90,000 words (coupling corpus), Sert tries to reveal the potential of using TV series in English as an additional language (EAL) classrooms. He focused on hyperbole in interaction through uncovering conversational sequences and embodied actions to show that the use of TV series can be an invaluable resource for language teachers. Students are exposed to multi-model texts that contextualise the materials used through various interactional, semiotic and linguistic resources.

Could you design a similar task which could be used to develop students' IC in your teaching context? What are the potential challenges of this task?

Summary

This chapter has examined the use of technological tools and applications to teach interactional skills. Although we have focused mainly on accuracy, fluency and interactional competence, it does not mean that these are the only things that we need to consider in developing students' interactional skills. Culture and social norms, for example, are key elements which need considering. There are other tools and applications we can use to develop these skills, and what this chapter has offered are just some examples to demonstrate the pedagogical thinking behind using technology to assist learning. Technology has many affordances that we can explore, and there is no single and correct way to use it in assisting learning. The key thing that we need to remember in designing a task is whether the technological tool is addressing the pedagogical purpose at hand and whether it is suitable for learners' cognitive and linguistic levels, as well as their cultural values. This will lead to the issue of appropriate use of technology and materials, which we will explore further in Chapter 8. In the next chapter, we will consider another set of skills: reading, writing and online literacy.

Student projects

1. Tecedor Cabrero, M. (2013) Developing Interactional Competence through Video-Based Computer-Mediated Conversations: Beginning Learners of Spanish. Unpublished PhD thesis, University of Iowa. Available at ir.uiowa.edu/etd/4918

   This PhD thesis examines the use and development of interactional resources during two video-mediated conversations by beginning learners. This project employs a combination of conversation analysis tools and quantitative data analysis to examine how these learners manage videoconferencing exchanges and develop their interactional capabilities in this new interactional setting through the use of turn-taking strategies, repair trajectories and alignment moves. This thesis aims to describe and explain how students construct, manage and maintain conversations via videoconferencing, and it aims to gain a better understanding of the links between technology-based social media and language learning. The project shows that (1) these learners are fully capable of participating competently in speaker selection to manage a conversation with a peer of similar proficiency level; (2) beginning learners orient to both the communication of personal meaning and the accuracy of their discourse during instructional videoconferencing exchanges, especially through the use of self-initiated self-repair; and (3) beginning learners primarily use acknowledgement moves.

2. Eftekhari, S. (2013) Student experience with technology-supported error correction for speaking in promoting accuracy and fluency in preparing for the IELTS. Unpublished M.Ed. dissertation, University of Exeter.

This dissertation is a qualitative explorative study into learning how to improve the spoken accuracy and fluency of three Taiwanese students in online IELTS (International English Language Testing System) classes. The researcher used Vsee (a group video-chat and screen-sharing software tool) to provide students with instant feedback in one-to-one tutorials. When students are speaking, the tutor can provide both verbal and written corrective feedback, which will be available for students to view after the task has been finished. The project shows that using a video-chat and screen-sharing software improves students' accuracy and fluency in speaking.

Annotated further reading

1. Ramírez Verdugo, M. D. & Alonso Belmonte, I. (2007) Using digital stories to improve listening comprehension with Spanish young learners of English. *Language Learning & Technology*, 11(1), 87–101. Available at llt.msu.edu/vol11num1/ramirez/

This paper examines the effects that digital stories may have on the understanding of spoken English by a group of six-year-old Spanish learners. A pre-/post-test design was used to investigate whether Internet-based technology could improve listening comprehension in EFL contexts. Findings indicate that the experimental group outperformed the control group in the final test administered.

2. Satar, H. M. & Özdener, N. (2008) The effects of synchronous CMC on speaking proficiency and anxiety: Text versus voice chat. *The Modern Language Journal*, 92(4), 595–613.

This article reports on a study investigating the use of two synchronous CMC tools: text and voice chat. The experimental design included three groups (text, voice and control), each consisting of 30 novice-level secondary school EFL learners. The data were collected through before and after anxiety scales and speaking tests, and closed and open-ended questionnaires. The results showed that the speaking proficiency of both experimental groups increased.

3. McKinnon, M. (online) Teaching technologies: teaching English using video. Onestopenglish website. Available at www.onestopenglish.com/methodology/methodology/teaching-technologies/teaching-technologies-teaching-english-using-video/146527.article

This is an article written for teachers who would like to know more about using videos in English language classrooms. It is practical and easy to follow. There are also related resources.

4. Tsukamoto, M., Nuspliger, B. & Senzaki, Y. (2009) Using Skype to connect a classroom to the world: Providing students an authentic language experience within the classroom. *CamTESOL Conference on English Language Teaching: Selected Papers*, Volume 5, 162–168.

This article describes how a Skype (web conferencing) project between a Japanese high school and a counterpart in the US benefited language learning. This project suggests that students speak more English during conference calls and prepare more eagerly for their lessons. Most importantly, the Japanese students clearly enjoyed speaking with American students through the Skype conferences. This paper also explored technical issues involved in setting up web conferences in a classroom.

4 Reading, writing and online literacy

Aims: This chapter reviews how technology can enhance reading and writing in second language acquisition and the development of online literacy. In particular, it draws on the literature concerning second language reading and writing and on technology-enhanced reading and writing to help the reader understand the potential applications of technology, including the use of Web 2.0 technologies such as wikis, blogs and social-networking tools. This chapter has three sections, as follows:

1. Writing and technology

2. Reading and technology

3. The development of online literacy.

Introduction

The use of technology in foreign language learning also appears to influence the development of writing skills and performance. Among the language skills, reading and writing are considered the areas on which teachers and learners spend most of their time. Reading well and writing well are vital skills for academic or operational success – reading can be an importance source for input, and writing is the form in which one expresses one's opinions, thoughts, ideas and arguments. In reading and writing activities, learners can develop the language proficiency required to conduct disciplinary or occupational tasks. It is perhaps why second language research has especially emphasised the development of reading and writing and why various technological tools have been considered in facilitating this. In this chapter, I will present ideas in relation to teaching reading and writing with the use of technology by considering both the approaches to reading and writing instruction and the pedagogical considerations of technology use. I will first consider writing approaches before discussing the role of technology in developing writing skills and then move on to discuss reading and online literacy.

Writing and technology

Writing is an important skill in second language learning. It is 'the combining of structural sentence units into a more-or-less unique, cohesive and coherent larger structure (as opposed to lists, forms, etc.)' (Grabe and Kaplan, 1996, p. 4). In second language pedagogy research, there is a debate as to whether the focus of writing should be on the product (text), the process (writer) or the genre (audience and context). In order to understand how technology helps writing, we need to consider different approaches.

Approaches to writing

Writing as a product

Writing as a product considers writing 'as grammar instruction, with the emphasis on controlled composition, correction of the product, and correct form over expression of ideas' (Susser, 1994, p. 36). In the 1960s, writing was viewed as a means of reinforcing speech patterns. It focused on sentence-level linguistic forms. Therefore, writing following this approach is preoccupied with constant concern about usage, structure or accurate form (Zamel, 1982, 1983) and is focused on the appropriate use of grammatical rules, vocabulary and mechanics. This approach follows a traditional model involving 'familiarization; controlled writing; guided writing; and free writing' (Badger and White, 2000, p. 153) as shown in Figure 4.1.

In this approach, teachers are the experts and examiners of linguistic knowledge (Mangelsdorf and Schlumberger, 1992) who help learners to identify and address their mechanical errors. Accuracy is more important than fluency (Raimes, 1985, 1991; Susser, 1994; Zamel, 1985). Teachers attend to 'surface-level features of writing' and 'read and react to a text as

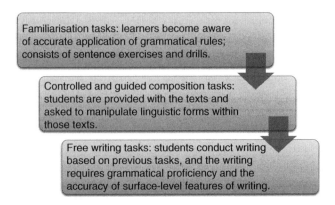

FIGURE 4.1   WRITING AS A PRODUCT MODEL

a series of separate pieces at the sentence level or even clause level, rather than as a whole unit of discourse' (Zamel, 1987, p. 700). The content or organisational issues are generally not addressed.

Writing as a process

Writing as a process views writing as a 'non-linear, exploratory, and generative process whereby writers discover and reformulate their ideas as they attempt to approximate meaning' (Zamel, 1983, p. 165). Process writing challenges the traditional view of teaching writing as developing learners' linguistic competence to produce a grammatical piece and instead focuses on developing an understanding of writers' cognitive processes in writing (Hyland, 2003). Process writing has a dual focus of raising awareness and implementing intervention (Susser, 1994, p. 34). First, it focuses on raising students' awareness of the nature of writing being a complex and recursive process. The writer is usually in an iterative process of generating, formulating and refining ideas through pre-writing, drafting, revising and editing procedures. The writer might have to go back to their original idea to make changes, revise the language to suit both the writing purpose and their audience, and format their writing (Zamel, 1982). Intervention refers to the guidance that the writer receives in a supportive and cooperative environment (Hyland, 2003). In second language writing, this means receiving guidance and feedback from teachers at different stages of writing, which includes pre-writing guidance in developing ideas and structure of writing, while writing feedback when students produce multiple drafts, and post writing feedback where the teacher usually provides a final evaluation. Because the focus is on process, students receive constant feedback during the writing activity, and the final product is not so heavily emphasised by the teacher. In this process, feedback covers the use of language, the relevance of content and the structure. The features of the approach to writing include pre-writing activities, multiple drafts, extensive feedback, peer review and delay in surface correction. However, there are problems with this approach, mainly in its theoretical grounding, its effectiveness in helping students to achieve better writing skills and a lack of consideration of writing as a social practice (Hyland, 2003).

Genre refers to abstract, socially recognised ways of using language. It is based on the assumptions that the features of a similar group of texts depend on the social context of their creation and use, and that those features can be described in a way that relates a text to others like it and to the choices and constraints acting on text producers (Hyland, 2003, p. 21).

Genre-based approach to writing

As a response to the issues identified in the process approach, **genre** approaches have gained attention in second language pedagogy (Hyland, 2003; Badger and White, 2000). This emphasises the need for students to be exposed to the target discourse community and link their practice to it.

There are three broad approaches to genre theories: the English for specific purposes (ESP) approach, systematic functional linguistics (SFL) model, and the new rhetoric approach (Hyon, 1996), each of them having a slightly different focus. Hyland (2003, pp. 21–22) summarises them:

- The new rhetoric approach studies genre 'as the motivated, functional relationship between text type and rhetorical situation' (Coe, 2002, p. 195). It focuses mainly on the rhetorical contexts in which genres are employed rather than on detailed analyses of text elements (e.g. Freedman and Medway, 1994).

- The ESP approach is more linguistic in orientation and sees genre as a class of structured communicative events employed by specific discourse communities whose members share broad social purposes (Swales, 1990, pp. 45–47).

- The SFL model (Halliday, 1994) stresses the purposeful, interactive and sequential character of different genres and the ways in which language is systematically linked to context through patterns of lexicogrammatical and rhetorical features (Christie and Martin, 1997).

Writing is viewed as a purposeful, socially situated response to particular contexts and communities. Therefore, writers need to use various linguistic and rhetorical options to accomplish different purposes in different contexts. In practice, the approach involves analysing target genres in terms of their linguistic and structural features (Johns et al., 2006), with multiple drafts. Badger and White (2000, p. 157) proposed an eclectic method: the 'process genre approach', which takes form, content, context and audience into consideration. So students need to use their linguistic knowledge (including grammar and vocabulary), writing skills (planning, drafting and redrafting) and contextual knowledge (context, audiences and the community practice) to produce content and also to follow rhetorical form used in specific contexts (e.g. essay writing).

Collaborative writing

Collaborative writing is the joint production of a text by two or more writers (Storch, 2011, p. 275). It is firmly grounded in several theoretical frameworks, among which are the interactional hypothesis (Long, 1996), output hypothesis (Swain, 1985, 1993, 1995), sociocultural theory (Vygotsky, 1978) and collaborative talk. The main ideas behind collaborative writing are as follows:

- When learners work in small groups, they engage in negotiations of meaning with the goal of completing the task at hand.

- Output is important in second language learning. The need to produce output is more likely to encourage students to engage in the learning process and encourage them to notice the gaps in their language production and their language use (Swain, 1993, 1995).

- When learners engage in a collaborative dialogue, they work together to solve problems at hand in a meaning-making process.

- Learning takes place in the social milieu, with scaffolded help from an 'expert'. SLA research suggests that peers can provide scaffolding for each other and that the role of the expert is fluid (Ohta, 2000) and is shared by learners pooling their expertise, which is defined as 'collective scaffolding' (Donato, 1994; Storch, 2002).

Collaborative writing has been popular for these reasons but also because it facilitates the joint cognitive development, or group cognition. Byrne (1988) proposed five steps for a writing process: gathering ideas, preparing an outline ('scaffolding'), writing a draft, correcting and improving the draft and writing the final output. This is also suitable for collaborative writing. Collaborative writing can be viewed as an attempt to reach mutual consensus, which, it has been suggested, is considerably better than individual understanding (Wells, 2000). Through collaboration, learning can be enhanced as a result of the act of doing things together, negotiating new meaning and learning from each other (Wenger, 1998). Collaborative writing has great potential: it provides students with an opportunity for reflective practice; it helps learners to focus on grammatical accuracy; and it promotes group autonomy in developing joint ideas.

Technology use in writing

New digital media have played a key role in the teaching of writing, and various tools have emerged in the past few years with the development of technology, especially Web 2.0 technologies. In what follows, we will focus on the use of some of the Web 2.0 technologies in writing.

Social networks

Students find it motivating to write for an audience of peers or the wider public (e.g. Godwin-Jones, 2003). So a social network can be used for real-life writing. There are many examples of these platforms – for instance, blogs (Wordpress, Blogspot), microblogs (Twitter, Posterous, Tumblr), Wikis (Wikipedia, Scholarpedia), social networking sites (Facebook, Academia, LinkedIn), photo-sharing sites (Instagram, Cymera), instant messaging (WhatsApp, WeChat, LINE), video-sharing sites (Keek, YouTube) and many more.

Students nowadays are experienced in using social networks where authentic interaction happens; thus the social networks can be used as learning platforms if planned carefully. Furthermore, there is evidence that social networking platforms can increase writing ability (Thanawan and Punchalee, 2012; Hatime and Zaynep, 2012; Wichadee and Nopakun, 2012). For example, Facebook can be used in order for a group of learners to share and exchange information (Kwong, 2007) or as a free writing tool.

Task 4.1: Does it work?

I am working with a group of learners, aged 17–19, who are learning English as a foreign language. In my class, I asked each student to have a Facebook account and use it for my free writing activity. Each student takes a picture every day and writes down what they think. They also have to visit each other's Facebook pages and leave comments.

Do you think students will be highly engaged in this activity? Why or why not? Apart from the potential restrictions of accessing Facebook in some parts of the world, can you think of any other constraints of using Facebook in improving writing?

It works, both in theory and in practice. Theoretically, Facebook is seen as a perfect platform because it fits with sociocultural theory insofar as knowledge can be constructed and fostered through collaboration, negotiation, active participation and community building. In practice, Facebook works because students are engaged in an activity that they are interested in: students already use it to connect and share information, and this task requires them to share only their thoughts, in English. The materials they share are genuine and relevant to their age and interests. So this meaningful education experience with Facebook provides students opportunities to interact with their peers, learn from each and develop higher order thinking skills. Obviously, care has to be taken in relation to using social networks. Apart from Internet safety and privacy issues, teachers also need to be aware of the possible unintentional cyberbullying of peers, leaving unfriendly comments or showing no interest in each other's contributions. Teachers might also need to guide students in terms of providing feedback and commenting on each other's entries. Establishing some ground rules before engaging with social networks in teaching and learning activities is important.

Blogs

Blogs have been used in developing various language skills – writing in particular (Bloch, 2007; Sun and Chang, 2012). They are different from other

Web 1.0 or Web 2.0 tools, such as discussion boards or wikis. Blogs include the following features: blogs

- are owned by individuals to publish their work and update it frequently, giving owners strong personal editorship;

- have archived features, which means users can go back to the content of their choice anytime;

- can be accessed by the public or a designated group;

- allow the writer and reader to share, create and interact virtually;

- allow other people to comment, which makes it an effective tool to combine both publishing and discussion in a writing task. Unlike essays or academic writing, blogs can be used to encourage students to write for a social audience and respond to other blogs.

Research suggests that blogs help increase the quantity of student writing and its lexical sophistication (Fellner and Apple, 2006). Dawns (2004) claims that integrating blogs into writing classes improves students' writing skills. Nadzrah and Kemboja (2009) point out that students write their compositions with specific purposes through blogging. When blogging, students work in an authentic but non-judgemental learning environment. It may be a friendly environment, especially for those shy and slow learners. Students are usually motivated by writing and publishing because they write for authentic audiences and because their writing can be accessed by a wider community. Other researchers have shown how blogs are used in developing second language writing skills (e.g. Armstrong and Retterer, 2008; Bloch, 2007; Lee, 2010; Noytim, 2010; Sun, 2009; Sun and Chang, 2012).

Case study 4.1:

Sun and Chang (2012) implemented blogs with six MA TESOL students and one MA linguistics student. They were required to have their own blogs on academic writing. The students were required to post 13 entries on their own blogs as well as 13 comments on their classmates' blogs: ideally, one entry and one comment every week. They were encouraged to reflect on their process of developing academic writing skills. The evaluation of blogs focused on the number of posts, rather than the content. And students were allowed to use either Chinese (their L1) or English, although 67 per cent of the language was in Chinese. The study suggested that the blog activity encouraged students to actively and reflectively engage in knowledge sharing, knowledge generation and the development of numerous strategies to cope with difficulties encountered in the learning process. Students also developed a sense of authorship.

In the above case study, Sun and Chang (2012) used blogs as an individual learning tool, which can also establish a community for students. Here, I would like to share a different example of using blogs in my teaching context. I teach a module called 'new technologies in language learning' in an M.Ed. TESOL programme. In my module, as a formative activity, students need to work in self-established groups to create their group blogs. The purpose of using group blogs in this module is to give students a small learning community where they can share knowledge, support each other and experience the use of blogs in writing activities. The group can blog anything they like that is associated with using technology for teaching and learning a second language. A group usually consists of four to six students, and they take turns to make entries and visit other groups' blogs. Their entries include sharing software, programmes, applications and tools for teaching vocabulary, grammar and skills. They also upload a podcast and evaluate it. Other materials include their reflections of using Mailvu and Voki, or videos and teaching plans of using multimedia materials. Figure 4.2 is an example of an entry from a student. As can be seen, the student is sharing a her ideas about using Mailvu in teaching, and Figure 4.3 is an example of comments made by other students. Clearly, they do not just share information; they also establish a community to learn together.

Analysis of group blogs over three years (2012–2015) shows that students enjoyed the group blogs, although the contributions from group members and comments on each other's entries varied. Students clearly found it to be a useful activity, and a good work culture within the group seemed to be the key. The group needed to build trust and a collaborative work ethos in carrying out the joint task. Because the group had to discuss their topics before they made the entry, they often found it difficult to find time to actually make the entry, owing to the pressure from other coursework.

Wikis

A wiki is defined as a "freely expandable collection of interlinked Web pages, a hypertext system for storing and modifying information – a database, where each page is easily edited by any user with a forms-capable Web browser client" (Leuf and Cunningham, 2001, p. 14). Wikispaces is a wiki engine where teachers or learners can open their own wiki pages (www.wikispaces. com).

Wikis offer not just a platform for people to collaborate but also is a work that might produce a community and is *sustained* by a community according to Ward Cunningham. Wikis have been implemented in writing tasks in different contexts (e.g. Kessler, 2009; Kessler and Bikowski, 2010; Oskoz and Elola, 2014, 2011a, b). There are some obvious advantages. First, wikis create a learning opportunity beyond classrooms. That means learners can meet to discuss

MailVu is also a great tool which you can communicate with students easily and help them with their pronunciation, speaking, and even listening skills. Educators can use it in Listening and Speaking classes so that teachers can see as well as hear students' homework.

Here are some quick ideas for MailVu in a listening/speaking context:

1 **Assigning Work:** Instead of repeating yourself over and over again in class, just send out a MailVu link to your Facebook/Twitter/etc.

2 **Homework:** Students can practice tongue twisters, free speaking, or comprehension responses on MailVu. That way you can see their enunciation as well as hear their speech.

3 **Collaboration:** Students can use MailVu to cooperate and collaborate with each other.

4 **Presentations:** Students can use the press/record/send ease of functionality to prepare, present, share their presentations quickly with others in a different environment than the traditional classroom.

FIGURE 4.2   AN EXAMPLE OF A BLOG ENTRY

topics after class when working on a wiki project. Second, the writing task can be less teacher dependent. Students pool each other's expertise in the project to jointly create knowledge. Third, wikis create a learning community that will benefit them in other activities. And finally, wikis present novel challenges, in terms of writing process, medium and writing product. In the writing process, knowledge is created and recreated as a result of collaborative work among a group of people (Wells, 2000). Also, the tracking system (history page) allows group members to track the changes made, who made them and when. This is not a pure writing process engaged in by individuals but a dialogic process that enables learners to relate their ideas to others' ideas. Research suggests that writing on wikis can contribute to raising learners' awareness of their audience, increasing the use of interpersonal meta-discourse (Alyousef and Picard, 2011; Kuteeva, 2011), improving structure and organisation (Oskoz and Elola, 2011a), the development of content (Arnold et al., 2009; Kessler, 2009; Lee, 2010) and increased grammatical accuracy and quality of writing (Storch, 2005). However, this does

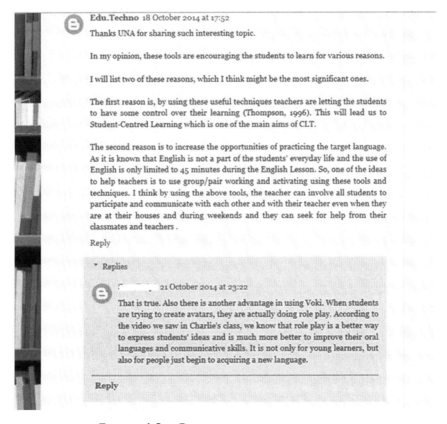

FIGURE 4.3   COMMENTS FROM OTHER STUDENTS

not mean that collaborative writing is beneficial for everyone, and there is evidence that some learners prefer individual writing tasks. Elola and Oskoz (2010) outline a number of reasons for this:

- Learners retain more control if they work individually.

- Learners can establish their own personal style.

- Learners do not need to depend on others' input.

- Learners do not need to negotiate a time to meet/work together.

- Learners are solely responsible for their own grades.

- Learners do not need to deal with technological issues.

Therefore, Elola and Oskoz (2010, p. 64) make the following suggestions for the use of a wiki in collaborative work:

> it is essential to (a) demonstrate to learners that integrating social tools goes beyond a classroom exercise (Levy & Kennedy, 2004; Ortega, 2009; Warschauer, 2004), (b) transform learners into critical users who understand how the application of technological tools can transform the learning environment (Blake, 2008), and (c) highlight the importance of seeing collaborative work as a practice that can be relevant to learners' future professional lives (Brown & Adler, 2008). The collaboratively created text should not be regarded as a combination of individual endeavours, but rather as the result of several contributions which together create one distinctive voice.

Case study 4.2:

Aydın and Yıldız (2014) used wikis in collaborative writing projects in foreign language learning classrooms in Turkey. A total of 34 intermediate level university EFL students were asked to accomplish three different wiki-based collaborative writing tasks (argumentative, informative and decision making), working in groups of four. The students participated in the wikis project for seven weeks. At the beginning of the semester, the instructor/researcher set up a class wiki for each class and held a training session before learners started to work on their projects. Learners were provided with detailed criteria regarding the grading of their wikis, which included an assessment of both individual and collaborative working skills. In this project, students clearly paid more attention to meaning than form.

Similarly, wiki projects have been implemented in teacher training projects (e.g. Kessler, 2009). In my own teaching, I taught a session on how to use wikis and invited my M.Ed. TESOL students to participate in a collaborative writing project: how technology can be used in teaching. There were seven steps in designing the project:

Step 1: A wiki project was established and a page was created by me in class using the virtual learning environment of the university. This showed students how a wiki project can be started.

Step 2: Students were grouped into three or four people, using a self-selection strategy.

Step 3: Each group started to work together to discuss the input they wanted to add to the topic.

Step 4: One group started to input their ideas, and then groups took turns to contribute to the wiki page (Figure 4.4 shows the project page after two groups input their contributions).

Step 5: All students started to read the contributions on the wiki page, including their own.

FIGURE 4.4 COMPARSION OF THE INPUT MADE BY TWO LEARNERS ON A WIKI WRITING PROJECT

Step 6: Groups then discussed what changes they wanted to make to the wiki page and started to make changes.

Step 7: The groups reviewed changes made further until no more changes were made.

Task 4.2: Comparing blogs with wikis

Now start a blog and create a wiki project using Wordpress and Wikispaces Education (see Chapter 1 for more information) for your writing course. And consider similarities and differences between them. As a teacher, when you implement wikis in teaching collaborative writing, what considerations do you need to take into account?

Among the Web 2.0 technologies, both blogs and wikis are unique in providing an environment for improving writing. When implementing these technological tools, there are issues that every teacher might want to consider:

- The teacher needs to develop students' awareness of the ownership of the authorship, especially in collaborative writing.

- Students need to be taught about responsible contributions to blogs and wikis, especially when controversial issues are debated. One must be aware of the possible responses from the readers.

- When designing the tasks, perhaps (grammatical) accuracy should be of less concern compared to the meaning and content of the writing. So teachers need to think about alternative assessments of the blogs or wikis (see Chapter 7).

- Students need to be aware of fair contributions to blogs and wikis among group members and how to acknowledge the help received from peers. It might be a good idea to have ground rules about collaborative work to make sure all opinions are listened to and respected.

There are of course many other issues we need to think about when we consider using technological tools. However, overall, blogs and wikis can bring students rewarding experiences and are worth exploring. Currently, the majority of collaborative writing/projects takes place among learners of the same class. Perhaps, then, the practicality and possibility of involving students from different geographic locations and cultures can be further tested and explored. This might provide students with a global perspective and novel opportunities for collaboration. Other options worth exploring include Google Docs (e.g. Kessler et al., 2012) and Wordles (e.g. Baralt et al., 2011).

Corpus

A corpus (plural: corpora) is 'a collection of texts, written or spoken, which is stored on a computer' (O'Keeffe et al., 2007, p. 35). Recent years have witnessed the popularity of the use of corpus in second language learning, in particular in vocabulary instruction and writing. When corpus technology is integrated in writing, it combines vocabulary, grammar and discourse patterns in the process. Corpus analysis, in combination with genre analysis, informs EAP materials (Flowerdew, 2002) and helps students to develop competence in specific academic domains in writing (Tribble, 2002). One of the advantages of corpus analysis is the access to natural and authentic texts in given contexts, and clearly the use of corpus analysis is beneficial for second language writing because the corpus can be used as writing material, a guide and a reference tool. Where corpus use is integrated into instruction, learners can increase lexical and grammatical accuracy, which contributes to a possible increase in the quality of their writing and in their confidence as second language writers (Yoon, 2008).

Each corpus is built with a specific purpose in mind and designed according to specific criteria. For example, if a student's aim is to check the language used in medicine, a suitable corpus could consist of relevant research articles written by experts and researchers in that area, not a collection of general academic writing. Corpora are accessed by using text analysis software, such as **WordSmith Tools** (Scott, 2008).

For a step-by-step screen shot of what WordSmith Tools do, see www.lexically.net/ wordsmith/step_by_step_English6/index. html?introduction.htm.

The search result can be saved for later use, edited, printed, copied to a word processor or saved as text files. Corpora have three main features:

1. Concordance: finding all instances of a word or phrase from the corpus. To use concordance, you need to specify a search word, which the function of *Concord* will seek in all the text files you have chosen. It will then present a concordance display, and give you access to information about collocates of the searched word.

2. Keywords: identifying keywords and locating them in a given text are the purposes of this programme. It compares the words in the text with a reference set of words usually taken from a large corpus of text. Any word which is found to be outstanding in its frequency in the text is considered 'key'. The key words are presented in order of outstandingness. For example, in a spoken corpus, 'OK', 'yes' and 'well' are very likely to be key words in social talk. The result produces the frequency of the word as it appears in the text, the percentage, its importance (how key is it) and its distribution.

3. WordList: listing the words in your text(s) in alphabetical order and by frequency.

Friginal (2013) used a corpus-informed approach to academic writing with a group of college-level students enrolled in a professional forestry programme. He explored the use of a concordance programme (AntConc) in fostering effective writing, in particular for (a) linking adverbials, (b) reporting verbs, (c) verb tenses, and (d) passive sentence structures. His research reveals that his Corpus Instruction group increased the frequency of using linking adverbials. The Corpus Instruction group increased their use of other transition words and phrases, especially *therefore, nevertheless, similarly, likewise, for example, in addition* and *on the other hand*.

There were four lessons, with lessons 1 and 3 dedicated to linking adverbials and tenses.

- In lesson 1, the instructor introduced the use of a concordancer, AntConc 3.2.1, and showed concordance lines of linking adverbials and patterns of verb tenses in the professional and student corpora. The learners were asked to nominate a particular linking adverbial or use of tense in sections of the research articles for concordancing, facilitated by the instructor. There were discussions of the patterns and mechanical conventions in using linking adverbials in technical reports (e.g. use of comma after 'however'; location [initial, middle, ending] of linking adverbials in the sentence).

- In lesson 3, students were asked to follow instructions in conducting hands-on concordancing of linking adverbials. A list of the most common linking adverbials in academic writing from the LGSWE (Biber et al., 1999) was provided as a guide to search for corpus patterns and frequencies. The students were instructed to copy and print concordance lines of linking adverbials that would be useful for them in editing their papers.

As this project showed, training students how to use corpus tools is very important in implementing corpus-informed curricula and student-centred learning. Students need to have access to relevant corpora (note that size is an important matter for a corpus), and they also need to have access to tools, such as WordSmith Tools or AntConc. They also need training to perform different analysis, with examples. This requires the teacher to be able to show students how to conduct analysis and searches and how to refer them to the available sources and tutorials online.

Task 4.3: Sorting out concordance

Use AntConc to perform a concordance search of the word 'suggest' using an academic corpus. Sort the concordance according to the left and the right contexts. Analyse the left and the right contexts of the node word 'suggest', one of the frequently used words in academic writing. You will have to write down ten collocations and explain what criteria your selection is based on. What can you find about the use of 'suggest' in academic writing?

Sketch Engine (www.sketchengine.co.uk/#blue) is another very useful tool for linguists, students and teachers to search for information in more than 80 languages. Sketch Engine uses multi-billion word samples of authentic text to help learners (and teachers) identify instantly what is frequent and typical usage in language and what is rare, unusual or emerging usage.

Unlike text search tools, Sketch Engine can determine parts of speech (noun, adjective, verb, etc.) and grammatical categories (singular/plural, present/past, passive/active, etc.), making it possible to quickly look up specific word combinations or even grammatical structures. Here I refer to two functions in specific that Sketch Engine performs: thesaurus and word sketch. Thesaurus is a function that provides similar words (or synonyms), whereas word sketch provides a word's grammatical and collocational behaviour. As an example, I chose British National Corpus and input 'suggest' to find out its synonyms (see Figure 4.5). The search provides both a list of words with their frequencies and a world cloud. When one clicks on each word,

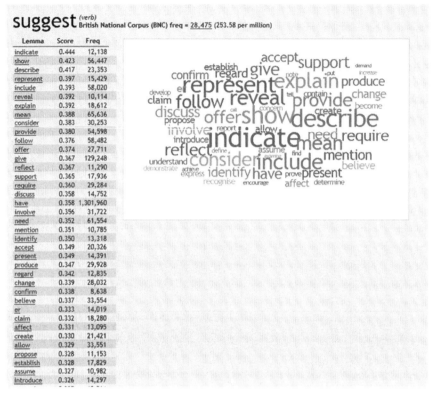

Lemma	Score	Freq
indicate	0.444	12,138
show	0.423	56,447
describe	0.417	23,353
represent	0.397	15,429
include	0.393	58,020
reveal	0.392	10,114
explain	0.392	18,612
mean	0.388	65,636
consider	0.383	30,253
provide	0.380	54,598
follow	0.376	58,482
offer	0.374	27,711
give	0.367	129,248
reflect	0.367	11,290
support	0.365	17,936
require	0.360	29,284
discuss	0.358	14,752
have	0.358	1,301,960
involve	0.356	31,722
need	0.352	61,554
mention	0.351	10,785
identify	0.350	13,318
accept	0.349	20,326
present	0.349	14,391
produce	0.347	29,928
regard	0.342	12,835
change	0.339	28,032
confirm	0.338	8,638
believe	0.337	33,554
er	0.333	14,019
claim	0.332	18,280
affect	0.331	13,095
create	0.330	21,421
allow	0.329	33,551
propose	0.328	11,153
establish	0.328	17,829
assume	0.327	10,982
introduce	0.326	14,297

FIGURE 4.5   THESAURUS FOR 'SUGGEST'

it also provides a comparison between the word and 'suggest'. Similarly, if I choose to perform 'word sketch', it gives me its grammatical collocation (see Figure 4.6).

Task 4.4: Explore Sketch Engine

Visit www.sketchengine.co.uk/ and explore the following functions of sketch engine (note that at the time of writing, you can register for a 30-day free trial): Word list; Word sketch; Thesaurus; Sketch diff; Trends. Think about how you can use this tool in a writing activity.

Because corpus is also used in lexicogrammatical teaching and in ESP and EAP contexts, I will consider the use of corpus in those areas in Chapters 5 and 6 respectively.

suggest (verb)
British National Corpus (BNC) freq = 28,475 (253.58 per million)

modifiers of "suggest" 3,105 0.11

collocate	freq	score
strongly +	190	9.25
strongly suggests that		
above	59	8.63
suggested above ,		
tentatively	21	7.67
tentatively suggest that		
otherwise	43	7.59
to suggest otherwise		
therefore	66	7.16
therefore suggest		
that	58	6.97
suggested that '		
first	63	6.90
was first suggested		
also +	448	6.89
also suggested that		
instead	20	6.85
suggests instead		
elsewhere	15	6.61
suggested elsewhere		
seriously	21	6.48
seriously suggested that		
below	13	6.37
suggested below .		
implicitly	9	6.37
perhaps	27	6.35
sometimes	35	6.30
it is sometimes suggested that		
even	90	6.30

objects of "suggest" 6,367 0.22

collocate	freq	score
possibility	54	7.38
way +	185	7.21
suggest ways		
link	41	7.09
solution	35	6.88
change	60	6.76
alternative	26	6.66
need	52	6.62
suggests the need		
existence	24	6.62
suggest the existence of		
reason	44	6.53
use	43	6.53
improvement	23	6.48
suggest improvements		
approach	31	6.46
degree	28	6.46
connection	23	6.44
presence	22	6.44
suggest the presence of		
date	24	6.40
affinity	16	6.29
model	26	6.27
method	28	6.25
role	35	6.22
relationship	28	6.21
idea	44	6.19
line	32	6.16
lines suggested by		

subjects of "suggest" 10,310 0.36

collocate	freq	score
evidence +	403	9.91
evidence suggests that		
study +	237	8.76
studies suggest that		
report +	255	8.63
result +	179	8.43
results suggest that		
finding +	104	8.19
. these findings suggest that		
research +	123	8.07
research suggests that		
name +	124	8.01
as the name suggests ,		
datum +	100	7.95
these data suggest that		
estimate	76	7.82
estimates suggest that		
experience	73	7.48
experience suggests that		
figure	87	7.46
figures suggest that		
theory	69	7.34
theory suggests that		
author	61	7.29
the authors suggest		
observation	53	7.27
observations suggest that		
survey	60	7.24
survey suggests		

"suggest" and/or ... 157 0.01

collocate	freq	score
do	6	5.42

prepositional phrases 1,512

collocate	freq	score
"suggest" by ...	614	0.02
"suggest" in ...	328	0.01
"suggest" to ...	276	0.01
"suggest" as ...	89	0.00
"suggest" for ...	87	0.00
"suggest" at ...	42	0.00
"suggest" on ...	25	0.00
"suggest" with ...	24	0.00
"suggest" from ...	11	0.00
"suggest" about ...	9	0.00
"suggest" if ...	7	0.00

pronominal objects of "suggest" 669 0.02

collocate	freq	score
itself	28	6.70
suggests itself		
themselves	29	6.15
suggest themselves .		
you +	280	5.59
I suggest you		
it +	305	5.08
suggested it		
them	10	1.73
suggest them		

pronominal subjects of "suggest" 5,036 0.18

collocate	freq	score
i +	1,363	5.89
i suggest		
it +	1,242	5.85
it is suggested		
he +	1,022	5.77
he suggested		
itself	16	5.64
itself suggests that		
we +	311	5.10
we suggest that		
you +	420	4.99
you suggest		
they +	345	4.86
they suggest that		
me	16	4.82
himself	8	4.74
she +	237	4.52
she suggested		
him	11	4.38
them	16	4.29
one	12	4.23
one suggested		
us	8	4.15

wh-words following "suggest" 264 0.01

collocate	freq	score
that	38	7.53
been suggested that		

FIGURE 4.6 WORD SKETCH FOR 'SUGGEST'

Case study 4.3:

Yoon (2008) has reported how students can integrate corpus use into their writing to become more independent and advanced writers. Their teacher worked with the six graduate advanced ESL learners in their academic writing course by incorporating the corpus approach into the curriculum as part of regular classroom activities. He used a free online corpus, the COBUILD Corpus, which is the largest general corpus available (www.collins.co.uk/Corpus/CorpusSearch.aspx). The corpus provides 'a concordance and a collocation sampler from which one can draw 40 randomly chosen concordance lines and see what are statistically the most frequent 100 collocates. The sampler offers instructions on how to conduct a search, though the concordance and collocate search process requires minimal technical skill' (Yoon, 2008, p. 33). The teacher required the students to search the corpus regarding their own writing problems and to email the search results to him on a weekly basis. He then combined those results on handouts regularly provided to the class so that students could benefit from each other's corpus searches. In addition, he usually began class sessions by commenting on writing errors that he found in students' drafts. He encouraged them to research the problems through the corpus. He also wrote feedback on their papers, directing them to search out solutions rather than correcting errors immediately. In so doing, he expected that the class would generate a useful lexicon that stemmed from their own errors.

Reading and technology

Urquhart and Weir (1998) argue that '(R)eading is the process of receiving and interpreting information encoded in language form via the medium of print' (p. 22).

Task 4.5: Why is reading important for ESL/EFL learners?

At a parent evening, a mum asked the teacher how she could help her son, Tom, improve his English. Tom is an EAL (English as an additional language) student and is a bit slow in learning English. The teacher said, 'there is only one way to improve – reading'. Could you explain, from the teacher's perspective, why reading is so important?

The most important reason is that reading can help a learner like Tom successfully learn the foreign language and improve his learning across subjects. The literature suggests a strong link between academic success and reading because reading is the most direct input to generate potential output (e.g. writing). For example, a reader can analyse the organisational structure of the materials they read and use that to improve their writing. Reading is also an effective way to build vocabulary because learners learn new words in specific contexts, which helps them to focus on both meaning and form.

Reading processes and approaches

Reading is an activity that involves 'decoding the written text on the one hand and efficiently processing the information gained on the other hand' (Hellekjær, 2007, p. 2). Reading is a set of complex and finely coordinated processes. As Grabe (2014) suggests,

> Reading comprehension involves abilities to recognize words rapidly and efficiently, develop and use a very large recognition vocabulary, process sentences in order to build comprehension, engage a range of strategic processes and underlying cognitive skills (e.g. setting goals, changing goals flexibly, monitoring comprehension), interpret meaning in relation to background knowledge, interpret and evaluate texts in line with reader goals and purposes, and process texts fluently over an extended period of time. (p. 8)

According to Grabe, 'all processes occur in working memory – which can be understood as the pattern of cognitive neural network activations at any given moment' (2014, p. 9). He further explains that reading abilities can be classified as lower- or higher-level processes and sets out what these two processes entails (ibid).

Lower-level processes include fast, automatic word recognition skills; automatic lexicosyntactic processing (e.g. recognising words parts, how words are formed and grammatical structure analysis); and the semantic processing of the immediate clause into relevant meaning units (or propositions). Higher-level processes involve strategies and resources for comprehension with more difficult texts: (a) form main idea meanings, (b) recognise related and thematic information, (c) build a text model of comprehension (an author-driven summary) and (d) use inferencing, background knowledge, strategic processing and context constraints to create a situation model of reading (a preferred personal interpretation) (Hannon, 2011; Perfetti and Adlof, 2012). Both lower- and higher-level processes are required for success in reading. By reviewing research in L1, Grabe drew conclusions:

- Training in phonological awareness and sounds that letters make helps reading development among children and beginner readers (Ehri, 2006).

- Vocabulary knowledge is highly correlated with reading ability (see Grabe, 2009; Grabe and Stoller, 2011), and there is strong evidence that L2 vocabulary links with reading (Qian, 2002; Droop and Verhoeven, 2003).

- There are strong relationships between (a) syntax and discourse awareness and (b) reading comprehension (see Grabe, 2009; Shiotsu, 2010).

- Strategic processing and metacognitive awareness during reading (e.g. inferencing and comprehension monitoring) influences reading comprehension.

Intensive reading is reading carefully to remember the details and understand all the words and meanings (Simensen, 2007, p. 149).

Reading can be classified as **intensive reading** or extensive reading, and it can be taught using top-down, bottom-up or interactive approaches. The bottom-up model uses predominantly low-level processing. So a learner starts with the smallest units in sentences (e.g. words) and then puts them together to decode the meaning of the larger units (e.g. sentences and paragraphs). Word recognition happens before comprehension. The top-down model relies heavily on higher-level processing when a reader uses syntactic and semantic knowledge that they had prior to reading (Grabe, 2009, p. 89). This very often involves guess and prediction. The reader relies on what he/she already knows about the topic and predicts what will be read. During this process, the reader can accept/reject his/her prediction when more information is accessed. This approach relies on the reader's skills to incorporate all the information and knowledge in order to understand the text. However, in practice, the interactive approach is perhaps more effective, given reading is not a linear process. The interactive approach draws upon aspects of both of the bottom-up and the top-down models to engage in an interactive process between the lower-level processing (bottom-up) and higher-level processing (top-down).

Technology use in assisting reading

Research studies suggest that technology improves reading skills (Lunde, 1990; Sanaoui and Lapkin, 1992; Beauvois, 1994). Specifically, the interplay of multimedia elements improves the learning how to read text written in a second language (Carman, 2003; Hagood, 2003; Mackay, 2003), and the integration of computer-mediated support also facilitates reading improvement for ESL learners (Williams and Williams, 2000; Stakhnevich, 2002), for example, online dictionaries, glossaries, graphics, blogs and discussion boards.

Multimedia reading materials

Dual-coding theory means human memory is composed of two independent but interconnected coding systems, with the visual system dealing with visual codes (images, concrete objects and events) and the verbal system dealing with non-visual codes (e.g. words). Although these are two separate systems, most information processing requires using both of them.

Reading is a meaning-making process in which the reader needs to activate both linguistic and contextual knowledge. Multimedia reading materials, including texts, graphics, video clips and audio resources, can assist this meaning-making process. The idea of using multimodal materials to support language learning is grounded in **dual-coding theory** and is widely approved. Akyel and Erçetin (2009) suggest that online glossaries support L2 online reading comprehension. Huang et al. (2009) report that L2 online readers predominantly use translation, dictionary and highlighting functions. Park and Kim (2011) show how L2 users employ various hypermedia resources and computer applications and functions (e.g. a spell checker) when reading online. Multimedia materials work with both adult and young learners. For young learners, images, sound and animations are strong motivators.

MeeGenius (www.meegenius.com/) is a website for young learners which contains various types of materials (see Figure 4.7). The learner can either

FIGURE 4.7   MEEGENIUS ONLINE READING

FIGURE 4.8   A SELF-DESIGNED WEBSITE FOR READING

choose 'Read it myself' or 'Read to me'. The books have texts, sound and illustrations to aid comprehension. The use of multimodal materials is recommended for every classroom with emergent readers (Bickart and Dodge, 2000).

Task 4.6: Design a task for Carol's class

Carol is teaching English in South Korea. Her class contains 35 seven-year-olds. They've learnt some basic English. Now Carol wants to use this website to keep her learners interested in reading. Visit the MeeGenius website and design two tasks for Carol's class.

There are many advantages of using websites in L2 reading instruction, with authentic and varied materials, texts, images, sound and graphic designs.

> **Task 4.7:** Analysis of a teacher's design of activities
>
> I had to deliver a topic on classical music to a group of 14–15-year-old students. I created a website (Figure 4.8) with a short introduction. I asked students to read the passage and then explore the hyperlinks I provided. Since the passage is not easy for students, I used L1 translation for some new words. I also provided students with sample music and a music website which they can access. Of course, there was a short quiz that they had to complete before they explored the external links. Students did this as independent learning in a computer room while I was supervising and monitoring the process.
>
> What are the strengths and weaknesses of designing a website to improve students' reading ability? Apart from reducing linguistic difficulty, what other roles does L1 have?

However, sometimes, teachers need to design their own materials in order to address students' learning styles and curriculum needs. The ad hoc design of websites requires technical skills, time and resources. WebQuest is a useful tool to address the need to design a specific website or study programme. If a teacher has knowledge of web design, he/she can also design a website using a web development tool, such as Dreamweaver.

Programmes

An efficient reader must be able to read fast. Together with rapid word recognition, accuracy in comprehension and incremental learning, a rapid reading rate contributes to the concept of 'reading fluency'. Grabe (2009) defines reading fluency as 'the ability to read rapidly with ease and accuracy, and to read with appropriate expression and phrasing. It involves a long incremental process and text comprehension is the expected outcome' (p. 291). For many EFL learners, perhaps one thing they can practise is their reading rate, in order to improve fluency. Spreeder (spreeder.com/app.php?intro=1) is a good tool to help learners to develop their reading speed, which can be used either independently or as a whole class activity. The reader sets the pace and increases it as they become more confident and competent in reading. The reader can control other variables, such as words per minute, font size, font colour and so on (see Figure 4.9). Apart from free apps and software, there is also paid software that is designed to increase reading comprehension as well as reading speed: for example, *7 Speed Reading*, *AceReader* and *The Reader's Edge*. Such software also provides exercises and tests, which help the reader customise their training.

Mobile-assisted reading

As mentioned in Chapter 1, mobile-assisted language learning (MALL) is now becoming more widely used in second language education, due to its

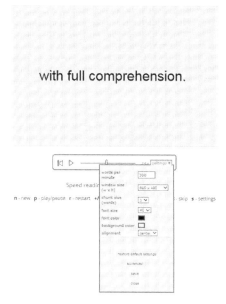

FIGURE 4.9   THE INTERFACE OF SPREEDER

advantages over other types of technological tools. For the first time, mobile devices allow learners to gain access to learning materials 'on the go' and support open, distance and informal learning opportunities (Chen and Chung, 2008). Mobile devices (e.g. smart phones, PDAs and tablets) with their increasing capabilities are a useful tool to help achieve educational goals such as supporting different types of learning needs (Cheung and Hew, 2009). Furthermore, mobile devices can offer informal, spontaneous, contextual and personal opportunities for learning (Sharples et al., 2009). Using mobile technology to teach vocabulary is the most common topic reported in research studies, whereas only very few studies have dealt with reading, writing or grammar.

Case study 4.4:

Wang and Smith (2013) reported an experiment on developing mobile reading for Japanese college students. In their programme, they recruited 10 advanced students to write materials for other students. Their materials were uploaded by the students and then were edited by university teachers. Each piece of text was no more than 140 words in length so that students could read it in two or three minutes on a small screen. The topics chosen for the mobile learning project were as topical and broad as possible – usually a short story, a joke or an anecdote. The text was annotated with Japanese translations, and vocabulary notes were placed at the beginning of the text to make readers aware of new vocabulary. All materials included both audio and visual content, to support the readings, so students could choose to read, listen or watch. Alongside the reading text, two types of grammar material were provided: grammar knowledge and grammar quizzes.

Task 4.8: Do you think this project works?

Look at Case study 4.4. If you were implementing this project with your students, do you think it would work? Why or why not? What changes would be needed to make it more suitable for your context?

The idea of this project was to engage students with reading and to develop their reading strategies by using mobile devices because students spend more and more time socialising on their mobile phones. So when students are encouraged to use mobile phones to read more successfully, the project should meet several conditions:

- The materials (reading texts) must be authentic and relevant to students. In this case, news which interests students would be more relevant than other students' essays.

- The teacher's involvement is important in successful implementation of mobile reading. So a follow-up discussion led by the teacher would be useful to keep students engaged.

- The goal of the reading should be clear. The focus should be placed on comprehension rather than on building vocabulary or improving grammar. So instruction on vocabulary and grammar should be a minor focus.

- Students are highly engaged with social networks nowadays, so make good use of the existing social networks. For example, a WeChat group (www.wechat.com) can be established for students to share news and relevant materials. Such an application makes it possible for students to make comments and interact with each other, not for academic purposes, but for social purposes.

Online literacy

Technological literacy is an essential component of the strategic toolbox for language acquisition (LeLoup and Ponterio, 2000; Richards, 2000; Hubbard, 2004; Godwin-Jones, 2000, 2010b). Digital literacies refer to 'the individual and social skills needed to effectively interpret, manage, share and create meaning in the growing range of digital communication channels' (Dudeney et al., 2013, p. 2). Digital literacies constitute a plural concept (Pegrum, 2009, 2011; Lankshear and Knobel, 2011; Kalantzis and Cope, 2012), which include not just individual skills or competencies but social skills that involve interpreting and creating both written text and visual and media resources. With the development of the use of Web 2.0 and mobile learning, we are also talking about attention literacy (Rheingold, 2009), personal literacy (Burniske, 2008) and mobile literacy (Parry, 2011). Although most digital communication still involves written language, the skills that a reader and a writer need to engage in digital communication are more sophisticated, as Dudeney et al. (2013) describe:

> Readers skim and scan extended texts, assess and analyse opinion pieces, and evaluate subtle cues of tone and intent in status updates. Writers carefully plan and compose blog entries, build persuasive arguments and counter-arguments on discussion boards, restructure and copy-edit their own and others' work on wikis, and express themselves succinctly in tweets. (pp. 7–8)

Reading online, readers encounter numerous hyperlinks, which possibly add cognitive load and slow down both reading speed and comprehension (Carr, 2010). Online reading therefore requires hypertext literacy: 'the ability to process hyperlinks appropriately and to use hyperlinks effectively to enhance a document or artefact' (Dudeney et al., 2013, p. 11). With regard to L2 reading, new literacy skills are required, which according to Park et al. (2014, pp. 162–163) are associated with five domains: '(1) identifying problems and questions, (2) locating information from multiple online resources, (3) critically evaluating information online, (4) synthesizing information online, and (5) communicating and exchanging information online'. These strategies parallel those found among L1 readers of English (Leu et al., 2004; Coiro et al., 2008; Mokhtari et al., 2008).

Task 4.9: How would you develop your learners' online literacy?

Now discuss with your friends and colleagues three ways to develop your (or your learners') online literacy. Are there other issues you need to be aware of when focusing on online literacy?

Developing students' new literacy skills for online reading involves a set of complex and interactive skills. The five areas above might require students to develop the following sub-skills:

■ Learners need to have an idea about what topics they would like to look for and what problems they need to solve by conducting an online search.

■ In order to acquire the appropriate sources to solve a problem, learners need to be able to identify and locate multiple online resources and multimodal materials.

■ Reading requires material selection, which further requires students to be able to evaluate materials they have located. Like reading print materials, students need to be critical and creative in dealing with online materials. The materials from authoritative sources are often believed to be more useful and trustworthy, but there are also materials produced by individuals which offer valuable opinions.

■ Online searches often result in abundant materials; therefore, the ability to be able to synthesise information available to individuals becomes critical. Closely related to this is the need to rapidly read and evaluate materials.

■ Learners might need to think about how they can make the best use of an online community in order to share materials and create knowledge together.

■ There will be security issues regarding reading online and downloading materials. There are also issues related to plagiarism and ethics when reading and gaining information online. Thus, the ownership of information also becomes an area that deserves attention.

Summary

In this chapter, we examined the role of technology in teaching writing, reading and a related skill: online literacy. Again, I would emphasise that technology can play various roles and is clearly beneficial to second language learners. However, the potential benefit of technology depends on how it is utilised in learning and educational contexts and how teachers implement technological tools. We will come back to this issue in Chapter 9. In the next chapter, we will examine more closely the functions of technological tools in teaching vocabulary and grammar.

Annotated further reading

1. Storch, N. (2013) *Collaborative Writing in L2 Classrooms*. Bristol: Multilingual Matters. Chapter 7, pp. 118–154.

This chapter discusses collaborative writing activities in computer-mediated environments, including first-generation web applications such as emails, chat-rooms and discussion boards and second-generation web (Web 2.0) applications such as podcasts, blogs, wikis, Google Docs and various social networking sites (e.g. Facebook, YouTube). The chapter focused mainly on the use of wikis in L1 and L2 contexts.

2. Evans, D. (n.d.) Corpus building and investigation for the Humanities: An on-line information pack about corpus investigation techniques for the Humanities. University of Nottingham. Unit 2: Compiling a corpus. Available at www.bir-mingham.ac.uk/Documents/college-artslaw/corpus/Intro/Unit2.pdf

This is a useful practical guide for anyone who is interested in compiling their own corpus.

3. Gilmore, A. (2009) Using online corpora to develop students' writing skills. *ELT Journal*, 63(4), 363–372.

This article describes how large corpora such as the British National Corpus and the COBUILD (Collins Birmingham University International Language Database) Corpus and Collocations Sampler were incorporated into a process-based writing approach to help develop students' writing skills. This article aims to familiarise readers with these resources and to show how they can be usefully exploited in the redrafting stages of writing. Gilmore also compared the use of these two online corpora in Japanese university writing classes.

4. Walker, A. & White, G. (2013) *Technology Enhanced Language Learning*. Oxford: Oxford University Press. Chapters 4 and 6.

This book can be used overall as a professional resource. It contains chapters dealing with various issues of using technologies in teaching languages. These two particular chapters are relevant to what we have discussed here about teaching reading and new literacies. Chapter 4 describes some skills involved in second language reading by comparing them with L1. It presents some of the challenges and opportunities of online reading. It also considers ways that technology can support the development of reading skills. Chapter 6 discusses how visual materi-als, activities and tools support language learning and support teaching new literacies where multimodal texts are used.

5 Technology for lexicogrammatical acquisition

Aims: This chapter focuses on the new technological tools in developing linguistic knowledge, in particular for lexis and grammar by reviewing evidence and proposing practices in second and foreign language classrooms. Researchers and teachers take different approaches to the acquisition of lexical items and grammar. In this chapter, a lexicogrammatical approach is applied but with different technological tools focusing on each area. In the summary section, future directions and challenges are also presented. This chapter has three main sections, as follows:

1. How vocabulary and grammar are learnt

2. Technology use in vocabulary and grammar teaching

3. Technology-enhanced lexicogrammatical acquisition.

Introduction

CALL has been used for some time now in facilitating the acquisition of linguistic knowledge and the development of language skills. Much research has been carried out to investigate how technologies can improve the effectiveness of language learning, in particular in developing knowledge of lexis, with slightly less attention having been given to grammar (Macaro et al., 2012). Situated in this context, we will examine some CALL tools for vocabulary and grammar acquisition by reviewing the evidence from CALL literature to consider why new technologies are theoretically appropriate in enhancing linguistic knowledge acquisition. The aim of this chapter is to help readers to understand how specific linguistic knowledge (i.e. vocabulary and grammar) is acquired and what technological tools are available to enhance the teaching and learning of such knowledge. First, I will discuss how vocabulary and grammar are learnt, in order to help the reader to make sense of the way in which some particular tools and applications are proposed to teach this knowledge. Then I will discuss how technology can enhance vocabulary and grammar learning, and I will present some ideas and examples. This is followed by further discussion of the lexicogrammatical approach and the future directions that teaching and researching vocabulary and grammar acquisition will go in.

How vocabulary and grammar are learnt

Vocabulary and grammar are very important language components, as Wilkins (1972, pp. 111–112) tells us: 'while without grammar very little can be conveyed, without vocabulary nothing can be conveyed'. For many language learners and teachers, vocabulary and grammar are the most important systems, as they are viewed as a foundation for developing communicative skills. Many English language teachers devote much time in developing their students' linguistic knowledge in these areas. This is especially true for foreign language learners, who normally study in an instructed environment, which does not provide them with many opportunities to acquire the target language. In such a learning environment, teachers emphasise the importance of learning vocabulary and grammar for both academic and social purposes. Language proficiency is often determined by one's linguistic knowledge (e.g. vocabulary and grammar) and skills (e.g. reading and writing). Many researchers have endorsed the importance of vocabulary and grammar in language learning. For example, Swan and Walter (1984) claim that vocabulary acquisition is the largest and most important task facing the language learner. Lewis (1993) goes further by arguing that 'lexis is the core or heart of language' (p. 89). Equally, grammar is an important component, especially in developing communicative competence (Canale and Swain, 1980). In terms of how grammar and vocabulary are learnt and what approaches should be used to teach them, there is constant debate on whether they should be considered as separate or interrelated.

Task 5.1: How did you learn grammar and vocabulary?

When you learned a foreign language, how did you learn vocabulary and grammar? Can you still remember how your teachers helped you remember the words and understand grammar rules? Was it useful and effective for you?

   If you ever used a technological tool to assist vocabulary or grammar learning, could you reflect on the effectiveness of the use of the tool/application?

You might come up with different methods and strategies of learning grammar and vocabulary, and your experience of successfully and effectively learning a language definitely helps you understand the theoretical considerations underpinning the acquisition of lexis and grammar. If we assume that every person is different, it is reasonable to then assume that their learning style, preferences and strategies are also different. But there is some evidence suggesting that some methods are more effective than others, although they have to be utilised in practice according to learners' differences.

A focus on vocabulary

Lexis 'refers to all the words in a language, the entire vocabulary of a language' (Barcroft et al., 2011, p. 571). Although vocabulary has conventionally been conceptualised as individual words, it has now become clear that lexis consists of individual words, sequences of words, collocations and fixed and semi-fixed expressions and idioms such as 'here and there', 'you know' and 'happy hour'. These sequences of words and collocations are taught and learnt as single lexical chunks because vocabulary learning frequently involves learning 'chunks' that are longer than individual words. It is important to note that lexical chunks can perform linguistic means to carry out language functions to facilitate clear, relevant and concise language use. They also help learners to achieve greater fluency in speech production and comprehension. As such, lexical chunks are considered as an essential part of vocabulary acquisition. What is worth mentioning here is lexical priming (Hoey, 2005), which is a new view of language, explaining the existence of combinations of words and why corpus linguistics works as a way of analysing language. According to Hoey (2005), we acquire vocabulary not only from explicit learning but mostly from contexts such as linguistic and contextual information and social interaction which we repeatedly encounter. Lexical priming gives us an idea why it is likely (or unlikely) that certain words stand in such relations to each other. Hoey states that

> Priming is the result of a speaker encountering evidence and generalising from it. [Primings come] from single focussed and generalising encounters. Language teaching materials and language teachers can provide essential shortcuts to primings. (2005, p. 185)

So it is implied that when we encounter a word or phrase, we store it along with all the words that accompanied it and with a note of the context when it was used. As such, we expect words to be in the units of other words (their collocations) and expect them to appear in certain grammatical structures.

Vocabulary knowledge is a complex construct which involves multiple knowledge dimensions, such as form, meaning, grammatical characteristics, collocations and several others (Nation, 2001). Vocabulary learning follows

Incidental vocabulary acquisition is generally defined as the 'learning of vocabulary as the by-product of any activity not explicitly geared to vocabulary learning' and is contrasted with intentional vocabulary learning, defined as 'any activity geared at committing lexical information to memory' (Hulstijn, 2001, p. 271).

two broad approaches: implicit learning and explicit learning. Implicit learning is the acquisition of knowledge about the underlying structure of a complex stimulus environment by a process which takes place naturally, simply and without conscious operations (Ellis, 1994, p. 107). Implicit learning is natural and meaning focused, which means vocabulary and grammar can be acquired through meaning-focused communicative activities such as reading and listening (Hulstijn, 2003). On the contrary, explicit learning is 'any activity geared at committing lexical information to memory' (Hulstijn, 2001, p. 271). It is the deliberate and intentional learning of vocabulary. In vocabulary acquisition, a distinction is frequently made which superficially appears to correspond to the implicit/explicit debate: that of incidental vs intentional vocabulary acquisition. Considering incidental learning, Waring and Takaki (2003) suggested that graded readers found small gains overall in vocabulary from reading, whereas van Zeeland and Schmitt (2013) found that considerable learning has taken place from listening, especially in the form recognition and grammar recognition tests.

Task 5.2: What learning is it?

My son plays computer games with his friends online. As a result of the game playing, they acquired some new vocabulary. Is this incidental or intentional vocabulary acquisition? Can you think of other examples for these two types of learning?

Schmitt (2008) argues that a more proactive, principled approach needs to be taken in promoting vocabulary learning, which will require contributions from learning 'partners' (p. 333). He lists four partners needed to make strong and active contributions to ensure the success of vocabulary learning:

- Learners can and are willing to be active over a long period of time.
- Teachers can provide guidance and support.
- Researchers can provide reliable information about vocabulary and learning techniques.
- Materials writers can deliver the research-based materials for teachers and learners to use.

In fact, these four partners cannot be separated, and they need to work together to make sure that vocabulary acquisition on the learners' parts is successful. Apart from highlighting the important partners in vocabulary learning, Hunt and Beglar (1998) proposed seven principles for vocabulary instruction:

Principle 1: Target frequent words. A minimum of the 3000 most-frequent word families that a learner needs to know to achieve some understanding of a text, and this figure could rise to as many as 8000 word families.

Principle 2: Provide opportunities for the incidental learning of vocabulary.

Principle 3: Provide opportunities for the intentional learning of vocabulary and engaging in deep processing.

Principle 4: Provide opportunities for expanding word knowledge.

Principle 5: Provide opportunities for developing fluency with known vocabulary.

Principle 6: Provide opportunities to encounter words in context.

Principle 7: Examine different types of dictionaries and teach students how to use them.

Schmitt (2008) provided additional points to be incorporated in vocabulary teaching as follows:

- Learners need an extensive vocabulary to successfully use a second language, and so high vocabulary targets need to be set and pursued. Research suggests that students need around 8000 words if they are comfortable with the demands of L2 reading or listening comprehension (Nation, 2006; Schmitt, 2008; Webb and Rodgers, 2009a, 2009b; Laufer and Ravenhorst-Kalovski, 2010).

- Vocabulary learning is a complex and gradual process, and different approaches may be appropriate at different points along the incremental learning process.

- At the beginning, establishing the meaning–form link is essential, and intentional learning is best for this. Using the L1 is one sensible way to quickly establish this initial link.

- Once this initial meaning–form link is established, it is crucial to consolidate it with repeated exposures. Providing learners with multiple encounters with words is important for vocabulary learning, for example, Zahar et al. (2001) suggested six to ten encounters when teaching vocabulary.

- It is also important to begin enhancing knowledge of different aspects of word knowledge. Some of these may be usefully learnt explicitly (e.g. knowledge of derivative forms), but the more 'contextualized' word knowledge aspects (e.g. collocation) are probably best learnt by being exposed to the lexical item numerous times in many different contexts.

- Make sure that learners maintain the maximum amount of engagement possible with lexical items.

A focus on grammar

Grammar concerns how words connect to each other in a sentence in ways that make sense. In grammar research, explicit and implicit knowledge is often referred to, and both dimensions relate to linguistic knowledge, but they are separate constructs (Ellis, 2005). As Ellis (2006) points out,

> *Explicit knowledge* consists of the facts that speakers of language have learned. These facts are often not clearly understood and may be in conflict with each other. They concern different aspects of language including grammar. Explicit knowledge is held consciously, is learnable and verbalisable, and is typically accessed through controlled processing when learners experience some kind of linguistic difficulty in using the L2. … In contrast, *implicit knowledge* is procedural, is held unconsciously, and can only be verbalized if it is made explicit. It is accessed rapidly and easily and thus is available for use in rapid, fluent communication. Most SLA researchers agree that competence in an L2 is primarily a matter of implicit knowledge. (p. 95)

Traditionally, grammar teaching has been defined with an overly narrow scope as the presentation and practice of discrete grammatical structures. However, grammar teaching is more complex than that and does not necessarily involve presentation or practice. Ellis (2006) offers a broad view on grammar teaching, stating that it

> involves any instructional technique that draws learners' attention to some specific grammatical form in such a way that it helps them either to understand it metalinguistically and/or process it in comprehension and/or production so that they can internalize it. (p. 84)

The current trend of learning grammar is one that combines form, meaning and functions (Larsen-Freeman, 1991). These three dimensions interact and should be considered together in teaching. That is, learning grammar perhaps should focus on not only mastering the rules but also considering the meanings and function of these rules in communication where social factors

Intensive grammar teaching refers to instruction over a sustained period of time (which could be a lesson or a series of lessons covering days or weeks) concerning a single grammatical structure or, perhaps, a pair of contrasted structures (e.g., English past continuous vs. past simple).

Extensive grammar teaching refers to instruction concerning a whole range of structures within a short period of time (e.g., a lesson) so that each structure receives only minimal attention in any one lesson (Ellis, 2006).

are important. Understanding intended meanings in a social context has more to do with the pragmatic awareness of a learner than with grammatical competence. So when we focus on grammar teaching, we do not just help learners to develop their grammatical competence or the accuracy of structure, including morphology and syntax; we also need to address pragmatics – the appropriateness of language use in a given situation. Clearly, grammatical development does not guarantee a corresponding level of pragmatic development, and there is no direct link between grammatical competence and pragmatic competence.

Research suggests that instructed learning is beneficial for grammar acquisition, but in order to be effective, grammar should be taught in a manner that is compatible with the natural processes of acquisition (e.g. Long, 1988). Grammar can either be taught **intensively or extensively**.

Ellis (2001) considered three broad types of form-focused instruction, namely 'Focus on forms', 'Planned focus on form' and 'Incidental focus on form'. Ellis (2006) outlined the differences of these three types of instructions as follows:

- Focus on form: refers to instruction involving a structure-of-the-day approach, and the primary focus of learning is on form (i.e. accuracy) and the activities are directed intensively at a single grammatical structure.

- Planned Focus on form entails a focus on meaning with attention to form arising out of the communicative activity. This focus is planned so as a predetermined grammatical structure can be elicited.

- Incidental focus on form means that attention to form in the context of a communicative activity is not predetermined but rather occurs in accordance with the participants' linguistic needs as the activity proceeds.

There is some theoretical disagreement regarding which of these types of instruction is most effective in developing implicit knowledge. Whereas some believe that focus on form is more beneficial and effective because learners are involved in meaningful communication (e.g. Long, 1988, 1991; Doughty, 2001), others argue that a focus-on-forms approach is more effective and appropriate (e.g. DeKeyser, 1998).

It is important to note that in both vocabulary and grammar teaching, the use and function of the language and its related context are emphasised. This view is in line with a sociocultural perspective of language learning. However, vocabulary and grammar teaching and learning are also highly influenced by other theories, such as cognitive learning theory, which emphasises the importance of the cognitive level of knowledge acquisition through enhancing a learner's noticing 'form' and by providing opportunities for practice.

Task 5.3: Link to the theories in Chapter 1

Now go back to Chapter 1 and read the learning theories again to see whether you can understand vocabulary and grammar acquisition from different theoretical perspectives. How do different theories understand vocabulary and grammar learning? Could you give an example to illustrate different theories?

Technology use in vocabulary and grammar teaching

Chapelle (2003, p. 56) takes the key concept of interaction and proposes three theoretical perspectives regarding technology use in language learning: the interaction hypothesis, sociocultural theory and the depth of processing theory. These different theoretical perspectives place different emphasis on how technology can facilitate language learning. Take human–computer interaction as an example: an interaction hypothesis would emphasise obtaining enhanced input; sociocultural theory would advocate gaining help in using the language; and the depth of processing theory would focus on opportunities for increased attention to language. So, the focus of human–computer interaction can vary based on different perspectives. From an interaction hypothesis perspective, technology can be used to obtain enhanced input through marking a grammatical form on the screen, modifying the difficulty level by providing images or adding elaborations to increase the potential for understanding. From a sociocultural theoretical perspective, language is closely related to the context in which it is used. For example, technology can be used to create various situations where the target language (a particular word) is used. The interaction between a learner and the computer can prompt attention to language, from the perspective of the depth of processing theory. Distinguished as they are, CALL designers and teachers review, select and apply these theories in an integrated way in practice and follow the principles of how language is learnt from an SLA perspective.

Benefits of technology for vocabulary and grammar learning

Technology affordances in facilitating linguistic acquisition have been widely recognised and acknowledged. In general, positive attitudes towards using TELL in facilitating lexis and grammar are reported in various studies (e.g. Can and Cagiltay, 2006).

Task 5.4: See the classroom extract below with the PowerPoint slide and respond to the following questions:

1. How is the teacher using technology to teach new vocabulary?
2. From this teacher's perspective, what are the reasons for using technology?

(showing a PowerPoint slide of the Loch Ness monster)

SS: (discussing in a low voice)

T: what's that?

S1: the monster of …

T: the monster of what?

S1: (in a low voice) lake.

T: lake, yes. It is a lake, but we always use this word (writing 'loch' on the blackboard). 'Loch' is a Scottish word: Loch's monster. Is it fact or fantasy?

Now, talk to a colleague and give the reasons why technological tools should be used to teach vocabulary and grammar?

Clearly in the extract above, the teacher is using technology to facilitate the understanding and acquisition of the new word by using multimedia resources. It provides learners with an opportunity of 'noticing' and using multisensory learning. So there are at least three reasons why technology can facilitate vocabulary and grammar acquisition.

Multimodal materials, including audio, visual and multimedia materials, can be developed and utilised in *enhancing linguistic acquisition*. Chapelle and Jamieson (2008, p. 7) illustrate this point:

(T)here are presentations of grammatical points. … [They might] include animation to make a point and practice exercises with feedback that allow students to test their understanding of the point. Perhaps because of their regular use of the Internet, students feel more engaged by interactive materials that provide feedback than they do with exercises in a workbook.

Multimedia is a combination of print, audio and imagery which can be used to enhance comprehensible input. Much research has been conducted on the use of multimedia for vocabulary learning (for a review, see Plass and Jones, 2005).

The use of multimodal learning materials not only helps retain learners' attention but also improves the learning outcome (Silverman and Hines, 2009). For example, **multimedia** presentations have a positive effect on vocabulary acquisition and retention (e.g. Tsou et al., 2002; Kim and Gilman, 2008; O'Hara and Pritchard, 2008; Silverman and Hines, 2009). In an experimental study, Nakata (2008) showed significant differences between students who learnt words through written lists and those who learnt words through the use of computers – the study has demonstrated the superiority of computers over lists. Similarly, Tozcu and Coady (2004) conducted a case study to examine the outcomes in vocabulary acquisition when using interactive computer-based texts as opposed to traditional materials with 56 intermediate-level students from various first language (L1) backgrounds. The study suggested that the experiment group who used computer-assisted courseware outperformed the control group in vocabulary knowledge, reading comprehension, and reading speed.

From a cognitive perspective, '*noticing*' is a necessary condition in successful SLA (Schmidt, 1990), and research on SLA suggests that learners benefit from any assistance that helps them focus on a specific form of language. As Schmidt (2001) claims, 'noticing' is 'the first step in language building' (p. 31). Research has shown that linguistic input increases when learners notice linguistic features, using techniques such as marking salience, modification or elaboration (Schmidt, 1990). Modification, making the input understandable to the learner through any means that 'gets at the meaning' – for example, images, L2 dictionaries and L1 translation – enhances linguistic acquisition. As such, technology presents itself as a useful tool for modification, in order to increase linguistic competence (Belz and Kinginger, 2003). Gu (2003) found that strategies of directing attention and memorising words are the most helpful in vocabulary learning. Provision of glosses to the new unfamiliar words can facilitate vocabulary learning by directing their attention to the meaning of those words (Liou, 2000). Among all the annotation types, research suggests that L1 is largely relied upon by learners (Davis and Lyman-Hager, 1997; Lomicka, 1998).

CALL applications can be used to attract students' attention and help them memorise words. Tozcu and Coady (2004) investigated the effect of direct vocabulary learning using CALL on vocabulary knowledge, reading comprehension and speed of word recognition and found that a CALL tutorial programme (New Lexis) assisted learners in gaining more highly frequent vocabulary, and they concluded that computer-assisted vocabulary instruction increased vocabulary learning. Torlakovic and Deugo (2004) investigated whether or not CALL systems could be used for grammar teaching by conducting an experimental study. The result suggests that the experiment group outperformed the control group.

In a Saudi context, AbuSeileek and Rabab'ah (2007) conducted an experimental study to compare computer-assisted grammar instruction with teacher-driven grammar (chalk and talk) instructional methods. Each method involves teaching verb tenses using two deductive approaches (a) the initial rule-oriented approach (involving initial presentation of explicit rules followed by illustrative examples) and (b) the structure-guessing approach (involving explicit presentation of rules in response to structure-guessing exercises). The results reveal significant differences between the four groups in favor of the computer-based grammar instructional method, and more specifically the structure-guessing approach except for the present perfect tense. Chenoweth and Murday (2003) also suggest that online grammar instruction results in high grammatical accuracy in writing.

However, studies also show that technology does not necessarily facilitate grammar or vocabulary acquisition. For example, in exploring the benefit of participation in chat or discussion forums, Coniam and Wong (2004) and Zhang et al. (2007) revealed no positive evidence of CALL in grammar acquisition. Proctor et al. (2007) found no evidence that a reading tutor had a positive effect (the Universal Literacy Environment) on vocabulary acquisition. Therefore, assumptions cannot be made that computers (technology) always enhance linguistic acquisition, and the positive impact of technology might be closely related to students' learning styles, appetites, motivations and other factors (e.g. the length of intervention).

As discussed in Chapter 2, technology can provide learners with *high-quality and authentic linguistic materials* and with a *context* for the study of language use. Language use in context is important in the processes of both grammar and vocabulary learning. Learners are able to see how vocabulary is used and collocates with other words and how a grammar rule is used in various situations to achieve different communicative purposes (e.g. through corpus linguistics). When experiencing language in real-life situations, learners will be able to apply in similar contexts the language skills that they have acquired.

Case study 5.1:

Horst et al. (2005) designed purpose-built on-line tools for vocabulary learning in an experimental ESL course for intermediate-level students at a Canadian university. The resources included concordance, dictionary, cloze-builder, hypertext, and a database with interactive self-quizzing feature (available at www.lextutor.ca).

The Word Bank involves learners in identifying important words to study, entering (i.e. typing) the words and their definitions along with example sentences into the bank, and using the gapped example sentences to review their own and their classmates' words. The sound feature allows students to hear the entered words and process the information in another modality. The concordancing feature enables learners to access to rich semantic, syntactic, and collocational information about a new word in the multiple sentence contexts located by the concordance (93).

Technology can *mediate* learning, through which learners can appropriate new understandings. For example, the use of videos, images and animations can help learners to understand abstract and difficult vocabulary. In some cases, the visual thesaurus can mediate the understanding of the relationship between words (e.g. synonyms and antonyms). Yoshii and Flaitz (2002) suggest that the more help learners receive (e.g. through images, sounds and animations), the better they acquire vocabulary. As such, online dictionaries and resources can be used as mediational tools to assist understanding.

Technology use in lexis teaching

In vocabulary acquisition research, Martinez and Schmitt (2010) note that 'the growing ethos among L2 pedagogy practitioners seems to be that technologies like computerized corpora, captioned videos, electronic games, and mobile phones can somehow enhance the learning an detaching of new words' (p. 26). A meta-analysis of 52 studies by Felix (2005) suggested positive effects of technology on English language learners in terms of vocabulary development, reading and writing. The earlier CALL programmes typically included language-learning activities, such as text reconstruction, gap filling, speed reading, simulation and vocabulary games. These programmes focused mainly on helping learners to remember the forms of vocabulary by providing them with different exercises that are strongly associated with explicit learning. The later programmes include the development of multimedia applications (Groot, 2000), the use of the Internet and Web 2.0 technologies. One common feature of these multimedia computer-assisted vocabulary-application or network-based learning programmes is the emphasis on learning vocabulary in context and understanding meanings through various activities. Also, they address learners' needs and learning styles through the use of multimodal materials and give learners as much freedom as possible to choose what to learn and how to learn.

Multimedia materials

Technology that uses visual referents (Jones and Plass, 2002; Nikolova, 2002) or games (J. Wood, 2001) has been shown to support vocabulary acquisition. Multimedia packages with vocabulary learning activities are the most popular type in language learning because technology-assisted multimodality provides a different (from the traditional paper-based input) but effective way for learners to engage with language input. Vocabulary learning rates are reportedly higher when computers are used than when print materials are used (Laufer and Hill, 2000). The use of visual texts improves learning, although the downside of using

Both reversed subtitle and captions proved to be more effective in assisting students in vocabulary learning, especially for recall and word recognition. However, subtitles should be used with difficult materials (Danan, 2004).

multimedia materials is that teachers need to spend more time on instruction (Kim and Gilman, 2008). Input from visual and auditory modality has been suggested to be effective, such as the use of on-screen text for videos (Sydorenko, 2010). There are three types of on-screen text: subtitles (L1 text, L2 sound), reversed subtitles (L1 sound, L2 text) and captions (sound is the same language as the text). In Chapter 3, we examined the role of captioned videos on the enhancement of communication skills. Captioned videos are in fact also beneficial for vocabulary learning. Sydorenko (2010) examined the effect of input modality (video=V, audio=A and captions=C, i.e. on-screen text in the same language as audio) and found that groups with captions (VAC and VC) scored higher on the written recognition than on the aural recognition of word forms, while the reverse applied to the VA group. The VAC group learnt more word meanings than the VA group. Similar results were reported by Montero Perez et al. (2014). So one of the direct pedagogical implications here is that teachers might want to use video (and audio) combined with captions to help learners develop better form–meaning links with new vocabulary. In that respect, Martinez and Schmitt (2000) pointed out that formulaic items may be ideally learnt through the medium of captioned video. This is especially true with formulae which are attached to certain social 'routines'.

Educational games

Many multimedia materials can be used to facilitate learning, and one of the most prevailing materials is educational games. Games are popular tools to enhance vocabulary learning. Interactive games can provide language learners with opportunities to practise language while playing. Because games are generally designed with reward and immediate feedback, learners can be motivated to achieve high scores. Games can also engage students with multimodal materials, including sound and visual animations. Digital games can offer opportunities for collaboration and interaction which might be difficult to achieve in other contexts (see Reinders, 2012). A good example is BBC Wordmaster: www.bbc.co.uk/worldservice/learningenglish/flash/wordmaster/

BBC Wordmaster (Figure 5.1) is an interactive game to test vocabulary skills. There are thousands of words to practise. The game gives the player a sentence with one word missing, and the player needs to beat the clock to complete the sentence with the letters provided. The player can also get help by clicking the 'definition' button, which will provide the definition of the missing word (Step 1). Once the individual letters are put in, the computer will provide the player with immediate feedback. If the correct letters are put

Step 1   Step 2   Step 3

FIGURE 5.1   BBC WORDMASTER

in within the time, the computer will provide the player with feedback on their performance (Step 2). Then the computer will take the player to the next step, which shows the completed sentence with the vocabulary high-lighted. The computer will also read the sentence aloud if the player clicks on the 'listen' button (Step 3).

Task 5.5: Design an activity

Go to BBC Wordmaster to try this game. Could you use it with your students? Design an activity and provide the rationales of your design.

Like many educational games, there are some pedagogical considerations for using this game in teaching:

■ This game places vocabulary learning in the context of a sentence, and it requires the learners to be able to understand three aspects of vocabulary, namely form, meaning and use.

■ The 'definition' function provides enhanced input in the form of modification.

■ The time limit motivates and challenges the player.

■ The immediate feedback on the correct letter helps the 'guesswork', and it provides comments and the score, which motivates the player.

■ The player can listen to the sentence with the target vocabulary highlighted. The highlighting is another form of enhanced input: marked input.

■ By playing a game, learners' involvement is maximised.

This game can be used either for whole class teaching or by individual learners out-side of class. Activities like this could encourage participation and collaboration.

Online dictionaries

CALL tools and applications must be utilised with a clearly defined role; for example, Kim and Gilman (2008) point out that an effective way to improve the learning of English vocabulary is to offer graphics that illustrate what the words mean. Therefore, visual tools should be more encouraged for lexical acquisition. Among visual tools, online (digital) dictionaries are becoming essential for language learning because of their advantages over the traditional dictionary:

- They are easy to access (as long as there is Internet access).

- They can be accessed and used by many learners at the same time.

- They include multimedia resources, meaning that learners can learn words by focusing on form, meaning and use at the same time.

- They are generally free.

- They include thesaurus tools.

One example is the Visuwords online graphical dictionary (www.visuwords. com/), which is a web-based visual dictionary and thesaurus tool which uses Princeton University's *WordNet* and a visualisation tool to build a visual network of words (Figure 5.2). Users can search for words to look up

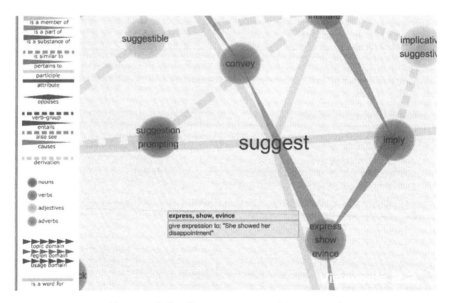

FIGURE 5.2 EXAMPLE OF HOW VISUWORDS'
ONLINE GRAPHICAL DICTIONARY WORKS

FIGURE 5.3   NINJAWORDS

their meanings and associations with other words and concepts in a visual interface. The diagrams produced by Visuwords show associations between word. This tool is especially useful for intermediate and adult learners since it requires analytical skills to identify the differences and similarities between words. This could be used as a self-study module to improve academic skills.

Some online dictionaries can also record personal search histories (e.g. *NinjaWords*) to help learners to build up an individualised word bank (Figure 5.3).

Online reading programmes

Apart from learning from formal instruction on vocabulary, learners tend to learn new words through reading or listening by deciphering unknown expressions through contextual use, root meaning, structure or similarity to known items (Godwin-Jones, 2010a). So reading is often used by teachers as a way to help learners to develop their lexical knowledge, especially when teachers are concerned about words' meanings. Gaining vocabulary knowledge through reading is theoretically more likely than isolated formal vocabulary instruction because vocabulary is presented in a context where it is used. Vocabulary learning through reading is not a new concept, but with its availability in e-books and other online materials and in reading courses, reading online (or with technology) has a new role in facilitating vocabulary learning.

Technology use in grammar teaching

Ellis (2006) indicates that grammar teaching requires structured input, explicit instruction, production practice and feedback about correctness.

Case study 5.2:

Huang and Liou (2007) constructed an online syllabus that provided comprehensible input and offered learners repeated contacts with target words for Taiwanese college learners. They selected 16 articles from issues of the Sinorama magazine (Taiwan Panorama, www.taiwanpanorama.com/en/index.php) to build an electronic corpus consisting of 5008 texts dating from 1999 to 2001. Then they implemented procedures as suggested by Ghadirian (2003), to ensure that target words appear frequently in the texts, using word lists as criteria for screening appropriate texts. They created two lists of target words apart from the General Service List (GSL):

1. The University Word List (UWL) (Xue and Nation, 1984) consists of 800 word families that are not included in the GSL or the HSF (High School Frequent Word List) but that are frequently found in academic texts (Nation and Kyongho, 1995).
2. The Sinorama High-Frequency Word list (SHF) contains 781 word families that are not in the GSL, HSF or UWL but that are frequently used in the 5008 Sinorama texts selected.

They conducted this reading programme with 38 college students over 12 weeks based upon vocabulary gains from a pre-test to a post-test. The results showed that learners improved their vocabulary scores after using the reading programme.

Doughty (1987) suggests that CALL can provide students with opportunities in all these areas. In particular, Hinkel and Fotos (2002) point out some important ideas that can be used in teaching grammar, including a discourse-based approach, explicit instruction and interaction. Chapelle and Jamieson (2008) explain that discourse-based grammar emphasises the context and situation in which the grammar is used. Presenting grammar examples within their relevant contexts provides a type of structured input (p. 39). Form-focused instruction directs students' attention to grammar by requiring students to produce the grammar form, receiving explicit instruction and feedback, analysing grammatical patterns or understanding language by comprehending grammatical relations. For grammar, interaction provides students with opportunities for form-focused instruction within the discourse. Next, I will focus on a few technological tools and applications regarding grammar instructions.

Websites

Web-based learning has become popular as a result of Internet access and flexible learning. Language teachers and CALL developers devote much

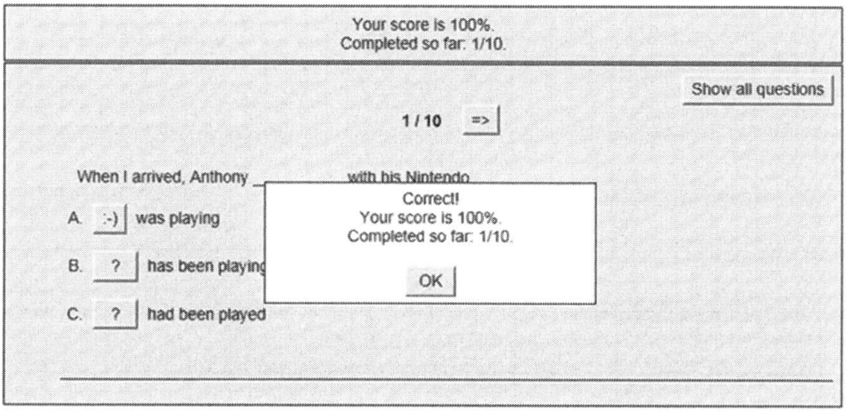

FIGURE 5.4   IMMEDIATE FEEDBACK ABOUT GRAMMAR

attention and energy to identifying language-learning resources for students and teachers to use in language teaching. Web-based learning is especially useful for independent and individual learning. For example, in Englishclub (www.englishclub.com/grammar/index.htm), learners can develop grammar knowledge and assess their own weaknesses and get immediate feedback (Figure 5.4).

Web-based mobile applications are an example of this kind of grammar teaching. Li and Hegelheimer (2013) have developed and implemented a web-based mobile application, *Grammar Clinic*, for an ESL writing class. Drawing on insights from the interactionist approach to SLA, the noticing hypothesis and mobile-assisted language learning (MALL), *Grammar Clinic* was designed as a series of outside-class grammar exercises in the form of sentence-level error identification and correction. It provides instant feedback for its exercises and includes a short grammar handbook. A total of 15 common grammatical error types are identified and used in this application.

Task 5.6: Think about disadvantages

I have outlined many benefits of using technology in teaching grammar and vocabulary. Are there any potential disadvantages to using websites to teach grammar? If yes, what are they? And how do we deal with them?

Despite the benefits of websites in supporting independent learning, there are some obvious shortcomings. When using websites to learn grammar, students need to have sufficient knowledge or awareness about their own learning styles and strategies and their ability to process information without assistance from the tutor. Teachers need to be aware that immediate feedback can also have a negative impact and might put off some learners.

Online chats

CMC has positive effects on language acquisition (Meskill and Anthony, 2005). In terms of grammar acquisition, this could be used as an informal learning tool where learners can participate in online forum discussions on grammar usage and functions. By participating in online discussions, learners not only identify gaps in their knowledge of grammar but also share what they know, to support other learners. There are many online forums available worldwide. For example, English Club Grammar Help (www.englishclub.com/esl-forums/viewforum.php?f=199&sid=94b54e43007fed1c8d eb3546849df4e7) allows learners to introduce a new post, view a post and reply to a post as they wish. Other examples might include the use of social networking sites as a means of promoting class discussions around grammar problems. They have the advantage of providing online, immediate language support, and they promote a more dialogic approach to learning about grammar.

Text-based online chat is beneficial to the development of grammatical competence because it promotes noticing problematic linguistic structures (Pellettieri, 2000; Lai and Zhao, 2006). Text-based online chat has great potential in increasing noticing, for two reasons: first, it gives the learner a longer processing time in receiving and producing the target language because the pace of conversation is controlled by the learners; second, it gives the learner opportunities to go back and forth with the conversation and 'notice' their language (Lai and Zhao, 2006). Apart from promoting meaning negotiation and raising collaborative learning (Kitade, 2000), online chat provides learners with opportunities to notice both their problematic output and the feedback from their interlocutors on the problematic linguistic forms, thus facilitating learning (Smith, 2004). Salaberry (2000) argued that 'the specific characteristics of the medium of communication represented in CMC may increase the chances that learners will focus their attention on both function and form, thereby increasing the likelihood that morphological development will occur in such an environment rather than in face-to face setting' (p. 19).

Instant messaging (IM)

Instant messaging systems are normally installed in the users' computers, and the majority of this software is free, (see, for example, Skype and Google Chat). They offer both text-based communication and audio and video chatting functionalities. Equally, such programmes are not limited to one-to-one

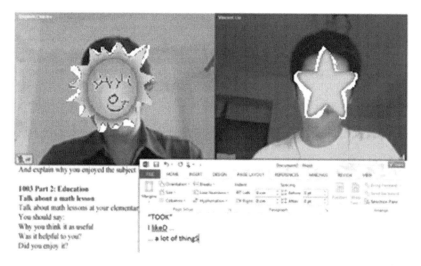

FIGURE 5.5   USING VSEE TO PROVIDE IMMEDIATE CORRECTIVE FEEDBACK

communication, but may be extended to multiple users. In relation to vocabulary and grammar acquisition, IM could be used as synchronous tutorials or to offer instant feedback. Vsee is freeware that enables videoconferencing and screen sharing, which can be used for giving students instant corrective feedback in grammar. Eftekhari (2013) conducted an exploratory study of using this tool to provide students with instant feedback during one-to-one tutorials and found that students were likely to take up the correct form after receiving feedback. This tool allows the student and teacher to conduct a virtual face-to-face tutorial. When students are speaking, the tutor can provide both verbal and written corrective feedback, which will be available for students to view after the task is finished (Figure 5.5).

A lexicogrammatical approach

Although vocabulary and grammar are often studied and researched as separate systems, it is difficult to separate them when considering language use since words often cluster to form grammatical patterns. A lexicogrammatical perspective treats lexicon and grammar as two inherently connected parts of a single entity (Liu and Jiang, 2009, p. 62). That is, when studying vocabulary, we look at not only collocation – which is how likely words are to occur next to each other – but also colligation – which is how words go together in grammatical rather than lexical patterns (McCarthy et al., 2010). In the field of SLA, lexicogrammatical acquisition has received much attention from

Concordancing does not provide 'correct' answers to grammar or lexical questions but helps learners to find an appropriate answer from many possible ones. That is, concordancing programmes makes grammar teaching more about making appropriate choices rather than following prescriptive rules.

linguists, researchers and teachers, and it is widely accepted that it is necessary in order to teach these language components explicitly, especially where English is learnt in an instructed environment. In this respect, corpus linguistics software is a useful tool to address the close lexical and grammatical connection which many words share. Two basic functions can be identified with a corpus:

■ Concordancing: the most basic and commonly used function of a corpus database is the 'Key Word in Context' feature, which shows how a searched word is used in the corpus. For example, the verb 'suggest' is searched with academic abstract corpus (174K words), and the result shows how 'suggest' is used.

■ Bar graph display: this illustrates how often a word is used.

Concordancing follows 'data-driven learning', which helps the learner to construct meanings and usage patterns based on discourse collected from published texts. It facilitates 'the marriage of grammar and rhetoric' (Kolln, 2007, p. xi), showing how grammatical choice is influenced by rhetorical context. Research shows the positive effect of concordancing on developing authentic materials (Chambers, 2007). It has been used in two ways in writing: as a source of materials for teachers and as a tool to help students to understand rules and patterns of language and raise their awareness of the use of language. However, caution is advised because the use of concordancing requires sufficient time, support, patience, enthusiasm and reflection from the teacher (Vannestål and Lindquist, 2007, p. 344).

The most basic and commonly used function of a corpus database is the 'Key Word in Context' feature, which shows how a searched word is used in the corpus. For example, the verb 'suggest' is searched using Corpus Concordance English (v.6.5) and AA Academic Abstracts that contain thesis and dissertation abstracts at master's and doctoral degree levels from universities in countries where English is the native language (174K words). The result shows how 'suggest' is used for academic purposes (Figure 5.6). Clearly, 'suggest' is followed by nouns and clauses (see the highlighted examples 022; 026). The concordance also indicates that 'suggest' is used in a particular way in an academic context (see 028–033; 040–044).

The main advantage of using corpus-based approaches in learning and teaching is that they provide opportunities for learners to access a large amount of natural language. Corpus linguistics presents a useful learning

FIGURE 5.6 CONCORDANCE FOR 'SUGGEST'

tool which promotes autonomy, individualised learning and authentic language materials. The use of corpora can help learners to understand relationships between words, both lexical (collocation) and grammatical (colligation). For example, Carter and McCarthy (2006, p. 431) list some of the most common particles that we use and the verbs they often collocate with:

■ go/hang/knock/mess *about*

■ forge/go/keep/move *ahead*

■ come/go/get/take *off*

■ break/come/go/put *out*.

MonoConc 2.2 or Wordsmith allows teachers to design their own corpora to teach grammar to reflect their pedagogical goals.

Learners can be encouraged to find the most frequently used words and how they collocate with other words either individually or collaboratively. Corpus tools thus are used as a study tool that enables learners to explore language patterns. The use of corpus can also help teachers to identify important or appropriate words students need to learn at a specific level or for a specific purpose. For example, students of business as a major will be able to identify the top 100 business words and see how they are used. In this respect, a corpus is also useful for looking at different registers of language – for example, we can compare how words are used in news reports, business documents and academic papers. We will also find that the grammar of words is different across registers. Corpus-based tasks can help learners with difficult aspects of vocabulary learning, for example, lexical chunks and idioms. Lexical chunks help the flow of the interaction and ensure speaker and listener understand each other in spoken discourse (McCarthy et al., 2010, p. 55) whereas the lack of knowledge of idioms can impede meaning. Lexical chunks, as well as idioms are important for both fluency and accuracy and the latter can be classified according to their grammar (McCarthy et al., 2010). A data-driven approach can be a useful way for studying both in context where learners are exposed to corpus data in the form of concordances. O'Keeffe et al. (2007) suggest that the study of large corpora makes us question these conventional divisions and helps us see how grammar and lexis interpenetrate and overlap in all kinds of ways. There are many free corpora and students and learners can also build their own corpus.

Case study 5.3:

Bloch (2009) has designed a web-based concordancing programme that uses an interface design to help students appropriately choose reporting verbs in academic papers. He created a database of sample sentences containing a variety of report-ing verbs, using articles from *Science* magazine (www.sciencemag.org). Two analogue corpora were created, and a third corpus based on student papers from previous sections of this class was also created in order to compare the distribution of the reporting verbs in student papers with the distribution in the science corpora. Each corpus contained approximately 300,000 words. These three corpora were then combined into one large corpus. MonoConc 2.2 was used to select possible sentences from this large corpus for inclusion into a single database. A total of 27 reporting verbs in 540 sentences were included in the corpus. The design of the interface followed principles of *accessibility* (the various ways the programme can be accessed), *simplicity* (ease of use of a programme and the ability of the programme to do only what it needs to do), and *functionality* (clear functions that do exactly what the designer wants them to do).

Future directions and considerations

Developments in CMC have resulted in language changing, particularly words and grammar rules. New words are created and new meanings are added to existing words. Grammar rules are changing too, with the emer-gence of e-grammar, which varies according to contexts and technologies (Herring, 2007). Grammar in CMC (especially text-based chat) is differ-ent from traditional spoken grammar in the way that it sometimes breaks/ modifies grammar rules. This change in language and the development of technology on language change has created considerable speculation and a growing body of research. For language-learning purposes, what is interesting is not only looking at the new meanings of words and accepting the modified rules and structure of utterances but also developing an understanding and knowledge of how words collocate – existing weak and strong collocations might change. What is also interesting is to look at colligation – how words go together in grammatical rather than lexical patterns. In this line of inquiry, we can see the greater use of learner corpora, perhaps a corpus of CMC language (see Farr and Riordan, 2015).

In the same way, technological tools are developing more and more to include social and affective aspects. Therefore, the role of learners' using these tools is becoming more central, meaning that technological tools are developing more and more as learning tools than as teaching tools. We can already see technological tools moving in this direction; for example, numerous applications are developed every day for independent learning. This shift will enable learners to develop more communicative and sociolinguistic competences.

The last issue with using technology in teaching vocabulary and grammar or other aspects of language learning is that a clear learning outcome needs to be defined. This works as a basis for pedagogy and the role of technology. For example, in grammar teaching, if practitioners focus on form and expect it to be a learning product, then technological tools, which can facilitate understanding grammar rules and provide exercises, are considered appropriate. On the other hand, if they focus on function, then a technological application which could provide students with real-life examples of language (e.g. videos and corpus) and context to use such a language is desired. Research suggests that technology is beneficial in vocabulary teaching, and there is not enough evidence about how grammar acquisition improves with the assistance of technology; therefore, it is necessary to develop both judgemental and empirical evaluations of CALL activities (Chapelle, 2001, 2007).

Summary

In this chapter, we have considered the use of technology in teaching vocabulary and grammar. Using technology to assist vocabulary and grammar acquisition involves more than just CALL materials. Li (2008, 2014) points out that teachers play an important role in integrating technology in language teaching because the teacher makes important pedagogical decisions in terms of what materials are used, how effective the materials are in prompting lexical and grammatical knowledge, how to maximise the benefits of technological tools and their own beliefs about the usefulness of technology in achieving pedagogical goals. Thus, the first and foremost question in mind should be the appropriateness of technology in pedagogical considerations (see Chapter 9). Again, the role of technological tools is also key. Without considering the role of technology explicitly in an activity or task, it is hard to understand how and to what extent technology can assist learning. In summary, there are many different ways that teachers can make use of technologies in facilitating lexical and grammar learning, and realising the full potential of technology relies on how teachers link their pedagogical goals to what technology can offer.

Annotated further reading

1. Reppen, R. (2001) Review of MonoConc pro and Wordsmith tools. *Language Learning & Technology*, 5(3), 32–36. Available at llt.msu.edu/vol5num3/pdf/review4.pdf.

     This review compares two concondancing tools: MonoConc Pro and Wordsmith. It is a useful guide for teachers who would like start to use concondancing programmes. It provides the reader with examples to understand how the programmes work.
2. Chapelle, C. A. & Jamieson, J. (2008) *Tips for Teaching with CALL: Practical Approaches to Computer-Assisted Language Learning*. White Plains, NY: Pearson Education. Chapters 1 and 2.

     This book is a professional reference, with practical classroom approaches, that is firmly grounded in CALL research. The chapters provide the reader with well-conceived and realistic approaches to language instruction, using examples in vocabulary and grammar learning. The chapters offer the reader an opportunity to link what the research says and what teachers can do in using CALL in facilitating lexis and grammar learning. The chapters include colour screenshots of authentic CALL software, along with descriptions, level information and notes. There are demonstration tips to show readers how to use various technological applications.
3. Nakata, T. (2012) Web-based lexical resources, in C. Chapelle (ed.), *Encyclopedia of Applied Linguistics* (pp. 6166–6177). Oxford: Wiley-Blackwell.

     Nakata's chapter outlines web-based lexical resources for teachers, students and researchers. It discusses in detail online dictionaries, word lists, vocabulary tests and software, corpora and concordancers, vocabulary profilers, guides for teaching and learning, and vocabulary quizzes. This chapter also provides researchers with bibliographies on vocabulary, online articles and lexical databases. It is a useful starting point for anyone who is interested in using the Internet in vocabulary teaching, learning and research.

6 Technology and ESP

> **Aims:** This chapter considers how technologies can support teaching English for specific purposes (ESP). It reviews the principles of technology use in ESP and offers some exemplary practice, covering five types of technological tools: corpus, web-based materials, computer-mediated communication (CMC), wikis and the 3D virtual world, in the contexts of both English for academic purposes (EAP) and English for occupational purposes (EOP). This chapter has four main sections, as follows:
>
> 1. ESP and its characteristics
>
> 2. Benefits of technology in ESP contexts
>
> 3. Principles for integrating technology in ESP
>
> 4. Technological tools for teaching ESP.

Introduction

ESP can be defined in terms of two basic goals: (1) the acquisition of content knowledge of a specific field; (2) the development of English skills required to perform in the discipline (Butler-Pascoe, 2009, p. 1).

Technology has always played a role in teaching English for specific purposes (**ESP** hereafter) (Arnó-Macià, 2012), although due to lack of awareness, teachers do voice concerns in using technology, because they are more comfortable with text environments, may be deficient in computer literacy and believe that technology does not necessarily deliver educational success (Virkus, 2008). The general observation is that apart from realising the benefits of technology and getting tips on how to integrate it into teaching, teachers need to be aware of the principles of using technology in teaching ESP.

The goal of this chapter is to introduce the principles of technology integration and to provide guidance for making it more practical in language classrooms than has thus far been the case. The chapter begins by defining and reviewing the characteristics of ESP and the benefits of using technology in language learning. It then introduces five general principles for integrating technology in teaching ESP, followed by some examples of ESP in English for academic purposes (EAP) contexts and for English for occupational purposes (EOP) contexts, such as English for business purposes (EBP). The chapter concludes with a brief discussion of various technological tools and apps that teachers can use in facilitating ESP learning.

ESP and its characteristics

ESP has a long history and is becoming more and more popular as globalisation continues to spread and as there is continued need for people to communicate within and across their disciplines internationally. The popularity of ESP has also witnessed the definition evolving, and as a result, different definitions have been used. There has been an ESP pedagogy shift from specialised vocabulary acquisition to language use in context. Currently, ESP is a learner-centred pedagogy which emphasises the importance of needs analysis. ESP learners need to understand authentic texts and how to communicate effectively in the situations they encounter in their discipline rather than mastering field-specific terminology (Smoak, 2003). This said, vocabulary is still an important learning element for ESP at least for two reasons: first, students would be able to understand concepts and phenomena in their disciplines better if they incorporated specialist language and terminology in their academic work (Woodward-Kron, 2008); second, students need to have specialised discourse competence to succeed in their studies and need to engage in group activities and their discipline communities (Hyland and Tse, 2007).

Defining ESP is not an easy task, since the requirement of English is different for different disciplines. Taking business and medical settings as examples, the communication skills and language genres are completely different because the purpose of communication is different. In a business setting, people use language to market their products or negotiate a deal, which requires skills of negotiation, whereas in a medical setting, understanding, listening with empathy and giving instructions are perhaps more frequent. Despite the different needs for language, there are several common important elements across disciplines concerning the use of language. As such, various definitions of ESP highlight the importance of contexts, materials and needs analysis, situational practice, cross-cultural issues and the authenticity of communication (Grosse and Voigt, 1991; Dudley-Evans and St. John, 1998; Grosse, 2002). For this reason, Arnó, Soler and Rueda (2006) argue that Dudley-Evans and St. John's (1998) extended and flexible definition can serve as a framework that can encompass various ESP contexts. Their definition is as follows:

Absolute characteristics

- ESP attempts to meet learners' specific needs.

- ESP makes use of underlying methodology and activities of the discipline it serves.

- ESP centres on the language (grammar, lexis, register), study skills, discourse and genre appropriate for these activities.

Variable characteristics

- ESP may be related to, or designed for, specific disciplines.

- ESP may use, in specific teaching situations, a different methodology from that of general English.

- ESP is likely to be designed for adult learners, either at a tertiary-level institution or in a professional work situation; it could also be for learners at secondary school level.

- ESP is generally designed for intermediate or advanced students; most ESP courses assume some basic knowledge of the language systems. (Dudley-Evans and St. John, 1998, pp. 4–5)

In order to understand how technology can facilitate teaching ESP, we need to unpack these characteristics. First and foremost, ESP is designed for learners with specific needs, which means needs analysis is the most important thing in teaching ESP. This point is emphasised by Belcher (2004) in her historical review of the field:

> Unlike other pedagogical approaches, which may be less specific needs-based and more theory-driven, ESP pedagogy places heavy demands on its practitioners to collect empirical needs-assessment data, to create or adapt materials to meet specific needs identified, and to cope with often unfamiliar subject matter and even language use. (p. 166)

So, broadly speaking, ESP concerns what learners need to know in their own work contexts. In other words, given the particular context in which English is used, the variant of English will change. Therefore, for ESP, the ultimate goal is to tailor language instruction to meet the needs of learners in specific contexts. Addressing learners' needs, which is referred to as 'the commitment to the purposes of the learners', is a goal shared by all branches of ESP (Belcher, 2009), and it includes learners' needs not only at the language level but also in terms of material and teaching aspects. According to Belcher (2009, p. 3),

> what the commitment to the purposes of learners entails is (1) first and foremost (before, during, and even after instruction), finding out what learners' needs are, then (2) developing or adapting materials and methods to enable needs-responsive instruction while concurrently (3) acquiring the expertise to function as needs-knowledgeable instructors. (Dudley-Evans and St. John, 1998; Robinson, 1991)

Second, the teaching in ESP must be authentic. Authenticity refers to authentic language materials and authenticity in tasks. ESP practitioners pay close attention to developing authentic materials based on the discourse in the taught discipline. This is also referred to as the target genre in which students engage in real-life work situations. Authenticity in task refers to how far the task is related to learners' real-life activities, as Ellis (2003) explains: 'authenticity concerns whether a task needs to correspond to some real world activity, achieve situational authenticity' (p. 6).

Third, closely related to authenticity and learners' needs is the appropriateness of the teaching methodology. ESP adopts the needs-based approach, and all aspects of learning and teaching are designed to address learners' needs. However, it is important to note that learners' needs vary according to the situations they are in, academic disciplines and/or the context in which they work.

Finally, it is worth noting that ESP deals with mainly adult learners who are at intermediate or advanced levels. It is a general assumption that ESP learners have achieved a certain level of English, and because ESP involves adult learners, in the course design, material development and pedagogical considerations, we need to take into account the cognitive as well as linguistic level of learners. This is why needs analysis, the authenticity of communication and materials, context, discourse genre, corpora, situational practice and cross-cultural issues and are important aspects of teaching ESP (Dudley-Evans and St. John, 1991; Hewings, 2002).

In discussing the delivery of ESP courses, Butler-Pascoe (2009) proposed that there are at least three models (p. 2):

1. ESP taught by English teachers using field-specific content;

2. field-specific courses taught by teachers in the disciplines using English as the language of instruction;

3. a collaborative model in which both English and field-specific teachers have joint input into the development and/or teaching of the course.

Task 6.1: Critical evaluation of these three models

Talk to your colleagues about these three models, and think about your own teaching context. What are the strengths and weaknesses of each model? Would any of them work in your work contexts?

When a teacher critically evaluates an approach or a method that they are going to implement in their working contexts, they will think about many issues, such as the materials they have, the language level of their students and their own expertise. When we examine these three models, we need to take sociocultural contexts into consideration. However, there are generic issues we can discuss despite the various social and cultural factors involved. The first model, where an English teacher teaches an ESP course using field-specific content, has been widely used in many EFL contexts. The major issue related to this model is that the teacher does not have expertise and experience in the discipline, which makes it difficult to realise authenticity in both material choice and task design. In this case, many ESP teachers follow the same approach in teaching a general English course, focusing on linguistic knowledge. Because teachers are unfamiliar with the field-specific contents, they have to spend more time understanding the materials, preparing lessons and developing content knowledge. The second model is the opposite of the first model, where the teacher obtains rich knowledge of the field but does not have knowledge or skills in teaching a foreign language. Subject teachers find themselves in a difficult situation where they have to balance the content and language input. Because of their subject background and expertise, the ESP course very often becomes another subject course, with materials written in English. Another issue which may be associated with this model is insufficient linguistic knowledge and metalanguage of the subject teachers. Due to a lack of linguistic knowledge and metalanguage to explain the language, some teachers find it difficult to be understood and to help learners efficiently process the materials. Considering the issues associated with the first two models, the third model is an ideal combination. However, it requires the language teacher and subject teacher to work together closely. They need to plan the lesson together, making sure that both content and language are covered at the appropriate time and that assessment reflects this. In reality, it is difficult to engage in such collaborative work because teachers are often placed in different departments and because there are many practicality issues.

Benefits of technology in ESP contexts

Technology has been used by ESP teachers for different purposes and used in all the three models of ESP instruction mentioned above (Butler-Pascoe, 2009). Technological tools are used to create suitable materials or relevant contexts for language learning (Arnó-Macià, 2012), to address learners' needs and to achieve positive psychological impact (Arnó, Soler and Rueda, 2006). The Internet and Web 2.0 technologies have had a strong impact on ESP teaching. The Internet enables ESP teaching to go 'beyond language learning by focusing on culture and social discourses' (Arnó-Macià, 2012, p. 91). Technology provides ESP teachers with a new tool to engage students in real-life communication, to bridge the intercultural gap, to collaborate in their professional community and to access up-to-date information relevant to their discipline. As discussed in Chapter 2, technology has many affordances to facilitate effective language learning in general. I will outline a few here that relate to ESP.

Technology enhances language learning

Butler-Pascoe (2009, pp. 2–3) lists 14 advantages of technology for ESP in the area of engaging students in the professional or academic environments, fostering understanding of the sociocultural aspects of the language, providing comprehensible field-specific input and sheltering strategies for language development, using task-based and inquiry-based strategies and authentic materials and so on.

Research suggests that multimedia presentation, including graphics and video clips, has a positive effect on vocabulary acquisition (e.g. Kim and Gilman, 2008; Silverman and Hines, 2009). For example, Rusanganwa (2013) investigated whether the use of multimedia can facilitate technical vocabulary acquisition with physics undergraduates in Rwanda and the results suggest that the effect of multimedia on the recall of the concepts taught is impressive. Technology is also reported to have improved writing ability (e.g. Mak and Coniam, 2008).

Closely related to linguistic acquisition is communication, the key purpose of second language learning. CMC has become popular to improve second language learners' communicative competence. It is true that email is becoming more important for written communication than other methods, and being able to communicate successfully and appropriately when using a computer is considered an important skill. The use of CMC technologies such as emails, online forums and Skype have benefited learners' real-life communication. Research suggests that email exchange encourages students to recognise that studying an L2 is more than just learning lexis and grammar but is also a powerful medium for communication (Warschauer, 2000b, 2003) and for engaging in authentic professional discourse. Of course, research studies also show the value of technology for development of intercultural awareness (Müller-Hartmann, 2000; Ware, 2005), especially with CMC and network-based learning (Kern and Warschauer, 2000). The Web 2.0 technologies even further develop opportunities for people from the same profession from different contexts to communicate and collaborate.

Technology assists in creating authentic contextualised materials

Technology is widely used as a language resource for authentic input and context to see how language is used. This is especially useful for ESP learners because an ESP course focuses on the authentic language learners' being able to apply language in real-life contexts in the workplace. In language learning, the authenticity of language materials and tasks are emphasised by various researchers, and using authentic language materials is encouraged whenever possible. As such, students are able to learn not only the kind of language they need but also how it is used. The underpinning theory is to experience, rather than acquire, the language. Designing materials for students' needs is perhaps the very first thing faced by many ESP teachers, and they are not simply teachers but also material developers due to a lack of availability of appropriate materials required or the lack of sufficient authenticity in common textbooks. The Internet is believed to serve well the authenticity of the text and the authorship of the language user – the two aspects of communicative language teaching (Kramsch et al., 2000). As such, the Internet is considered as an authentic resource for natural, context-rich and cultural-specific materials (Herron et al., 2002). These materials are not restricted to textual resources but also include rich audio and visual materials (e.g. YouTube). The multimodal representations and availability of up-to-date information and tasks in different discourse communities provides authentic language materials for teachers and resources for students to complete their tasks and projects. As I mentioned before, corpora have been used by ESP teachers to develop suitable materials for their learners. The availability of academic and occupational corpora enables both teachers and learners to access the authentic language used in their targeted context, and by analysing corpora, learners' needs can be addressed.

Technology can mediate thinking

Technology can also be used as a mediational tool (Li, 2014), especially in network-based learning and computer-supported collaborative learning.

Mediation is how people use 'culturally constructed artefacts, concepts and activities to regulate the material world or their own and each other's social and mental activity' (Lantolf and Thorne, 2006, p. 79). In an ESP context, learners not only engage in the ways of thinking underpinning the discipline but also develop their own cognitive and metacognitive strategies because of the authentic tasks they conduct and the authentic audience with which they communicate. The multimodality of technology materials can mediate ideas, thoughts and thinking processes through images, sounds and videos. Even in text-based chat rooms, the use of emoticons and emojis can help express thoughts and emotions. The mediational role that technology plays in network-based learning is vital. Students from different cultures and backgrounds can take advantage of computer tools to represents their thoughts and to bridge gaps in intercultural communication.

Technology provides a learning environment for interaction

Interaction lies at the heart of language learning, and technology can provide learners with an environment where they can engage in authentic interaction: for example, interactions between learners and their professional community can be promoted through the use of a particular technological tool, such as a forum or online discussion board. The kind of interaction in which students engage in such a learning environment is a real-life situation, as the task is genuine and language is authentic. With the development of network-based learning, project-based CALL between learners is also popular in assisting students to develop their IC. For example, in the context of German as a foreign language, Chun (1994) has argued that the use of network-based activity facilitates developing IC as learners '[g]enerate and initiate different kinds of discourse, which in turn enhances their ability to express a greater variety of functions in different contexts as well as to play a greater role in managing the discourse' (p. 18).

Technology facilitate self-directed learning

Carter (1983) proposed three features common to ESP courses: (a) authentic material, (b) purpose-related orientation and (c) self-direction. For Carter, 'ESP is concerned with turning learners into users' (ibid, p. 134). In order for self-direction to occur, the learners must have a certain degree of control over when, what and how they study. Technology in this sense offers a great opportunity to realise self-direction. For example, in a self-access learning environment, students are able to access the learning materials and direct their own learning at their own pace. This not only involves students' developing learning strategies and gaining competence in language skills (e.g. listening) but also provides them with an opportunity to control the pace and direction of learning. In this context, technology can 'support self-paced instruction and to support self-paced review of concepts' (Roblyer, 2006, p. 48).

Technology motivates and engages learners

Technology can be used as an effective tool to engage, motivate and regulate learners. In particular, motivation has been central to discussions about technology in language learning in general (Braine, 2004; Schwienhorst, 2007). Because of the authenticity of the task, materials and interactional opportunities, learners are more motivated in engaging with learning tasks and content (see also Chapter 2).

Principles for integrating technology in ESP

Based on the above discussion of benefits of technology, I propose five basic principles in integrating technology in ESP.

Principle 1: understanding the benefits and roles of technology

Teachers need to be aware of the benefits of technological tools for language learning. Technology in general has a positive impact on language learning, but technology does not do everything, and different tools have different functions. For example, some tools are more appropriate for developing collaborative learning (e.g. the use of wikis, blogs and other Web 2.0 technologies), whereas other tools are more suitable for helping students to develop their linguistic knowledge and skills (e.g. the use of software, videos and applications). Some tools are more useful to help engagement in real-discourse communities (e.g. online discussion forums and social networks), and others are good for identifying students' needs (e.g. corpora). Knowing the theoretical underpinnings of different technological tools helps the teacher to realise the potential of technological tools.

Principle 2: linking technology to learners' needs

ESP adopts a learner-centred approach, and learners' needs are the top priority in designing and teaching a course. Westerfield (2010) argues that there are three things teachers need to do. First, teachers need to understand

What learners need	How technology can help (examples)
Communication skills	CMC tools (e.g. online discussion board, emails and videoconferencing) can be used to engage students in real-life discourse
Academic writing	Corpus analysis of published academic work to identify how to use linking words, reporting verbs and tenses
Collaborative experience	Wikis, project-based CALL
Engage in professional community	The use of social networking

TABLE 6.1   LINKING TECHNOLOGY TO LEARNERS' NEEDS

the learner's specific needs for English, taking their specific situations into consideration, and the teacher assesses how technology can help them both achieve the best learning outcome for the learner. Table 6.1 provides an example to illustrate how to link technology to learners' future needs.

Second, teachers need to understand the current learners' language situation – that is, what the learners can do now and what they want from the course. The current knowledge can be assessed through corpus analysis of student work (oral and written) and comparing this with the academic or professional corpus.

Third, teachers need to know what technological environment a student will be in (e.g. one computer classroom, network-based classroom, self-access centre or a distance learning), the student's available resources (e.g. Internet access and software) and the student's level of experience in using technology in learning.

Principle 3: integrating technology into, rather than adding it to, teaching

Technology needs to be integrated as part of pedagogy rather than as an 'add-on' to the existing situation. 'Integration' emphasises pedagogy, which means technology is used to achieve pedagogical goals. Therefore, teachers need to be aware of their pedagogical beliefs (Li, 2008). Research suggests that teachers use technology according to their underlying beliefs about teaching and learning (see Table 6.2 for an example of teachers' beliefs about writing tasks and the use of technology). Only by understanding their own beliefs could teachers integrate technology into their teaching routines rather than adding it on as a supplementary tool.

'Integration' also means that technology is integrated into assessment. For example, for each pedagogical goal, teachers need to have a reliable, measurable

Teacher's pedagogical belief	Main technology use
Writing is a means of reinforcing speech patterns (product-based)	■ Grammar and vocabulary exercises on a website ■ Use feedback tools (e.g. track changes in Word) for peer reviewing, focusing on local feedback, such as tense, spelling and grammar
Writing is a process of constructing personal meaning (process-based)	■ Accessing web database ■ Composing with the word processor ■ Using mind map tools ■ Collaborative web-based writing projects ■ Small group use of prompted writing and grammar software
Writing is an important academic and professional skill (content-based)	■ Using a corpus to analyse academic and professional discourse ■ Using academic and professional websites ■ Online referencing sites (e.g. dictionaries and libraries)
Writing is viewed as a text understood by the reader	■ Blogs and wikis ■ Online discussion (e.g. wikis and blogs) ■ Email exchange

TABLE 6.2 AN EXAMPLE OF TEACHERS' PEDAGOGICAL BELIEFS AND THE USE OF TECHNOLOGY

and clear assessment method. Mueller (2010) calls for authentic assessment, which means real-life tasks that demonstrate meaningful applications of essential knowledge and skills. In this aspect, an email task with different purposes could be used to assess students' (internal and external) communication skills.

Principle 4: considering the role of a teacher

Clearly, technology is transforming the means of teaching and learning – and as a consequence, the role of the teacher. One of the factors influencing teachers' use of technology innovatively is the understanding of a teacher's role (see Chapter 9). Teachers need to be aware of the different roles that they perform when different kinds of technology-supported activities are implemented. The challenge is to give control to learners, allowing them to explore their agency in learning. Technologies in many situations can be used

Teacher role	Activity	Technology
Organiser	Students work together on a collaborative writing project	Wikis
Audience/reader	Students present their views and opinions about topics in their field	Blogs
Guide	Students develop a vocabulary project for their discipline	Corpus
Participant/facilitator	Students initiate and participate in discussion	Online forum
Evaluator	Students produce oral and written work (with multimodal materials)	Digital recording software and Microsoft Office package

TABLE 6.3   TEACHERS' ROLES WHEN USING TECHNOLOGY: AN EXAMPLE

as a learning tool, and the teacher needs to realise this and thus explore how they might support and facilitate this learning process rather than trying to be the controller of this process, as in traditional knowledge-transmission classrooms. To illustrate, I present some different roles that teachers can perform in activities where technology is used (see Table 6.3).

Principle 5: enhancing authenticity of both language and task

Teachers can use technology as a tool to access authentic materials so that students are experiencing and learning the authentic discourse they are expected to encounter in their profession. Any tasks should resemble the kind of tasks that students are expected to carry out in a real-life work or study environments, such as discussing a project with a senior colleague or solving a problem with peers. Technology can to some extent give students an authentic environment: for example, in Second Life (a free 3D virtual world where users can socialise, connect and create using free voice and text chat), law students can have a virtual court room, and business students can set up virtual business.

Task 6.2: Find the principles

Find an example where technology is used in ESP and analyse whether these five principles are applied. Are there other principles underpinning the design of technology-enhanced ESP learning?

Technological tools for teaching ESP

In this section, I present some ideas for integrating technologies into teaching ESP. These ideas can be approached from the perspective of a discipline's goals, from the perspective of learners and teachers and as language skills or technological tools. Since these ideas can be applied across disciplines and involve different language skills, I choose five different kinds of technological tools to explore how they can be integrated into teaching and learning.

Corpora

In many academic writing contexts, vocabulary acquisition and grammatical structure appear to be important features, and many investigations have been done in these areas (see Chapter 5). In recent years, the use of corpora in academic and technical writing has become a more common focus of research. As Friginal (2013) suggests, the 'future direction of teaching writing for specific purposes will include corpus-based textbooks, materials and data' (p. 209).

Hamp-Lyons (2011, p. 96) writes that '[o]ne valuable development for the EAP classroom has been the use of corpora and concordances, through computer systems, to allow EAP students to conduct their own mini research projects ... providing students with hands-on exercise in figuring out how language works'. There are at least three ways that a corpus can be used in ESP. First, a corpus can be used to develop writing. Yoon (2011) suggests two functions of a corpus in assisting this aspect: as a research tool and as a reference tool. ESP or EAP teachers could use the corpus to search how a vocabulary item is used. I have already given an example in Chapter 5 regarding the use of 'suggest' in an academic context (see Figure 5.6). Here, I show another example where I used corpus concordance English (v.7) with BNC Law (2.2 million words). The result shows how 'argue' is used (see Figure 6.1). Clearly, 'argue' in legal writing is often used with the modal verbs: can, could, may, might or must (010–019, 022–035), and is followed by clauses (014–033). The way 'argue' is used reflects the writing practice in the legal field.

There are various free corpora available to use to find searchable text samples of writing across academic disciplines and registers. For example,

Corpus concordance English www.lextutor.ca/concordancers/concord_e.html
Corpus of contemporary American English (COCA)
www.americancorpus.org
the Michigan corpus of upper-level student papers (MICUSP) (2010)
search-micusp.elicorpora.info/simple/

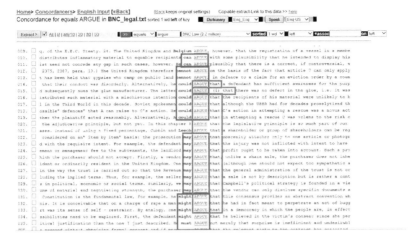

FIGURE 6.1   AN EXAMPLE OF A CORPUS SEARCH FOR 'ARGUE'

A corpus can also be used as a reference tool for students to solve writing and language problems. This can be done through concordancing for linguistic references in terms of collocations and lexicogrammar and for revisions of their writing, particularly self-correcting errors. Students could compare their essays with a corpus to do revision after the teacher has highlighted the problems (e.g. Gilmore, 2009).

Case study 6.1:

Friginal (2013) investigated the use of corpora to develop the research report writing skills of college-level students enrolled in a professional forestry programme in the United States, focusing in particular on a set of selected linguistic features: linking adverbials, reporting verbs, verb tenses and passive sentence structures. Students' work is compared with published forestry articles to find differences in these areas, and subsequent treatment was offered to students to improve in these areas. The study showed the positive impact of using corpora to address students' writing problems: the use of linking words and reporting verbs. Students can identify the linking words and reporting verbs from their own writing and check how they are used in academic writing corpora. In this way, students are able to understand how to use these vocabularies more appropriately and accurately, hence improving writing overall. This can be done either in or outside class.

Second, a corpus can be used to study key lexis. For example, students can check and discuss how **the top 100 key business lexical items** (words and phrases) are used in context. This would enhance the authenticity of vocabulary acquisition. That is, students do not learn the words and phrases alone but

The top 100 key business lexical items (words and phrases) can be accessed through Mike Nelson's business English lexis site at: users.utu.fi/micnel/business_english_lexis_site.htm.

understand them in contexts. This could be a task outside class and each student can be responsible for two to three words and present them in class. In this way, students not just engage in independent learning but also learn from each other.

Third, a corpus can be used by teachers to develop materials. Evans (2012) offered insights into designing email tasks for business English classrooms by analysing data from Hong Kong's service sectors, including 50 email chains comprising 406 separate emails. He recommends a simulation-based approach in designing email tasks, in which students are given 'clearly defined and differentiated roles in a particular business context, and a task that stimulates collaboration and conflict, both internally and externally (Evans, 2012, p. 210).

Task 6.3: Designing an ESP

Design an ESP task using a corpus. Outline the reasons why you want to use a corpus, your target students and the situation. Identify the corpus and make a plan. What are the advantages of a corpus in your design?

Web-based materials

Authentic materials are important for teaching ESP, for which the Internet is useful resource base. There are many interesting EA/SP websites which can be used to address both teachers' professional needs and learners' needs. For example, *Arlyn Freed's ESL/EFL ESP* website (www.eslhome.com/esl/esp/) offers a range of topics, including business English, medical English, banking and finance English, dentistry English, engineering English and science English. For each category, there are useful links which users can explore for either getting materials for lessons or self-studying. *ESP on the web* is another website (www.unav.es/espSig/esponweb.html) which contains lots of material for teachers and learners. It provides different categories of ESP, including ESP associations, resources, discipline-specific sites and articles on the web. From here, teachers can guide students to explore resources in the student's own discipline. These websites can also be used by students for independent study, especially in revising and expanding their knowledge in the discipline. From these sites, students can also access the discourse of the community and participate in activities (e.g. online discussion).

Wikis

Wikis serve as powerful mediating artefacts for collaboration (Lund, 2008) because they let participants 'collaboratively generate, mix, edit and synthesise subject-specific knowledge within a shared and openly accessible digital space' (Wheeler et al., 2008, p. 989). Although wikis have been popular in collaborative writing (see Chapter 4), very little attention has been given to the use of Web 2.0 collaborative technological tools in EA/SP (but see Alyousef and Picard, 2011; Bradley et al., 2010). A wiki can be used as a collaborative tool for an ESP project. Students can work collaboratively to create a discipline page. For example, students studying commercial law could have a wiki page about unfair commercial practices where they not only collaborate with their group members to co-construct knowledge but also invite people outside to contribute to their page. This kind of collaborative activity is not restricted by location or time.

A wiki can also be used for academic writing purposes. When students co-construct texts, they not only focus on what they want to write but also understand other members' perspectives. In this way, they develop flexibility and an awareness of multiple perspectives. For example, in English for legal purposes, students could be writing a report about human rights together and understand how human rights are understood in different contexts and issues around these perspectives.

A wiki project can also be used for students to collaboratively solve writing problems (e.g. Li and Zhu, 2013). In the writing process, students can be guided to use a 'discussion' page to discuss issues they encounter and support each other to solve problems. Because students can view the 'history' page, they can see what revisions/changes have been made and can critically reflect on their own writing.

CMC

There are different kinds of CMC tools, one of the most important ones for all disciplines being email. Nowadays, employees in almost all disciplines which require collaborative work need to exchange information and ideas through emails (Angouri and Harwood, 2008). Studies in the ESP literature have also emphasised that email has become an integral part of organisational communication (Louhiala-Salminen, 2002). As Evans (2012) indicates,

> email plays a crucial role in binding together flows of internal and external activities that are directed towards the resolution of problems, the formulation of plans or the execution of decisions. Email is thus an important means of working

towards these goals, enabling professionals to exchange and discuss information and ideas quickly and conveniently with colleagues and clients. (p. 210)

Emails can be used to address the issue of lack of intertextuality in traditional business textbooks and to raise business students' awareness of writing as an ongoing and dialogic process (Evans, 2012). By analysing emails in authentic contexts, students can identify the differences between email writing and other types of communication (e.g. letter and telephone conversation). Language teaching can focus on style and register, but at the same time, pragmatic and cultural awareness can be raised in the communication. Email tasks can be designed for students through email analysis (see Evans, 2012). For example, in business disciplines, students need to write emails to organise a meeting for the unit, make queries about a product, liaise with international partners regarding a contract and submit a report to the line manager about a project. These tasks can be designed with the help of real business partners.

Task 6.4: Reflection

Engaging students in their professional community is a good idea. What are the potential issues of getting students to practise in real-life situations? And how can we address these issues?

3D and virtual worlds

3D virtual worlds, including online role-playing games, give learners an opportunity for immersion in the environment and a sense of investment in learning. This immersion and investment is particularly relevant to foreign language learning, especially for specific purposes. Communication in virtual worlds can take both verbal and nonverbal forms (Robbins, 2007). Verbal communication is typically established synchronously in the text-based chat format, whereas nonverbal communication can be established through avatar appearance, posturing and gestures (Robbins, 2007). Virtual worlds now are used by educators for simulating the real world to train people in various professions, such as nurses, border guards, midwives and so on. The same 'places' can be used for role playing with ESP students (Godwin-Jones, 2005) and real interactions with people (Thorne, 2008).

Second Life (SL) is a free online synchronous 3D (or multi-user virtual environment, MUVE for short) virtual world, which is appealing to educators because it is customisable and immersive and has a range of communicative tools within the environment. One can enter SL by creating a digital representation of oneself (an avatar) and downloading the viewer from the SL website (www.secondlife.com).

SL, like other virtual worlds, has unique characteristics which make the platform similar to the real world:

- Anything can happen in SL, apart from dying (e.g. shopping).

- SL has its own currency (Linden $) and its own time zone.

- Communication media include text chat, instant messaging, voice chat and notecards.

- All communication can be logged for future use.

English City is a virtual city created on SL where all the language classes take place. Students can go there to learn English by total immersion in real-life scenarios, for example visiting a doctor, supermarket or a lawyer etc. Immerse Learning (formerly called Languagelab.com) is another good example of using 3D and virtual environments for learning.

SL is particularly useful for ESP because students can experience how professionals operate and communicate in authentic situations. They are immersed in the virtual world and learn by taking part in the activities. Another useful feature is that students can improve English by visiting their professional communities and also establish their own clubs or classrooms.

Task 6.5: Explore Second Life

Visit SL and design an activity for an ESP class of your choice. Then ask yourself, is SL the best place for this activity? Could you do it in a face-to-face conventional classroom?

In ESP courses, blended learning has been adopted early because it gives learners flexibility regarding where and when they learn (Arnó-Macià, 2012). So in practice, all the tools mentioned above can be integrated in blended learning.

Summary

Computer technologies can benefit language learning in many aspects, but it depends on how they are utilised. Warschauer (2004) suggests that teachers will make the best use of computers in the classroom when students are encouraged to perform the most real tasks possible, taking advantage of the power of modern technological tools. This chapter further emphasises the view that integrating technology, authenticity, technological benefits, learners' needs, pedagogical beliefs and teachers' roles are the most important principles. In the ESP context, teachers need to take a flexible approach in programme design, study material, location, forms of communication and types of interaction (Collis and Moonen, 2002). Technology can be brought in to help teachers to realise flexibility in all of these dimensions. This chapter also considers the various benefits that technology can bring to language learning and outlines some suggestions and practices in how technology can be integrated into teaching ESP in general, drawing on both a literature review and my own practice. Of course, this chapter is only one glimpse of what technology can do and how we can use it to facilitate ESP learning. Many innovative ideas can be explored by teachers themselves through working out principles for the context they are in.

Annotated further reading

1. Butler-Pascoe, M. E. (2009) English for Specific Purposes (ESP), innovation, and technology. *English Education and ESP*, 1–15.
   This paper explores ways in which technology can facilitate ESP by examining the challenges of ESP instruction and exploring the benefits of technology-mediated ESP learning environments. It examines two ESP courses that reflect the benefits and principles of technology-enhanced ESP teaching and gives suggestions for the role that ESP practitioners can play.
2. Kern, N. (2013) Technology-integrated English for Specific Purposes lessons: real-life language, tasks and tools for professionals, in Motteram, G. (ed.), *Innovations in Learning Technologies for English Language Teaching*. British Council.
   This chapter provides an overview of using technology in ESP, with some case studies. The author discusses the nature of ESP and the role of technology in ESP lessons, tools and tasks.

Resources

Some general corpora of English are accessible online:

(a) The *Collins Wordbanks Online* English corpus contains 56 million words of contemporary written and spoken text. It contains 36 million British written texts, 10 million American written texts and 10 million American spoken texts. The corpus is accessible at www.collins.co.uk/Corpus/CorpusSearch.aspx
(b) The *British National Corpus* (*BNC*) contains 100 million words of contemporary British English of which 90 million are written and 10 million are spoken texts. The corpus is accessible at sara.natcorp.ox.ac.uk
(c) *MICASE* (the *Michigan Corpus of Academic Spoken English*) contains 1.8 million words of (transcribed) academic speech, recorded at the University of Michigan between 1997 and 2001. The corpus is accessible at micase.umdl.umich.edu/m/micase/

Part C

Feedback, Materials and Teachers

7 Feedback and alternative assessment

> **Aims:** This chapter considers feedback supported by technologies from both theoretical and practical perspectives. Issues and problems when technologies are used in giving feedback and assessing students are also considered. Feedback and assessment tasks, and examples, are used to illustrate how a teacher can tailor existing assessment techniques to cater to the new learning style. This chapter has three main sections, as follows:
>
> 1. Focus on feedback
>
> 2. Focus on assessment
>
> 3. An alternative assessment.

Introduction

Computer-aided assessment (CAA) covers a range of assessment procedures and is a rapidly developing area as new technologies are harnessed. CAA refers to any instance in which some aspect of computer technology is deployed as part of the assessment process. Some of the principle examples of CAA in language learning are as follows:

- interactive exercises and tests completed on a computer;

- use of computers to produce coursework, such as using a word-processor;

- on-screen marking of students' word-processed writing;

- using a spreadsheet or database to keep a record of students' marks;

- use of email to send coursework, marks and feedback to students;

- use of webpages to set tasks for students and to provide tutor support;

- use of plagiarism detection software.

These are just some examples of CAA, not a comprehensive list. In this chapter, we will examine CAA in two broad areas: feedback and assessment that includes tests. Here I deliberately separate feedback from assessment (tests) to reflect the nature of its purposes – feedback is designed primarily to help students to improve their work, whereas assessments (tests) are designed to evaluate their learning outcomes. The goal of this chapter, therefore, is to provide (both pre-service and in-service) teachers with the knowledge and skills to use technology-enhanced feedback and assessment in teaching. This chapter first discusses (effective) feedback and the potential benefits of technology in providing feedback, and then it moves on to CAA, with a focus on tests. Finally, this chapter considers alternative assessments that teachers might need to be aware of, especially when they consider assessing students over a period of time.

Focus on feedback

Feedback on student language production is important for language learning because students rely on teacher feedback to improve. Feedback can come in various forms and is also closely related to learners' motivation and how learning is defined or conceptualised. Feedback can be understood from different perspectives: for example, Keh (1990) defines feedback as 'input from a reader to a writer with the effect of providing information to the writer for revision' (p. 294). Narciss (2008) defines it as 'all post-response information that is provided to a learner to inform the learner on his or her actual state of learning or performance' (p. 127). Hattie and Timperley (2007) define it as 'information provided by an agent with respect to one's performance or understanding' (p. 81). What is clear from these definitions is that feedback is designed to provide an understanding and evaluation of performance through offering some guidance and information for some improvements. Hattie and Timperley (2007) went further to clarify the relationship between feedback and performance:

> A teacher or parent can provide corrective information, a peer can provide an alternative strategy, a book can provide information to clarify ideas, a parent can provide encouragement, and a learner can look up the answer to evaluate the correctness of a response. (p. 81)

Clearly, students need to use the feedback they get in order to improve what they are learning. By receiving feedback, they can 'confirm, add to, overwrite, tune, or restructure information in memory, whether that information is domain knowledge, meta-cognitive knowledge, beliefs about self and tasks, or cognitive tactics and strategies' (Winne and Butler, 1994, p. 5740). This said, learners only benefit from good feedback. Therefore, developing an effective feedback strategy is clearly important. Although when we talk about feedback, we refer to both oral and written work produced by students, we will talk about mainly written work since it is the main area that technology can be of help.

Effective feedback

Traditionally, feedback is provided by the instructor, and such feedback serves three purposes: to check if their intended message is expressed properly; to encourage the learners; and to help the learners realise the ambiguity of their work (e.g. writing) (Sommers, 1982). Ellis et al. (2002, p. 430) proposed that even in communicative tasks, teachers should not be limited to being only a communicative partner. They need to pay attention to form. By receiving feedback, learners are able to notice the gap between their knowledge and the correct linguistic form. Explicit feedback can also help students understand why their language production is correct or incorrect, and research suggests that this can lead to learning better grammar (Nagata, 1993). In this area, computer-assisted feedback can provide immediate, accurate, consistent and individualised feedback (Tsutsui, 2004).

In writing, feedback has long been appreciated for its potential in support-ing learning and for increasing student motivation (Arndt, 1993; Hyland and Hyland, 2006b). Feedback can be both qualitative and quantitative and should motivate the writers to produce improved revised drafts. Although not all feedback leads to improvements (e.g. Bangert-Drownset et al., 1991; Kluger and DeNisi, 1996), appropriate and good feedback should have a positive effect on students' writing (Gibbs and Simpson, 2004). Because students rely on the feedback they get to improve themselves, there are some basic principles for effective feedback, which I will list here.

- Feedback should provide information specifically relating to the learning process so as to assist learners in understanding what they are learning and what they have just learned.

- Feedback should be sufficiently frequent.

- Feedback needs to be timely. Delayed feedback might not be as effective for students' development as timely responses would be, especially the local and explicit feedback.

- Students benefit from individualised feedback, or feedback that they can see has relevance to their specific learning.

- Feedback should be tailored to students' language levels.

- Feedback should motivate and empower students.

- Students might be able to act on the feedback.

- Feedback should be appropriate for the purposes of the task.

As discussed in Chapter 1, sociocultural theory emphasises the knowledge co-construction through communication between members of the social community. In this case, learners can improve and re-construct their knowledge by using guidance and information from the expert (teacher). The extended version of this theory, in particular, supports dialogic, meaningful interaction and mutual scaffolding between reviewer – either teacher or peer – and writer in producing meaningful texts. One type of feedback of this kind is peer feedback, which commonly involves students commenting on each other's writing. Peer feedback is usually organised in pairs or small groups. Students can do peer feedback activities in either a written, an oral or a computer-mediated mode (e.g. CMC) (Liu and Hansen, 2002). Using peer feedback is not meant to replace teacher evaluation, nor can it identify all the strengths and challenges in a piece of writing. However, when integrated into the writing task, peer feedback can be a useful learning tool (Memari Hanjani and Li, 2014).

The role of technology

In this section, we will explore how technology can be utilised to provide students with timely, accurate and individualised feedback. When considering feedback, we should refer to the automated writing evaluation (AWE), computer-based feedback that dates back to the 1960s, when Page Ellis developed Project Essay Grade (PEG). Since then, AWE has been explored in various contexts to support learning. However, Hegelheimer et al. (2016) urge for more studies to be done in order to evaluate the use of AWE tools in classrooms and beyond. Opinions on the utility of AWE tools and their potential effects on educational practices vary (see Ericsson and Haswell, 2006; Shermis and Burstein, 2013). However, AWE is not the focus of this chapter, because of its scope. We will explore tools that benefit everyday feedback and that teachers might find it possible to integrate into their teaching.

With the development of information technology, ways of providing and giving feedback have shifted from traditional feedback to computer-mediated feedback. Social networks (e.g. blogs) have enormous potential that can encourage critical engagement (Selwyn, 2009). For example, using blogs can engage learners in peer feedback. Dippold (2009) and Gedera

(2012) employed blogs in their ESL writing courses to allow students to use the authentic target language with a real audience. Their studies showed that students improved their writing skills and became more independent and reflective learners. Blogs can also encourage students to actively participate in the learning process by providing a friendly and less threatening environment (Hyland and Hyland, 2006a). Research also suggests that online feedback improves learners' work more than face-to-face peer feedback (Liu and Sadler, 2003; Hatime and Zeynep, 2012; Wichadee and Nopakun, 2012). In the next section, we will examine a few tools closely, in relation to providing feedback to written work.

Microsoft Word

The importance of feedback in writing lies in its role in the evolution of a piece of writing as feedback informs the writing process by permeating, shaping, and moulding it (Arndt, 1993). There are some advantages to using Microsoft Word's review functions to provide feedback on a piece of writing: (1) varieties of feedback can be included (e.g. direct and indirect feedback; feedback on **local** and **global errors**; comments, suggestions and encouragement); (2) feedback is clear in terms of its presentation; it's easy for the reader to read and follow; (3) the function of the 'comment' makes the feedback process *dialogic*; (4) it is easy for teachers to use and carry out – physically, the instructor does not need to carry heavy assignments; (5) using track changes in the writing makes it convenient for learners to identify their errors and analyse typical errors in the editing process; and (6) the deletions, insertions, questions and comments provide learners with opportunities to notice their linguistic deficiencies. Writing instructors face a wide range of options to respond to students' papers. They can correct the errors directly or indirectly, pointing out the flaws by underlining, coding, circling and highlighting them and requiring the students themselves to find the accurate forms. They can also provide general feedback on content and organisation by giving text-specific comments, asking questions, making suggestions and providing solutions (Raimes, 1991). Finally, they may want to include and encourage peer evaluation as well as self-evaluation in their writing courses.

Next I will show how to use Microsoft Word to give feedback. There are two things teachers can do with Word: track changes and comment. The track

> An error can be one of two types: local or global. Local errors are mainly linguistic and minor in that they do not significantly hinder the comprehensibility of the text. Global errors, on the other hand, cause a reader to misunderstand a message or to judge it as incomprehensible (Ferris, 2003). Local feedback addresses mechanics, linguistic and vocabulary mistakes; global commentary concentrates on ideas, content, clarity and organisation of a written text (Montgomery and Baker, 2007).

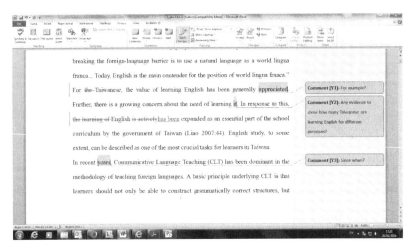

FIGURE 7.1 A SCREENSHOT OF FEEDBACK PROVIDED THROUGH MICROSOFT WORD

....
Recasts are corrective feedback provided with a reformulated answer.

Metalinguistic feedback is a comment or information about something without reformulating it.
....

changes function shows the direct corrections on a document, whereas comments provide students with indirect feedback, often requiring the revision of content, organisation and complex language issues (see Figure 7.1 for an example). Comments can include **recasts** and **metalinguistic feedback**, as well as feedback on organisation and content.

The following are the steps to use Word for feedback (the first step can change the name of the person who provides feedback to make it more anonymous if desired):

1. Set user name (**Tools → Options → User Information**).

2. Show **Reviewing** tool bar (**View → Toolbars → Reviewing**).

3. Click on the **Track Changes** icon on the **Reviewing** toolbar.

4. Type the corrections directly into the text of the document.

5. Highlight some text and then use the **Insert a Comment** icon on the **Reviewing** toolbar to make longer comments.

Task 7.1: Practise giving feedback

Now follow the steps provided above to give feedback on a piece of writing by your students. Then analyse what kind of feedback you provided and if possible, ask your students what feedback is the most effective.

Case study 7.1:

AbuSeileek and Abualsha'r (2014) implemented a computer-mediated corrective feedback process in an EFL writing course. They used the 'track changes' feature of Microsoft Word 2010, which strikes through deletions and marks insertions in a different colour. They also implemented recasts and provided metalinguistic feedback, to compare them with the tracked changes. They found the tracked changes offer the most effective way to provide feedback, measured by students' writing performance.

The Markin Programme

Markin is an on-screen marking and annotation software, which runs on Windows. It has a built-in feature allowing users to translate the programme's menus and messages into different languages – the translation can be saved and shared with other users via a Markin Interface File. It now has non-Roman languages such as Mandarin, Japanese, Hindi and Urdu, as well as European and Scandinavian languages. Markin can be used in three steps.

1. Import students' work (by copying and pasting from the document that students submitted).

2. Mark the text using annotations, comments, feedback and grades. Markin provides a comprehensive set of tools for the teacher to mark and annotate the text (see Figure 7.2 for an example).

3. Save the marked work and return it to the students.

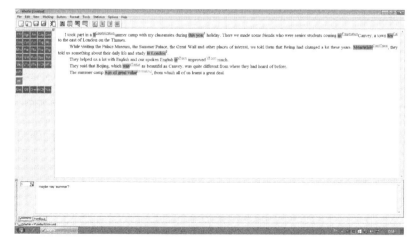

FIGURE 7.2   AN EXAMPLE OF USING MARKIN TO MARK STUDENTS' WRITING

Different from the functions in the Reviewing (or Review) panel in Word, Markin has a collection of annotations to help the teacher to give feedback to students, the majority of which offer indirect feedback using metalinguistic comments. This is a good tool to provide students with an opportunity to engage in thinking about their problems and working out a solution. This tool can also be used in peer feedback once students are familiar with the annotations. However, if students have insufficient metalinguistic knowledge, there is a risk to using this tool because students might struggle to offer and follow feedback. We already know that accuracy of peer feedback varies because student knowledge varies among different levels. Historically, peer assessors have not been regarded as 'knowledge authorities', thus leading to more reticence in accepting a peer's judgement or advice (Hanrahan and Iasscs, 2001; Strijbos et al., 2010). This means that when using Markin in peer feedback, the teacher needs to make sure students not only have linguistic knowledge (e.g. grammar, vocabulary) but also metalinguistic knowledge.

Screencast tools

Screencast software has now become popular for enabling clear and effective feedback, such as Jing and Snagit (go to www.techsmith.com/education-tutorial-feedback-snagit.html for a Snagit tutorial). The screencast tools basically record what happens on the assessor's computer screen as well as through audio commentaries.

Task 7.2: Advantages and disadvantages

Compared to the traditional feedback method, what are the advantages of video-recording feedback? What about disadvantages?

The screencast tools feature several advantages:

- Learners understand feedback better because the content of the video-recording is almost like having a conversation with the students: the teacher can talk them through the problems in their writing.

- The teacher can provide more feedback by talking and referring to the screen rather than writing down all the comments.

- The feedback is perceived as more personal and positive.

- The feedback is individualised for each student, which potentially enables students to engage in critical reflections in learning.

- The feedback provided for students can be used as learning sources – students know exactly what to work on.

The Jing video-recording tool from TechSmith has been gaining a lot of popularity in the last couple of years, and it can be used in three steps:

1. Download Jing for free onto your computer.

2. Open the student's writing on screen and record a short (five minutes max) video of what you are doing on screen: correcting/highlighting texts along with an audio commentary.

3. Send the link to the student once you have finished.

Task 7.3: Try it

Now try Jing or Snagit. Is it easy to use? What are your concerns when using the software?

There are also weaknesses to giving individualised feedback using screencast software. For example, when the teacher has a large number of students, offering personalised, detailed feedback for each student might be problematic because of the time constraints.

Electronic feedback is rapidly gaining popularity as an option due to the recent advances in technology and more availability of computer facilities as well as instructors' and students' increased computer literacy. At present, many teachers welcome these developments and integrate computer technology into their classrooms, and students receive feedback on their electronically produced and submitted work from their tutors, their peers or the computer itself (Hyland and Hyland, 2006b). However, teachers need to carefully consider students' target needs and abilities as well as both the rationale behind and the constraints of using computer-based feedback. It might be a good idea to combine both traditional and technology-based feedback, especially when peer feedback is used (Liu and Sadler, 2003). The two methods could complement each other, enhance students' motivation, lessen their anxiety and increase their involvement in the activity (Liu and Sadler, 2003, p. 222).

Focus on assessment (tests)

Apart from providing students with feedback, teachers often need to assess students through tests. Advances in technology make it possible to have computerised testing programmes. Computer-based tests have advantages over the traditional paper-based tests. First, they save administration time and lower costs. Second, they usually have higher validity. Third, they motivate learners in many cases because in some diagnosed tests, computers are able to provide immediate feedback.

Chapelle and Jamieson (2003) outline challenges for language teachers in considering technology-enhanced assessment. The first challenge is to define the purpose of a test. They argue that terms such as 'placement', 'proficiency' and 'achievement' may work for the public, but teachers need a more systematic, thorough and accurate way of considering the purpose of English language assessment because the purpose of the assessment is critical for choosing or developing a good test. In considering the purposes of assessment, teachers need to think about the inference that test users want to make based on test scores, the use of the test results and potential impact (e.g. as a motivating factor) of the test. The second challenge is to understand what a test measures, which determines the validity of a test. Chapelle and Jamieson argue that test validity depends on how a test is used. As they rightly point out, 'an important part of English language teachers' expertise includes a more thorough understanding of principles of assessment'.

Popular technological tools and applications in addressing feedback include websites, software and other applications. There are many websites that house online tests, where learners can take the tests and get immediate feedback. It is believed to be a useful way to help students to identify their weaknesses. Apart from using existing tests online, teachers can also develop exercises and quizzes using authoring tools or programmes.

Authoring tools

Authoring tools are programmes that allow users to create interactive materials with different kinds of media using predetermined templates (Níkleva and López, 2012). Hot Potatoes and Quandary are two examples. Hot Potatoes is a set of six authoring tools created by the University of Victoria. It is a programme that allows teachers to create interactive web-based exercises of several basic types. The six tools are as follows:

1. JQuiz can be used to create question-based exercises, including multiple-choice and short-answer quizzes.

2. JCloze is suitable for creating cloze and fill-in-the-blank exercises. The blanks generated by this programme can also be substituted for a drop-down menu.

3. JCross creates crossword puzzles.

4. JMix creates exercises in which students unscramble a sentence. It is a programme that can be used to review grammar and sentence structure.

5. JMatch is used to create matching exercises in the format of standard style, drag/drop and flashcard.

6. The Masher is a programme that can be used to bring all of the exercises above together by creating a unit. It can also add hyperlinks to connect all of the activities.

Exercises or tests can be easily created by entering the data (text, questions, answers, etc.) into a template, and the software creates the webpages for post-ing on the site. They support the inclusion of links, reading texts, images and media files in the learning materials, though these materials must be obtained from other sources. Hot Potatoes exercises can be designed follow-ing the steps outlined below:

1. Design Hot Potatoes activities (to learn how to design each exercise, go to http://hotpot.uvic.ca/wintutor6/tutorial.htm for a tutorial).

2. Create/export those activities into HTML format (follow the command as shown in Figure 7.3 or press F6).

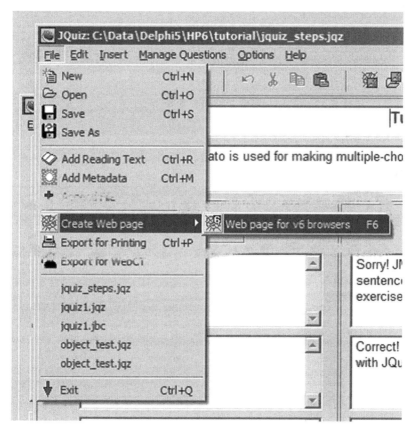

FIGURE 7.3   CREATE/EXPORT WEBPAGE
(Reproduced with kind permission from Laurence Anthony, 2017)

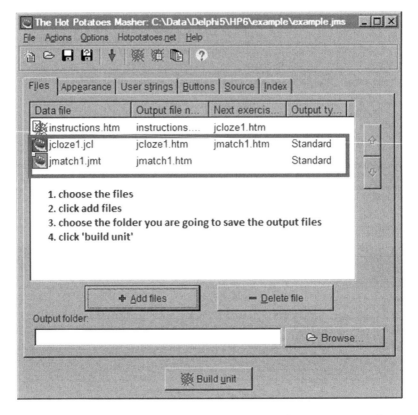

FIGURE 7.4   USE THE MASHER TO BUILD UNIT (WITH ADAPTATION).
(Based on' Laurence Anthony, 2017)

If teachers want to bring all activities together, they need to follow these next two steps (go to http://hotpot.uvic.ca/wintutor6/mashertutorial.htm for help):

i. Choose each Hot Potatoes file (as shown in Figure 7.4 below with .jcl for cloze, .jmt for matching) or choose the exported HTML files (as shown in Figure 8.4 with jcloze1.htm or jmatch1.htm).

ii. Choose Build Unit, and then a home page called 'index.html' or 'index. htm' will be created.

3. Upload the file to a website (a personal space, such as a blog, can be used) or the Hot Potatoes web server (http://login.hotpotatoes.net/) (Figure 7.5). Note that an account is needed on the Hop Potatoes website for the latter option.

FIGURE 7.5 UPLOAD FILES IN THE MASHER
(Reproduced with kind permission from Laurence Anthony, 2017)

Task 7.4: Do it yourself

Now open the Hot Potatoes tutorials (http://hotpot.uvic.ca/wintutor6/tutorial. htm) and start to create an exercise. You can choose to do any of them or more than one (and then bring them together in the Masher!).

Vargas and Modernas (2014) discuss the possibility of using Hot Potatoes as a valuable resource in the design of customised exercises and didactic units for reading comprehension courses in developing both student and teacher autonomy. One way to engage students is to ask them to create mini quizzes using the software, and then the teacher can use the quiz with the class (see Figure 7.6 for an example of crosswords). Having students create exercises may allow the individuals to not just memorise the language points but also think about how to use them through the creation of the exercise (Erben et al., 2009). Winke and MacGregor (2001) observed that a negative aspect of Hot Potatoes is that it makes mostly form-focused activities. Teachers therefore need to be aware of the shortcomings of the programme in promoting more task-based learning.

FIGURE 7.6 A CROSSWORD EXAMPLE

Online exam software

There is also all kinds of software for online exams that can help teachers create quizzes/exams online, such as Quizworks (www.onlinequizcreator.com) and QuizStar (http://quizstar.4teachers.org). These online tools enable the teacher to design ad hoc quizzes with very little technical knowledge.

Task 7.5: Explore an online quiz creator

Go to one of the above websites and try to create a quiz for your students. What are your considerations in creating the quiz?

There are many advantages of using online exam software to create tests and quizzes:

- Teachers do not need to have any technical skills or knowledge.
- It is online and the link can be embedded in a personal space (e.g. blogs).
- Students can take the quiz on any device (e.g. tablet, phone or computer) and at any time.
- Teachers can create various question types, such as multiple choice, free text, fill in the blank, video and audio.
- The software produces results for each student and also for the whole class, to give a teacher an overall idea of the performance of the whole class.

Of course, those who have technical skills might want to design an ad hoc test to meet their students' needs and learning styles.

Task 7.6: Pedagogical thinking

I have designed an online grammar learning and testing suite for one of my classes. When students log in to the system, they can take an initial test on a topic. As soon as they submit their test, the computer provides them with immediate diagnostic feedback (e.g. 'you need to work on …'), as well as follow up exercises and grammar explanations. After reading the explanations, the students are given a follow-up exercise on the areas they need to improve and then another comprehensive test to finish the topic. When they complete the final test, the computer gives them feedback but also gives them a choice to ask the teacher about the items that they do not understand (see Figure 7.7).

Now consider the underlying design of this test. What was my purpose in designing the test? And what advantages does this web-based test have over the traditional paper-based test?

Student log-in page

英语在线测试

学生登录

姓名 ▭
学号 ▭

进入

Initial test

必要性

第 1 题

It _____ be difficult to learn Tibetan.
A. shall
B. must
C. should
D. need

◯ A ◯ B ◯ C ◯ D 确定

Test result and recommended follow-up exercises

17	The plant is dead. I _____ it more water. A. will give B. would have given C. must give D. should have given	D ✓	D
18	- Where is my pen? -- You _____ it. A. might lose B. would have lost C. should have lost D. must have lost	D ✓	D
19	She didn't answer the doorbell. She _____ have been at home . A. ought not to B. might not C. mustn't D. couldn't	B ✗	D
20	You shouldn't _____ the ticket without asking me first. You _____ yourself the money. A. buy, could save B. have bought, could have saved C. have bought, could save D. buy, could have saved	D ✗	B
学生姓名：guest		题目总数：20	做对题数：8

根据测试情况，你需要做以下练习：

必要性 能力、允许 推测 意愿、请求

Grammar knowledge page before the follow-up exercises

3) ought 的用法：

• 表示应当、应该
⊕ Parents ought to send their children to school when they reach seven years old.
当孩子满七岁时，家长应当送孩子去上学。
⊕ You shouldn't judge a stranger always by the clothes he wears.
你不应当总是以貌取人。

注意：
在大多数情况下，ought to都可以被should代替。ought to语气较should重，

Final test where students can choose to ask the teacher if they need to

答题结果

题号	类别	题目内容	答题结果	正确答案	提交
320	测试	Although he tried, he _____ not make it. A. would B. should C. might D. could	A ✗	D	问教师
323	测试	Peter _____ come with us tonight, but he isn't very sure yet. A. must B. may C. can D. will	D ✗	B	问教师
324	测试	You _____ to the meeting this afternoon , if you have something important to do. A. needn't to come B. don't need come C. don't need coming D. needn't come	C ✗	D	问教师

FIGURE 7.7 A FLOW OF THE INDEPENDENT TEST ON GRAMMAR

The design of grammar test in Figure 7.7 is based on the following assumptions:

- The computer can cater for an individual's need in terms of grammar topic. Not every student has the same difficulty in understanding the topic, and therefore the computer can address individual students' needs.

- The computer can give students immediate feedback after they submit the test. The feedback will be diagnostic to give students a summary of not just how well they have done in the test but also what they should work on.

- The computer refers students to a designated area to learn grammar knowledge, where they can read explanations and see examples.

- The computer programme follows up with a further exercise after students read the explanations, to test their understanding and further diagnose whether students need more help.

- The computer also provides students with opportunities to raise questions with the teacher by clicking on the 'asking the tutor' button.

- The computer produces a summary sheet for the teacher that shows how well the group has done on individual items so that the teacher knows not only individual performances but the overall performance of the group. In this way, points of difficulty can be identified with the help of the computer.

An alternative assessment

In this chapter, I also want to introduce the concept of alternative assessment, which is different from tests, described above. Among the various forms of alternative assessment, the e-portfolio has become popular in recent years. The e-portfolio is a desired option for learners who learn and grow up with technology. An electronic portfolio, according to Barrett (2004, p. 271)

> uses electronic technologies, allowing the portfolio developer to collect and organise portfolio artefacts in many media types (audio, video, graphics, text). A standards-based portfolio uses a database or hypertext links to clearly show the relationship between the standards or goals, artefacts and reflection. The learner's reflections are the rationale that specific artefacts are evidence of achieving the stated standards or goals.

E-portfolios provide teachers with an opportunity to assess students with qualitative and longitudinal methods, which summarise learning and proficiency over time. Godwin-Jones (2008) suggests that e-portfolios can bridge the gap between formal instruction and informal learning, and the design of the e-portfolios should be mainly about presenting and documenting learners' work. In this process, learners should determine how best to do this. Barrett (2011) proposed several steps in building an e-portfolio:

1. Establish the purpose: define the purpose for the portfolio.

2. Collection/classification: decide what artefacts are collected and how to categorise them.

3. Reflection: focus on reflection on action, as well as reflection in action.

4. Connection/interaction/dialogue/feedback: an opportunity to gain some feedback.

5. Summative reflection/selection/evaluation: summarise the learning process and provide a meta-analysis of the learning experience as represented in the reflections (e.g. blogs).

6. Presentation/publishing: decide what part of the portfolio is included.

Barrett (2011) gives an example of using Google Apps to create an e-portfolio, with Google Docs to collect and store materials and blogs, or the Google site to write reflective journals, and then the Google site to present the e-portfolio.

Task 7.7: Create a document in Google Docs

Create a document, and then write down your portfolio context and goal. Then share it with your colleagues. Try editing the document collaboratively.

Mobile devices (e.g. smartphones) can also be exploited for the e-portfolio purposes (see https://sites.google.com/site/mportfolios/home/introduction for more information). Teachers should be creative in terms of tools to create e-portfolios because the key to the e-portfolio is reflection rather than technology.

Summary

In this chapter, we considered the role of technology in feedback and assessment. Technology definitely has affordances for flexibility, convenience and multimodal presentations in assessment and feedback. However, it is up to the teacher to explore these affordances and adapt the technology in their own contexts. In the next chapter, we will explore principles of evaluating e-learning materials.

Annotated further reading

1. Hegelheimer, V., Dursun, A. & Li, Z. (eds) (2016) Automated writing evaluation in language teaching. *CALICO Journal Special Issue*, 33(1).

    The journal issue includes conceptual and empirical research on AWE tools development, AWE tool classroom implementation and resulting pedagogical implications. It represents a good complement to existing books on AWE.

2. Casal, J. E. (2016) Criterion online writing evaluation. *Computer-Assisted Language Instruction Consortium*, 33(1), 146–155.

    This is a review of a product *Criterion* for online writing evaluation, created by Educational Testing Services. It uses the e-rater scoring system. It is a good introduction and evaluation of the product for anyone who would like to seek new ideas on evaluation software.

3. Walker, A. & White, G. (2013) Technology-enhanced language learning. *Oxford University Press*. Chapter 9: 'Assessment'.

    This chapter provides a basic introduction to assessment and how technology can support assessment – for example, through using authoring tools, e-portfolios and audio feedback. It also discusses the drawbacks of technology in making assessments.

4. https://sites.google.com/site/eportfolioapps/

    This Google site was set up by Helen Barrett to show teachers how to use Google to create an e-portfolio. There are instructions on how to use the different elements of Google Apps to maintain e-portfolios. It is suitable for anyone who is considering starting to use e-portfolios.

8   E-learning material evaluation and design

Aims: This chapter considers e-learning material evaluation by examining different evaluative frameworks. It also gives the reader 'hands-on' experience evaluating materials for their classrooms and provides support in understanding the principles of designing appropriate materials. This chapter has three main sections, as follows:

1. Understanding material evaluation

2. Frameworks for evaluating e-learning materials

3. Contextualising CALL tasks and material.

Introduction

Technology is developing at a rapid rate, and a large amount of material is produced for language learning and available for free. On the one hand, it is great for teachers to have access to various types of language materials. On the other hand, the rapid growth of online material makes it difficult for teachers to choose the right resource for their students. In this environment, almost 'all teachers need to know how to use the Web as a resource for current authentic language materials in written, audio, and visual formats' (Chapelle and Hegelheimer, 2004, p. 305). It has been increasingly important therefore for teachers to evaluate these materials systematically before they adopt them in classrooms (Chapelle and Hegelheimer, 2004; Fotos and Browne, 2004). Developing frameworks or criteria to evaluate electronic materials and technology-enhanced activities is thus one of the most important activities prior to integrating technology into teaching. Great efforts have been made in this area (e.g. Hubbard, 1988; Chapelle, 2001). The purpose of this chapter, therefore, is to develop teachers' awareness and skills in evaluating and adapting e-learning materials. The chapter begins by defining material evaluation with special attention to e-learning material evaluation. It then introduces three frameworks for evaluating e-learning materials followed by some examples. Finally, the chapter offers guidelines for teachers to contextualise and adapt CALL tasks and materials to address their learners' needs and learning styles.

What is materials evaluation?

Hubbard (2006) proposed three stages of evaluating CALL materials, namely selection, implementation, and assessment.

Materials evaluation has been defined by Tomlinson (2003, p. 15) as 'a procedure that involves measuring the value (or potential value) of a set of learning materials'. Regarding language learning, **evaluating CALL materials** relates to how teachers make subjective judgements about the effectiveness of materials in addressing the needs of the teacher and students (Tomlinson, 2003).

Evaluations can be carried out pre-use, in-use or post-use. Usually we are concerned with pre-use evaluation because teachers need to know whether it is appropriate to implement the materials in their class. Having said that, in-use and post-use evaluations are also important in establishing how successful learning materials are (McDonough and Shaw, 2003, p. 71). There are several established theoretical evaluative frameworks (e.g. Cunningsworth, 1995; McGrath, 2002; McDonough and Shaw, 2003). With regard to e-learning materials, 'evaluation refers to the process of (a) investigating a piece of CALL software to judge its appropriateness for a given language learning setting, (b) identifying ways it may be effectively implemented in that setting, and (c) assessing its degree of success and determining whether to continue use or to make adjustments in implementation for future use' (Hubbard, 2006, p. 1). Although in this definition, Hubbard refers to e-learning materials as CALL software, the process can be applied to any computer programmes and accompanying content, dedicated CALL or tutorial CALL programmes, as well as web-based materials and applications.

Characteristics for good language materials

It is important for teachers to know the characteristics of good language learning materials and to use these characteristics to guide how they select materials. However, determining what characterises good language learning materials depends on context and various conceptions.

Task 8.1: Reflect

Now reflect on your learning and teaching experience. Could you come up with a list of characteristics for good language materials?

If I ask teachers to come up with a list of characteristics for good language materials, they might come up with different lists. But no matter what grades teachers teach, what kind of learners they work with or what materials (e.g. textbooks) they have at hand, good materials should have the following characteristics:

1. They should provide learners with a context to learn language. That is, the materials should give learners authentic examples of how language is used in various real-life contexts. Both written and spoken language elements should be considered in the materials.

2. They should have a clear connection to the learner and should be appropriate to learners' general interests and to learners' cognitive and linguistic levels.

3. They should clearly explain grammar rules and vocabulary use.

4. They should have coherence in content, language presentation tasks and activities.

5. The materials should focus on language use in communication.

6. The materials should be well presented and easy to use.

These characteristics can be utilised as principles for evaluating materials, and an evaluative framework should address the issues around these areas.

Frameworks for evaluating e-learning materials

When using technology, teachers are concerned about issues of 'appropriate materials' for language classrooms (Li, 2008). When we consider evaluating materials, it is a widely accepted belief that e-learning materials are harder to evaluate since they differ from the traditional print materials, such as textbooks. So perhaps it is useful to consider two issues before we start to evaluate materials. First, how are they different from print materials? Second, why is it difficult to evaluate e-learning materials?

There are abundant materials available for teachers to use online, but the task of selecting suitable ones is quite difficult, for many reasons. First, e-learning materials (both Internet-based and courseware) have a complex structure, which means that teachers usually are not able to skim through them in the way they do with textbooks. They are not able to see the overall structure or the connections between different materials. Second, textbooks are usually developed by ELT authorities and written by experienced researchers and teachers, and the textbooks often go out for peer review before the final production. However, e-learning materials can be written

Task 8.2: Print vs e-learning materials

In what aspects are print and e-learning materials similar and different? Use the table to help you to think about this question.

Some considerations:	E-learning materials	Print materials
Does it have transparent structure?		
Can you skim through the content or orangisation?		
Can you get a full version to review in advance of making a selection?		
Is it accessible by all the learners in class?		

and published by anyone, and the quality varies. Even for those developed by authorities and researchers, or commercial companies, it is hard for teachers to get a free copy before they consider adopting it in their teaching. Third, e-learning materials are multimodal, meaning that materials contain not only text and images but also hypertext, hypermedia and multimedia elements. The multimodal dimensions make the evaluation less straightforward. These materials are often designed with different purposes; therefore, teachers cannot use one set of criteria to evaluate different types of materials. Fourth, there are not well-established, research-based and well-tested criteria, and there is little agreement about essential criteria among researchers. Yang and Chan (2008) have criticised the existing evaluation criteria, claiming that many of the existing website evaluation criteria are not specific enough and lack emphasis on evaluating the teaching of the four skills. Yang and Chan pointed out that most of the criteria do not provide a complete set of criteria for one or all language-learning aspects; most are entirely based on theory without including the needs of teachers and learners, and most are not validated by empirical research. Finally, in addition to the amount of time and effort involved in evaluating materials, expertise in evaluation for teaching purposes is required. However, many teachers are novice technology users themselves and do not possess the required knowledge and skills in assessing e-learning materials. Many teachers have taught from textbooks for years, and they find it difficult to transfer the knowledge and skills of evaluating print materials to assess e-learning materials. In fact, research suggests that many teachers do not receive sufficient training for incorporating technology, including evaluating materials for teaching purposes.

Task 8.3: Levels of experience with CALL

Read the following two quotes. To what extent do you agree?

'Language teachers who are not accustomed to looking at CALL software may perceive its purpose very differently than those who are more experienced' (Bradin, 1999, p. 159).

'Teachers with low level of CALL expertise are less likely to appreciate and understand the range of opportunities and activities that well-designed courseware might offer' (Li, 2008).

Evaluating teaching materials effectively is a vital professional activity for all EFL teachers (McDonough and Shaw, 2003). In Cunningsworth's (1995) words, 'careful selection is made, and that the materials selected closely reflect the aims, methods, and values of the teaching program' (p. 7). After evaluating materials, language teachers should adapt or modify them to suit their own teaching situations (Chapelle and Hegelheimer, 2004). There are several known factors that can be brought into the evaluation process: learners' characteristics such as learning styles, preferences and attitudes towards e-learning materials; technical infrastructure, access to technology, teaching objectives and tasks; teachers' competence and confidence in using technology and their pedagogical beliefs.

A variety of resources and evaluation methods have been applied to select materials and courseware (e.g. Robb and Susser, 2000). Levy and Stockwell (2006) present three major types of CALL material evaluation: checklists or forms, methodological frameworks and SLA research-based criteria.

Checklists

According to Hubbard (2006), **checklists** contain a series of questions or categories for judgement, and the evaluator will make a response based on information gathered through the reviewing process. There are many checklists available online, such as 'Evaluative criteria for computer-delivered language learning systems' developed by the National Foreign Language Resource Center in Hawaii (www.nflrc.hawaii.edu/networks/NW31/) and 'Language Learning Website Review Form' (Son, 2005) (http://eprints.usq.edu.au/820/1/Son_ch13_2005.pdf).

The majority of evaluative frameworks used in the literature use checklists, in the form of questions or categories. Survey is also popular (e.g. Yang and Chan, 2008).

Task 8.4: Evaluate materials using a checklist
Choose a checklist from one of the above websites and use it to evaluate a piece of software or a website. Consider the following:

1. To what extent does the checklist help you evaluate the material for your teaching context?
2. What are the advantages and disadvantages of using a checklist?
3. How are you going to adapt the checklist if necessary?

The advantages and disadvantages of checklists have been pointed out by various researchers (e.g. Susser, 2001; Hubbard, 2006). The advantages of using a checklist to evaluate software, an application or a piece of web-based material are that (1) checklists are usually systematic and comprehensive; (2) they are cost and time effective; (3) the evaluation is straightforward, and both teachers and learners can use them; (4) the results are easy to understand, replicate and compare (McGrath, 2002, pp. 26–27); and (5) they can be easily adapted to suit the specific needs of a learning situation.

Of course, checklists do come with disadvantages. First of all, pre-existing checklists can become dated, and the criteria used may not be transparent or based on assumptions shared by everyone (McGrath, 2002). Second, teachers often need to adapt the checklist because of cultural issues and its appropriateness for the given teaching context. Third, a checklist might not be comprehensive in scope. Fourth, the review might be very superficial since the questions asked tend to be closed. The opportunity to make an in-depth review is very limited when using checklists. In defending checklists, Susser (2001) has pointed out that they do not have to be accepted but can be adapted and updated for particular purposes because they do provide teachers with a useful tool to recognise the variety of elements that make up a software application and to trigger reflection on some of their own assumptions of CALL. One such an example is a study by Ngu and Rethinasamy (2006). They developed a checklist to conduct a post-use evaluation to assess the effectiveness of using a CALL lesson instead of a conventional lesson to facilitate learning English prepositions in Malaysia.

Methodological frameworks

Methodological frameworks are descriptive rather than judgemental. A methodological framework is an integrated description of the components of CALL materials. As Hubbard (1988) puts it, 'rather than asking a specific set of questions, a framework provides a tool through which an evaluator can create his or her own questions or develop some other evaluation scheme' (p. 52). The first CALL material evaluation framework following the methodological approach was designed by Phillips (1985). It considered categories for the

*Richards and Rodgers (1982) speci-
fied three characteristics of language
teaching methods:*

*Approach: underpinning theory of
language learning;*

*Design: consistent with approach
but detailed operational dimensions
in teaching, such as tasks, methods,
teaching objectives, and the role of
the teacher and learners;*

*Procedure: classroom techniques to
realise the design.*

CALL programme, describing language learning dimensions such as language difficulty, learner focus (i.e., skill area – listening, speaking, reading or writing), and language focus (i.e., lexis, grammar and discourse). Built on Phillips' system and integrated with one developed independently by Richards and Rodgers (1982) for describing and analysing **language teaching methods**, Hubbard (1988) developed a methodological framework by adapting the approach, design and procedural constructs into a CALL environment and established the categories for evaluating CALL materials as 'teacher fit, learner fit, and operational description', respectively. Hubbard (2006) believed that a methodological framework is descriptive and more comprehensive in nature. He proposed six areas to examine when evaluating CALL materials (p. 10), as outlined below (see Table 8.1).

Task 8.5: Teacher fit

One of the criteria in this methodological framework is *teacher fit*. Now reflect on your own teaching beliefs: what is language? And how is language learnt? When you use technology, what would you like the technology to do?

Hubbard's methodological framework certainly is useful in describing the software or application and providing an in-depth analysis. It has been used by the *CALICO Journal* for learning technology reviews of software and applications (see the detailed version of the methodological framework at *CALICO Learning Technology Review Guidelines* available at the journal website).

Task 8.6: Critique the methodological framework

Go to the CALICO review site and use the methodological framework to evaluate the same material you evaluated when you used a checklist.

Then compare the advantages and disadvantages of the methodological framework and reflect on whether there is anything you found difficult.

One obvious disadvantage of the methodological framework is that conducting the review is time consuming. Sometimes teachers might find it difficult to conduct the review thoroughly. This might require teachers to be innovative and collaborative in reviewing e-learning materials. That is, teachers can work together and make their evaluation available to other

Areas of examination	Explanation	Example:
Technical preview	enable the system that the software or app requires and determine whether both the teacher and students have access to it	Will it run on the machines the students will be using? Do students have access to the network or the web?
Operational description	understand how the software or app works	Does it require user input?
Teacher fit	figure out whether the approach underpinning the design of the software or app matches the pedagogical beliefs of the teacher	What is language, and how is language learnt? Is the language learning for a communicative purpose?
Learner fit	determine how well the software or app addresses the students' needs, proficiency level, learning preferences, styles and interests	Does it present linguistic challenges for learners?
Implementation schemes	learn how the software or CALL materials can be integrated into learning	Do students need training?
Appropriateness judgements	make a decision based on the quality and degree of teacher fit, learner fit and the costs and benefits of implementation	Do I adopt, adapt or reject the material?

TABLE 8.1 A METHODOLOGICAL FRAMEWORK IN EVALUATING E-LEARNING MATERIALS

teachers (e.g. through the *CALICO Journal*). Collaborative evaluations of materials make sense for two reasons: first, a majority of teachers rely on recommendations from their colleagues (Robb and Susser, 2000); and second, this enables many teachers to learn from each other how to evaluate materials in a community.

SLA-based approach

In the interest of formulating perspectives from instructed SLA in a manner that would guide CALL evaluation, Chapelle (2001) proposed five principles for evaluating CALL, as summarised below:

1. CALL evaluation is situation specific.

2. CALL should undergo both **judgemental and empirical evaluations**.

3. CALL evaluation criteria should come from instructed SLA theory and research.

4. The criteria should be applied relative to the purpose of the CALL task.

5. The central consideration should be language-learning potential.

Chapelle (2001) described the use of these criteria for guiding both judge-mental and empirical evaluation of CALL materials. Judgemental evalua-tion is based on an individual's logical analysis, whereas empirical evaluation is based on analysis of observed data from a group of individuals.

Based on these five principles, Chapelle (2001, 2007) proposed a framework encompassing six criteria, including language-learning potential (focus on form), meaning focus (focus on meaning of the language), learner fit, authenticity (how authentic the learning is in relation to real-life situations), positive impact (e.g. motivation, autonomy and engagement) and practicality (resources available). The following outlines the meaning of each (see Table 8.2 for examples of questions regarding learner fit, meaning focus and authenticity from Jamieson et al., 2005):

- *Language-learning potential* is the degree of opportunity present for ben-eficial focus on form.

- *Meaning focus* is the extent to which learners' attention is directed towards the meaning of the language.

- *Learner fit* is the amount of opportunity for engagement with language under appropriate conditions given learner characteristics.

- *Authenticity* is the degree of correspondence between the learning activ-ity and the target language activities of interest to learners outside of the classroom.

- *Positive impact* is the positive effects of the CALL activity on those who participate in it.

- *Practicality* is the adequacy of resources to support the use of the CALL activity.

Unlike the methodological framework, the SLA research-based framework was designed for what Chapelle refers to more generally as 'CALL tasks', encom-passing a broader set of options, including computer-based language testing and computer-based SLA research. In one of the evaluation projects by Jamieson, Chapelle and Preiss (2005), they adopted a case-study approach to offer an example of a context-based evaluation. They did this by operationalising

Criteria	Operationalizations	Desired responses to support claims for quality
Learner fit • appropriate difficulty for learners to benefit • appropriate for characteristics of learners	• Is the material at an appropriate ability level? • Are the student characteristicsas anticipated? • Is the material at the appropriate difficulty level?	• Yes, intermediate • Yes, young adult, self-motivated • Yes, somewhat difficult
Meaning focus • Learner's attention primarily focused on meaning	• Will students understand or remember content?	• Yes
Authenticity • Correspondence to CALL and language outside classroom	• Is the language in LEO3 needed for outside of class? • Is it like that used outside of class?	• Yes • Yes

TABLE 8.2   AN EXAMPLE OF QUESTIONS RELATING TO SOME OF CHAPELLE'S CRITERIA
(This is part of the table: Reproduced with kind permission from Criteria for CALL Quality, Operationalizations as Questions, Desired Responses. Jamieson, Chapelle & Preiss, 2005, p. 100)

criteria for CALL evaluation and administering the instruments to three groups of stakeholders in a community college ESL class in New York. One teacher, 42 students and four developers were involved in the evaluation of Longman English Online (LEO). The results suggested a good agreement among stakeholders and overall positive evaluations, and they identified some areas for improvement in the materials and the evaluation instruments.

Task 8.7: Evaluate and reflect

Use Chapelle's framework to evaluate the e-learning materials you or your colleagues have identified. Focus on the questions that you will need to ask in order to address each category of the criteria.

How does contextual information affect the questions you might ask for each category?

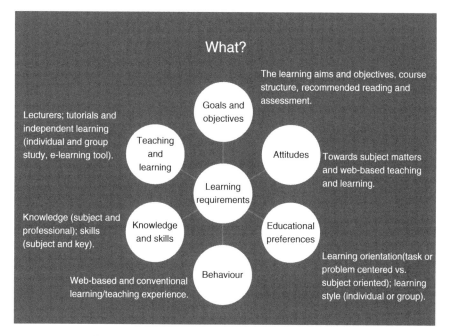

FIGURE 8.1 KEY ELEMENTS FOR CONSIDERATION IN
THE PROCESS OF CONTEXTUALISING MATERIALS

Contextualising and adapting CALL tasks and materials

Because of the differences in learners, learning styles, educational values, pedagogical goals and availability of technology, teachers find themselves in a position to consider adapting and modifying materials after evaluating them. Before adapting or contextualising materials, teachers need to think about key elements in their teaching situation, including learning goals and objectives, their own beliefs and attitudes, educational preferences, learners' behaviour, knowledge and skills required and finally the nature of learning and teaching. These areas and detailed explanations are presented in Figure 8.1.

Here, I propose two approaches in adapting e-learning materials. The first one is a technology-based approach and the second one is an activity-based approach. I will briefly outline each approach below.

Technology-based approach

The technology-based approach, as its name suggests, requires the teacher to modify technical aspects. For example, for video or audio materials (e.g. podcasts and films), teachers can edit the materials to meet their needs. This includes adding subtitles, providing captions with key words and

WebQuest is an inquiry-oriented lesson format in which most or all the information that learners work with comes from the web. The model was developed by Bernie Dodge at San Diego State University in February, 1995. More information about WebQuest can be found at www. webquest.org

slowing down the speed of the speech. Teachers can also make technical changes to other types of materials, such as **WebQuest**. WebQuest published a flow chart to walk teachers through the steps to adapt an existing WebQuest to meet their needs (see Figure 8.2, and the detailed explanation can be found at http://webquest.org/sdsu/adapting/index.html).

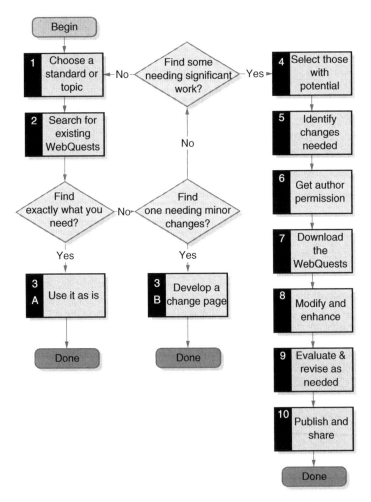

FIGURE 8.2   ADAPTING AND ENHANCING EXISTING WEBQUESTS.
(available at www.webquest.org) (Reproduced with kind permission from Bernie Dodge)

Task 8.8: Modify a WebQuest

Modify a WebQuest you are interested in using in your own teaching context (you might want to use this iPod project as an example: (http://questgarden.com/53/74/2/070721171535/)

Then reflect on the problems and issues you have had in adapting this e-learning material.

Activity-based approach

The activity-based approach is more common than the technology-based approach because it requires fewer technical skills. For this approach, changes can be made regarding *scope, complexity and difficulty level* of the task, as outlined below:

- *Scope* is the range of activities that can be maximised to include all language skills and knowledge. For example, a podcast can be used for developing both listening and speaking skills, but the teacher can also extend the activity to focus on vocabulary and reading.

- *Complexity* refers to 'the result of the attentional, memory, reasoning, and other information processing demands imposed by the structure of the task on the language learner' (Robinson, 2001, p. 28). A task's complexity level can be enhanced when learners are pushed to be more accurate and when the complexity of L2 production in a communication task increases.

- *Difficulty level* concerns the learners' perceptions of task demands, as these are affected by *affective* and *ability* factors. The task difficulty level is perceived to be reduced if students are highly motivated and engaged. In contextualising and adapting e-learning materials, teachers can work on one or more of the above mentioned aspects.

Task 8.9: Adapting a material
Visit the podcast sample exercises and worksheets at the bottom of this text-box. Now consider adapting these activities for your learners. Which aspects do you need to work on to contextualise the materials?
www.podcastsinenglish.com/pages/freesample.shtml

Principles for adapting materials

There are strong reasons to consider Chapelle's materials evaluation criteria when adapting materials, including the fact that language is based on context and oriented according to situations; that accurate, complex and realistic language use must be accurate; that differences and perceptions among learners are important; and that the environment must be practical. Based on these criteria, it can be suggested that the use of CALL to achieve effective language learning may follow the principles discussed below, and adaptation of materials should address these aspects:

- It must specify a language-learning feature as the target/purpose of the activity. In designing CALL activities and implementing CALL applications in teaching, teachers need to be aware of the specific linguistic outcome or purpose of that activity. The kind of question the teacher needs to ask is 'is it form, meaning or use that this activity is about?'

- It must understand SLA research and link it to the use of CALL materials and pedagogy. From an SLA perspective, teachers need to understand why and how technology can be used to focus on form.

- It must situate materials, activity and language learning in a specific context, bearing in mind sociocultural and educational contexts. This principle includes the availability of technology, preparedness of teachers and learners in using technology (e.g. technology confidence and competence), curriculum and testing requirements.

- It must specifically address learners' needs and levels from both linguistic and cognitive perspectives. By considering a learner's needs, interests and level, the full potential of CALL materials and applications may be realised.

- It must link what is being learnt (vocabulary and grammar) to the context in which it is used. Students need to see the relevance of what they learn, in real-life situations. This could be done either by analysing real-life materials where a particular language item is used (e.g. TV series) or by giving students opportunities to use the learnt language to carry out an authentic task.

- It must provide conditions to assist students to appropriate the use of the language. Technology can be used as a mediational tool to facilitate conceptual understanding (either grammar structure or lexis acquisition). In terms of the latter, for example, an animation or visual of a less common lexical item, such as 'concierge economy', can be used to assist learners to understand not only the meaning but also the potential impact of it, which contributes to a deeper understanding.

- It must raise student interest in engaging in learning; involvement and motivation play a major role in successful learning. As discussed in an earlier chapter, one of the affordances of technology is its positive impact on motivation, engagement and participation (see Chapter 2). For example, web-based learning instruction can produce authentic learning environments where a task-based approach is employed to increase participation (Thomas and Reinders, 2010).

Summary

In this chapter, we have considered three different frameworks for evaluating e-learning materials. Of course, there might be other frameworks emerging as a result of the development of pedagogy and technology. When evaluating materials, the focus should not be placed on the technological; instead, it should be on the pedagogical aspect. The questions every teacher should be asking are, therefore, how is technology being used to assist learning, and what aspects of learning could be encouraged by using technology? In the next chapter, we will consider the role of technology and teachers in technology-enhanced learning, as well as the key factors that influence teachers' use of technology.

Annotated further reading

1. Ngu, B. H. & Rethinasamy, S. (2006) Evaluating a CALL software on the learning of English prepositions. *Computers & Education*, 47, 41–55.
   This article is an example where researchers assessed the effectiveness of using a CALL lesson to facilitate learning English prepositions at Bario, Malaysia. The authors applied tests and questionnaires to address their research focus.
2. Jamieson, J., Chapelle, C. A. & Preiss, S. (2005) CALL evaluation by developers, a teacher, and students. *CALICO Journal*, 23(1), 93–138.
   The authors provide a good example of using the SLA research-based framework (Chapelle, 2001) to evaluate a professionally developed software programme for second language learning. This involves three groups of stakeholders, namely the teacher, students and courseware developer. An explanation of the evaluation framework (with relevant questions for each section) is presented and applied in this study.
3. Hubbard, P. (2006) Evaluating CALL software, in L. Ducate and N. Arnold (eds), *Calling on CALL: From Theory and Research to New Directions in Foreign Language Teaching*. San Marcos, TX: CALICO.
   This article provides an overview of three frameworks introduced in this chapter, with a particular focus on the methodological framework developed by Hubbard (1988, 1996). It provides a detailed account of the evaluative framework and its workflow. The framework is attached as an appendix.
4. Susser, B. (2001) A defense of checklists for courseware evaluation. *ReCALL*, 13(2), 261–276.
   This paper examines the role of checklists as a device for evaluating CALL courseware. It covers in detail the main objections to the use of checklists for courseware evaluation, such as accuracy, objectivity and reliability. The author examines these claims one by one, finding either that the criticism is unjustified or that it applies equally to any form of courseware evaluation.

9 Language teachers and new technologies

Aims: This chapter reviews the literature on teachers' attitudes towards using technology in language teaching and considers factors contributing to technologies in teaching. This chapter also examines the roles of teachers in the technology-enhanced learning environment. Finally, it presents a framework for integrating technology in teaching and advice to teachers on how to take an active role. This chapter has five sections, as follows:

1. Language teachers' attitudes towards integrating technology in teaching

2. Factors contributing to technology use in teaching

3. The role of teachers in technology-enhanced language teaching

4. The role of technology in learning

5. A framework for integrating technology in teaching.

Introduction

If integrated properly, technology can benefit both language teachers and language learners by creating a more interactive language classroom, motivating learners and providing authentic language input taken from 'real-life' situations (Warschauer and Healey, 1998; Lee, 2000). However, the realisation of this potential depends on how teachers use the technology (Cabanatan, 2003; Li, 2014) and on the skills and attitudes of teachers regarding the effectiveness of its integration into the curriculum (Bitner and Bitner, 2002). In this chapter, I will examine language teachers' attitudes towards using technology in teaching and the factors contributing to the implementation of technology. I also consider the various roles of teachers in the implementation of technologies in teaching and a framework for integrating technology into teaching. First, I will briefly re-examine the benefits of technology.

Research suggests that teachers do realise the benefits of technology, such as facilitating the sharing of resources, expertise and advice and providing both better networking opportunities and better management of their students (Bushweller, 2000; Li, 2008). The Teacher Workload Study conducted by PricewaterhouseCoopers (PwC) (2001) estimates that using technology in teaching could save between 3.25 and 4.55 hours per teacher per week. However, it further reports the conditions for reducing workload, such as coherent planning and deploying technology on a school-wide basis; high quality software and web-based resources for teaching; and high quality training. Egbert et al. (2002) suggest that technology use in the classroom can improve working processes, by increasing students' productivity, enhancing the variety of classroom activities and including up-to-date resources. As Brinton (2001) emphasises, 'whatever the approach, language teachers seem to agree that media can and do enhance language teaching' (p. 459).

Language teachers' attitudes towards using technology in teaching

Recognising the important role that teachers play in using technology for educational purposes, much work has been done to investigate teachers' attitudes towards, and beliefs about, using technologies in the classroom (e.g. Lam, 2000; Baek et al., 2008; Li and Walsh, 2011b). A possible rationale for such work has been the view that initiatives to promote technology uptake in teaching are more likely to succeed if teachers' attitudes and concerns are understood and the potential contributing factors are considered.

Task 9.1: Your attitudes

What is your attitude towards technology and using technology in teaching? Now consider the following statements (Table 9.1) and give a mark on each statement (strongly agree: 5; agree: 4; not sure: 3; disagree: 2; strongly disagree: 1 – for items with shade, you need to score each of them as follows: strongly agree: 1; agree: 2; not sure: 3; disagree: 4; strongly disagree: 5).

These statements are part of the questionnaire from Li (2008). They were designed to reveal teachers' attitudes and perspectives to integrating technology into EFL teaching and learning. The items in this section consist of attitudes towards technology itself and towards technology knowledge and skills that teachers need in order to successfully integrate technology into teaching, towards the benefits that technology can have for teachers and learners and finally towards using technology to assist teaching.

What are your top ten statements? Compare your results with a friend or colleague and discuss your responses to the items.

	Strongly agree	Agree	Not sure	Disagree	Strong disagree
1 I would like to know more about ICT.					
2 ICT helps me find lots of relevant information for teaching.					
3 ICT reduces my workload					
4 I enjoy working with computers for teaching purpose.					
5 A computer is an important tool to assist learning.					
6 I think ICT will change the way I teach.					
7 Using computers saves me time.					
8 Computers can make learning fun.					
9 I don't think computer have any real effect on students' learning.					
10 Using computers makes lesson preparation time-consuming.					
11 I was forced to use computers in teaching.					
12 Using computers to teach is trendy.					
13 Using computers in teaching has positive effects on learning.					
14 Students will be more active and motivated when using computers.					
15 I use computers only in open class for observation.					
16 It is interesting to learn using ICT.					

TABLE 9.1   EFL TEACHERS' ATTITUDES TOWARDS TECHNOLOGY USE SCALE

17	I have only basic computer skills.
18	I am not sure how to teach students to use ICT.
19	ICT helps students acquire new knowledge effectively.
20	I am afraid to make mistakes in front of my students when I use ICT.
21	I have attended a CPD (continuing professional development) programme using ICT.
22	I do not feel supported in using ICT.
23	ICT encourages students to work together.
24	Students get distracted by technology.
25	Some students are as scared of ICT as me.
26	I don't have the appropriate ICT skills to use it effectively.
27	I don't get support from my school for using ICT in teaching.
28	ICT helps me communicate with colleagues.
29	I improve my subject knowledge through using ICT.
30	ICT training does not change my use of ICT in the classroom.
31	I don't need ICT to help with my subject knowledge enrichment.
32	ICT does not go with my subject.
33	I have enough ICT knowledge already.

TABLE 9.1 CONTINUED

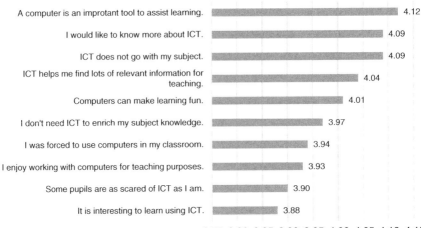

FIGURE 9.1   TEACHERS' ATTITUDES TOWARDS USING ICT IN EFL TEACHING

Li (2008) surveyed 400 EFL teachers in China about their attitudes and found out that English teachers held overall positive attitudes towards using computers to assist teaching, in spite of their experience of using technology. Figure 9.1 illustrates the overall attitudes of these teachers.

As evidenced in the literature, teachers' attitudes are likely to be influenced by background factors. Li (2008) highlights a few:

- Teachers who work in the city are more open to the idea of using technology for teaching purposes than are those who work in rural areas.

- A significant difference was found between teachers' overall attitude towards using computers in teaching and access to computers in the classroom, the office and the computer lab for teaching purposes. Teachers with access to computers hold more positive attitudes towards using them for teaching purposes.

- Computer training is highly correlated to positive attitudes. Those who had prior training are more likely to use technology.

- Age makes a difference. Younger teachers (e.g. under age 45) hold more positive attitudes. Clearly there is an assumption in the literature that younger teachers engage in more playful practices (Robinson and Mackey, 2006; Tan and McWilliam, 2009).

- Teaching experience affects teachers' attitudes. Teachers who have more than 20 years' experience are less positive than those who have less than 20 years' experience.

- Department size influences teachers' attitudes. Teachers from smaller-sized departments hold more positive attitudes towards using computers in teaching than teachers from bigger-sized ones.

- School category affects teachers' attitudes. Teachers from city key schools[1] hold more negative attitudes towards using computers in teaching than those from regular schools.

Task 9.2: What factors influence attitudes?

Now consider the factors affecting teachers' attitudes. Do they make sense in your own context? Besides those factors, what are some other factors that affect teachers' using technology, in your context?

Factors contributing to technology use in teaching

Despite positive attitudes held by teachers in a range of educational settings across different countries, in terms of the actual use of technology, teachers are reluctant technology users (see, for example, Li and Walsh, 2011b; Yang and Huang, 2008).

Technology Acceptance Model

The literature indicates that teachers' beliefs about the potential outcome of the usage or the perceived usefulness of the technology and its ease of use are crucial factors influencing their willingness to employ technology. This has been termed the Technology Acceptance Model (TAM) (Davis et al., 1989). The model implies that if teachers perceive computer use to be important in enhancing teaching and learning, they will have a positive attitude. And a positive attitude results in their using technology.

---

[1] Schools in Beijing are usually categorised into three groups: 'key school', 'district key school' and 'ordinary school' based on the students' academic achievement, facilities of the school and ratio of the graduate entering university. Key schools are the best schools in the city; district key schools are the best schools in the district, except for the key schools; and ordinary schools are the rest of the schools.

Task 9.3: TAM

Search the literature and find a study which adopts TAM. Read and critically review the TAM in understanding teachers' use of technology. If you have a colleague that you can collaborate with, then read the article and do the critical analysis independently before you compare notes.

TAM is undoubtedly useful in researching attitudes towards technology and has been widely applied in different contexts. However, research has also reported other relevant issues. Li (2014) offers a list of suggestions based on empirical research of EFL teachers, including accessibility of resources, time, technology competence and confidence, sociocultural contexts and pedagogical beliefs.

Access to resources

Loveless et al. (2001) claim that pedagogy can express a dynamic interaction between learners, teachers and knowledge. Educationalists are convinced from research evidence that technology helps to reduce teachers' workload (Becta, 2002) and enables teachers to express their 'epistemological stance' (Becker and Ravitz, 1999; Moseley et al., 1999). However, the complex systems of policy, practice and assessment present a wide range of factors that influence the uptake of technology in educational contexts (Cox et al., 1988; Selwyn, 1999; Li, 2008).

In the literature, the most widely reported influences on teachers' use of technology are external factors such as *access to technology* and *resources*; much research has suggested that teachers are often frustrated by these factors. Furthermore, research highlights the importance of the level of technology usage in technologically well-resourced schools (e.g. Pelgrum, 2001; Becta, 2004; Li, 2008, 2014) because how teachers use technology is often restricted by the availability of computers, especially when teachers want to involve students. One might argue that there are many effective uses of technology in any computer classroom (e.g. Tamela et al., 2000), but if teachers do not believe that they have enough control over the work environment, they might not have the autonomy to be able to explore the environment. Resource accessibility also applies to relevant software, courseware and electronic resources. Teachers traditionally rely on textbooks, and if they are to use e-learning materials, then they need to be able to evaluate and adapt those materials to their learners' needs (Chapelle, 2003) (see also Chapter 8).

Time

A lack of time is another external factor which hinders the likelihood that teachers will use technology. Jones (2001) notes that even if the teachers receive training, both technical and pedagogical, they still might not find enough time to put this into practice. However, this might be interpreted as teachers' recognising that computers do not save time or reduce workload (Burston, 1996). Teachers very often believe that CALL activities take time away from what they need to do. In fact, one of the criteria for effective CALL integration is that it is efficient (Egbert, 2001), but many teachers are unable to efficiently use CALL in their classrooms. One of the reasons is lack of knowledge and skills to match CALL activities to their pedagogical purpose and to evaluate such materials.

Technology competence and confidence

Besides resources, technology competence and confidence are important factors. Teachers are not prepared to integrate technology into their teaching if they do not feel confident and competent in using technology. Anxiety levels correlates to teachers' uptake of technology in teaching, as well. For example, Thao (2003) reported that EFL teachers in Vietnam were not confident in giving proper instruction, designing activities and solving the problems that occurred in teaching when they used computers. Lam (2000) reported a similar result: American ESL teachers lacked confidence in computer skills and knowledge about teaching through computers. Technology knowledge and skill is well recognised in the literature (Pelgrum, 2001; Snoeyink and Ertimer, 2001). Training is one of the most important means of improving teachers' competence and confidence, and such training needs to be ongoing and needs to cover both technical and pedagogical aspects. In training, contextual factors such as learning style, test, curriculum and culture should be taken into consideration, as teachers must see how to fit the technology into their teaching contexts. Because teachers are more likely to incorporate technology that aligns with either their value beliefs (Zhao et al., 2002; Ottenbreit-Leftwicha et al., 2010) or their students' needs

Sociocultural theory understands teacher learning as an ongoing, long-term and complex developmental process where teachers have opportunities to participate in social practice. Teachers are offered scaffolded help, opportunities to interact and internalise ideas and a supportive community in which to identify themselves. There are many ways to implement a sociocultural approach to teacher education, and one effective way is through the collaborative dialogic approach.

(e.g. achieving high exam results), professional development programmes are more likely to be effective if they are oriented towards these beliefs and needs. Kessler (2007) suggests that traditional teacher education programmes need to be revised in order to integrate teacher CALL training in a variety of pedagogical classes. A new approach might be the one that fits with the **sociocultural perspective of teacher learning**, where teachers actively engage in educational activities, forming part of a community of practice and having opportunities to reflect on and theorise based on their learning (Johnson, 2006, 2009; Wright, 2010). Such learning is effective because it is 'situated in authentic learning contexts' (Egbert et al., 2002, p. 122). A **collaborative dialogic approach** is effective because it emphasises the interaction and collaboration between teachers in making links between the content of learning and classroom practice. It is important to have 'hands-on' practice with technology during teachers' professional education, which can help develop foundational knowledge about skills to teach with the use of technology (Fleming et al., 2007; DeliCarpini, 2012). Teachers will see immediate applications of such carefully tailored professional development programmes in their teaching situations in order to meet their students' specific needs.

Case study 9.1:

The following are three examples that followed a sociocultural approach to teacher learning. What are the strengths and weakness for each approach?

1. Meskill et al. (2006) reported a study where novice teachers, experienced teachers and doctoral students worked together on implementing innovative collaborative CALL projects. Novice teachers brought in technology skills, whereas experienced ones provided the pedagogical expertise, and the doctoral students served as their mentors.
2. Hanson-Smith (2006) put forward Webheads in Action, which is an online community where in-service teachers can peer-mentor each other. They share information, reflect on their experiences through online presentations and engage in technology enhanced learning projects.
3. Schocker-von Ditfurth and Legutke (2002) reported a collaborative project between student teachers and in-service teachers. The student teachers prepared an online project for the in-service teacher's classroom and then accompanied the in-service teacher to the classroom to deliver the lesson. They then returned to the university to reflect on their project.

Technical support is an important factor in technology integration. PwC (2001) proposes that technical support is a major factor that can affect the effectiveness of technology in reducing workload, and various research suggests that technical support is crucial to the smooth flow of a lesson (Wang and Coleman, 2009; Li, 2008, 2014). One way to forestall the need or reduce the likelihood of needing to call technical support is to involve students in the process of integrating technology. For example, Hruskocy et al. (2000) suggest that students acting as 'technology experts' in class might aid the integration of technology.

The sociocultural context

Sociocultural contexts play an important role (Mumtaz, 2000; Cuban et al., 2001). This includes the macro context, such as the curriculum, culture of learning, the testing system and so on, and the micro context, such as the expectations of colleagues and school leaders, school culture and norms. In some countries, exams play an important role in many aspects of people's lives; therefore, teachers and learners might face heavy pressure from examinations. Such pressure plays a central role in shaping whether and how teachers use technology. The 'washback effect' of tests can have a heavy influence on teaching methods and students' approaches to learning (e.g. Xiao et al., 2011). So technology integration depends on whether the examination system is altered to reflect the proposed innovation with technology. One of the clear aspects for teachers and policymakers to think about is the multiple assessments of learning and the need to move away from simply linguistic acquisition and towards developing students' interactional and intercultural awareness and competence.

The micro context, including schools as organisations and support from colleagues, can be influential, either positively (Li, 2008, 2014) or negatively (Lam, 2000). Lam (2000) pointed out in her study that the top-down implementation of technology might cause resentment and avoidance from teachers, but Li (2008, 2014) argues that in a society that highly values the expectations of others and recognises its leaders, support from school leaders and local education authorities is crucial. Recognition from the organisation and colleagues was vital for the teachers because they see it as validation of their behaviour. Wang and Coleman's (2009) study in a Chinese university context presents a similar view, where it was confirmed that a teacher-led top-down approach is more appropriate in a Chinese context than a more learner-oriented Western approach would be. Therefore, in designing technology integration, the sociocultural context needs to be taken into consideration.

Pedagogical beliefs

Another important factor influencing teachers' uptake of technology is pedagogical beliefs. Pedagogical beliefs are associated with what teachers

think, believe and do in instruction, all of which influence their acceptance and uptake of new approaches, techniques and activities (Donaghue,
2003). Cuban (2001) points out they play a crucial role in teachers' decision
making regarding when and how to use computers. Moreover, pedagogical
beliefs arguably play a more important role than external factors. Li (2014)
identified three issues about teachers' beliefs that are worth considering in
integrating technology. First, it is important to examine these beliefs in relation to the context in which they work. Rather than trying to impose ideas
of technology integration, teachers' own understandings about the usefulness
of technology in their daily teaching schedules need to be understood and
taken into consideration. Second, it is important to develop teachers' ability
to evaluate resources and think critically about the usefulness (or the role) of
technology in their own classrooms in order to facilitate their fully exploring
the potential of a given technology and to develop their own technology-
enhanced pedagogy. That is, teachers should be encouraged to ask, what do
I want to achieve by using technology and what is the best way to achieve
my pedagogical goals? Engaging teachers in critical reflection can be realised
through the use of video clips of their teaching because teachers can use
them to reflect on their beliefs with the use of video evidence. This type
of critical reflective approach to technology integration is vital. Third, it is
important to raise teachers' awareness of the multiple roles that they play in
technology-integrated classrooms so that they can shift their thinking from
an exam-oriented approach to a student-centred one.

Teachers' openness to change influences their willingness to integrate
technology into the classroom (Mumtaz, 2000; Baylor and Ritchie, 2002).
Resistance to change is the opposite of the concept of 'innovativeness', which
Hurt, Joseph and Cook (1977) define as a personality characteristic indicating
the degree of willingness to change. In terms of innovation, Marcinkiewicz
(1993–1994) suggests that self-competence and innovativeness are most
closely related to computer use. It is believed that teachers' dislike of change
is one of the main barriers for technology integration into classroom
practice. It is understandable because, on the one hand, teachers have to
acquire the fundamental skills to operate computers but more importantly,
on the other, because they have to modify the way they teach (Fabry and
Higgs, 1997). Findings from a quantitative investigation by Niederhauser
and Stoddard (1994) suggest that teachers who view the computer as a tool
(relating to a constructivist approach) are more innovative with technology
in the classroom than those who view it as a teaching machine (a behaviourist approach). More discussion about the role of technology will come later.

Teachers' 'personal beliefs about using technology will greatly influence
the use of a particular technology' (Sugar, 2002, p. 13), and their personal
beliefs in a teaching context are influenced by their teaching philosophy.

It is suggested that successfully integrating technology into teaching and learning depends on transforming teachers' beliefs and philosophy (Windschitl and Sahl, 2002). This requires teachers to make some changes, including in their roles in the classrooms. Levy (1997) suggests there must be a fit between teachers' philosophies of both teaching and learning language and what they see as the capabilities of technology to facilitate and motivate technology integration. Research shows that teachers who use computers in a classroom do so because they consider that the functions of technology facilitate effective teaching and learning or that they assimilate innovative practices by using technology according to their current beliefs (Higgins and Miller, 2000). Teachers adapt technology to fit current teaching patterns rather than making modifications to their instructional ways. Unless teachers are 'presented with evidence that shows positive effects of the new teaching method of quality of learning outcomes', they will not change their practice to use technology (McMeniman and Evans, 1998, p. 1).

Technology use is powerfully mediated by the interplay of institutional and individual values of what constitutes good teaching (Windschitl and Sahl, 2002). The conception of what effective teaching is and what learners need is heavily shaped by the macro and micro contexts they are in – for example, broad cultural effects on the value of teaching and learning, as well as school culture. On the one hand, some research has shown a strong connection between in-service teachers' beliefs and their use of technology in the classroom (e.g. Ottenbreit-Leftwicha et al., 2010; Li, 2008, 2014). Teacher belief and classroom practice exist in a 'symbiotic relationship': beliefs both shape and are shaped by ensuing practice (Li and Walsh, 2011a). Teachers who are more constructivism-oriented use technology more often and in various and powerful ways than those who are more instruction-oriented (Bai and Ertmer, 2004). On the other hand, experimenting with technological tools also has a strong influence. The adoption of technology can have an impact upon teachers' thinking about effective organisation and management of learning (Dwyer et al., 1991) and upon teaching strategies and assessment activities (Sandholtz et al., 1997).

Kern (2006) notes that the 'rapid evolution of communication technologies has changed language pedagogy and language use, enabling new forms of discourse, new forms of authorship, and new ways to create and participate in communities' (p. 183). If this is correct, then we have to investigate the broad ecological context that affects language learning and use in today's society as well as teachers' understanding about using TELL. First of all, the English language has become a language of international communication for many purposes, and it is the most internationally studied foreign language as well as the dominant language of education, commerce, communication, science, technology and entertainment; therefore, the nature of foreign language learning may have changed, where in now requires better communicative abilities rather than simply linguistic competence. Second, this is apparently a new way to think about learning (Rosenberg, 2001). Hadley and Sheingold (1993) propose that 'integrating the computer has turned a teacher-centred classroom into a student-centred one, with the teacher acting more as a coach than information dispenser, and with more collaboration and work in small groups going on' (p. 277). Foreign language learning may have changed, requiring better communicative abilities rather than linguistic knowledge. Therefore, some transformations must take place in EFL classrooms, including in the approach to teaching, the roles of teachers and students, the interactions between them and assessment. Third, Jones (2001) claims that computers are not 'free standing' or 'regarded as a self-access operation' (p. 361); as a result, the teacher's role remains undiminished.

The role of teachers in technology-enhanced language teaching

Teachers play an important role in pedagogical decision making and at every stage of learning. In a traditional classroom, a teacher plays the role of materials evaluator and selector, task designer and executor, learning outcome assessor and knowledge provider. However, in technology-enhanced teaching, teachers might perform different roles to ensure that technology is successfully and effectively used for pedagogical purposes. In an online learning environment, Berge (1995) and Liu et al. (2005) identified four different roles of a teacher (see Table 9.2).

Goodyear et al. (2001) proposed eight different roles for teachers based on a 48-hour workshop in the United Kingdom and the United States:

1. The process facilitator lays of a range of online activities that enhance student learning.

2. The adviser-counsellor works with learners and offers advice.

3. The assessor provides grades, feedback and validation of learners' work.

4. The researcher is concerned with student engagement in production of new knowledge of relevance to the content areas being taught.

5. The content facilitator is concerned with facilitating learners' growing understanding.

6. The technologist makes, or helps make, technological choices that improve the environment available to leaners.

Roles	Descriptions
Pedagogical role	Teachers play this role to facilitate educational processes for students' understanding of critical concepts, principles and skills.
Technical role	Teachers make students feel comfortable with the system and software programme used for online courses. Support includes referring students to technical support resources, addressing technical concerns, diagnosing and clarifying problems encountered and allowing students sufficient time to learn new programmes.
Social role	Teachers promote a friendly environment and community to support cognitive learning processes. Such social functions include developing harmony, group cohesiveness and collective identity. Teachers in this role need to encourage participation, give sufficient feedback and reward, attend to individual concerns and use a friendly, personal tone.
Managerial role	Teachers conduct organisational, procedural and administrative tasks associated with the learning environment. Tasks in this role include coordinating assignments, managing online discussion forums and handling overall course structure.

TABLE 9.2   THE ROLE OF TEACHERS

7. The designer creates online learning tasks.

8. The manager administrator is concerned with issues of learner registration, security, recordkeeping and so on.

Although these eight roles are slightly different from what Berge (1995) suggested, we can see that teachers play different roles in technology-enhanced learning environments, but they do share some similarities. Generally speaking, teachers need to play several key roles. First, teachers need to play a *technical role* (Alvarez et al., 2009), which requires confidence and competence in using technology, in order for them to offer technical advice to students and resolve technical problems when necessary. This is a really challenging role, as many teachers do not feel they have enough competence. For example, Kollias et al. (2005) conducted an online project (Technologies for Collaborative Learning Project) with teachers from four countries and found that teachers might be overwhelmed by the student need for technical advice even though they can usually face the challenge. Second, teachers need to be *pedagogy experts* in integrating technology in task design. They need to be clear about their pedagogical purposes, the benefits and affordances of technological tools and applications and how everyone can together realise the pedagogical purposes by utilising the affordances of technology. Technology should not be an add-on, or supplementary. Third, teachers need to be a *materials evaluator*, who can evaluate resources based on students' needs, learning styles, language-learning principles and technology affordances. Fourth, teachers need to be *facilitators* who provide students with opportunities to learn and develop, rather than only knowledge providers. This view is in line with the sociocultural perspective of learning where teachers play the role of an expert, scaffolding the novice (a learner). This role also involves providing students with guidance which teachers sometimes might find challenging if they are new to a technology-enhanced learning environment. In technology-enhanced learning mode, especially when they have to work online and conduct collaborative work (e.g. in a wiki environment), learners might need a lot of guidance (Kollias et al., 2005). This means that teachers not only need to be aware of various roles that they need to play but also need to negotiate these roles. Further, teachers inevitably take the role of *activity planners*. Designing a task or activity for technology-enhanced language learning requires teachers to be able to link student needs, learning preferences and styles, materials, technology affordances, teaching objectives, teachers' pedagogical beliefs and assessment. Task design is perhaps the most important element for successful technology-enhanced language learning. Closely related to the role of facilitator is the *manager* or *monitor* role that teachers have to take. Finally, sometimes, teachers need to perform a *social role* to maintain the cohesion of the learning community (Alverez et al., 2009; Onrubia and Engel, 2012). This role in traditional classrooms is rare, but it is important in online environments.

Task 9.4: Analyse characteristics of good language teachers

Now take an activity that you have designed before or that you borrowed. Evaluate it by talking about the various roles that a teacher might play at different stages of the activity. Make a note of characteristics that a competent teacher working within technology-enhanced pedagogy should have.

Are there particular characteristics that a teacher has that makes him/her competent and confident in working within a technology-enhanced pedagogical framework?

The various roles a teacher has to play make teacher education/development more complex. Clearly, teachers need to understand and develop competence in understanding and utilising multimodal materials and communication channels, including texts, audio and visual representations, synchronous and asynchronous communication channels, social networks and virtual worlds. Teachers need to develop knowledge about the differences between face-to-face and technology-enhanced learning environments. In talking about applying telecollaboration, Müeller-Hartmann (2012) discusses the essential and crucial role of the teacher: '(teachers) need to develop competences in the central areas of multiliteracy or multimodal competence … intercultural communicative competence and task-based language teaching … to effectively implement technology into their teaching' (p. 12).

The role of technology

As early as 1997, Levy (1997) conducted a comprehensive survey of experienced CALL practitioners to find out how they conceptualise and use the computer. One common view from 104 participants was that CALL should be 'based on learners' needs and the curriculum, rather than on the computer itself' (p. 124). The literature to date has overwhelmingly reported the supplementary role of the technological tools.

Lam (2000) interviewed ten L2 teachers to find out that technology-based language teaching was interpreted as a teaching activity, and technology played a supportive and supplementary role or acted as an aid/tool for the teacher. Cuban (2001) reported that teachers use technology to prepare teaching materials, and they make only small adjustments to their classroom practices rather than revolutionising their beliefs. Zhong and Shen (2002) reported the emergence of technologised language classrooms in China and argued that the appearance of technological tools in classrooms had not brought any changes to teaching. However, according to Kern and Warshaur, computers play multiple roles in language teaching, from 'a tutor that delivers language drills and skill practice' and 'a space in which to explore and creatively influence Microworlds' to 'a medium of local and global communication and a source of authentic materials' (2000, p. 13). To interpret these multiple roles in teaching, Li (2015) observed some classrooms and summarised the functions and roles that technology can assume. It can act

- as a tool to create a context where language is used for real-life purposes or more interaction;

- as a mediational tool to better understand a linguistic term or a concept;

- as an authentic resource;

- as a workspace for students to conduct learning or a platform that holds learning materials;

- as a tutor that provides feedback and gives instruction;

- as an effective tool to motivate and engage students;

- as an organisational tool.

One of the important things in realising the multiple roles of technology in teaching relates to whether and to what extent the technology is integrated into teaching.

Technology integration framework

TPACK is developed based on Shulman's (1987) Pedagogical Content Knowledge framework (PCK). Shulman proposed that expertise in teaching is based on the development of three knowledge bases: subject matter knowledge, pedagogical content knowledge and general pedagogical knowledge, and he emphasised the 'intersection of content and pedagogy'.

Mishra and Koehler (2006) have proposed a framework to incorporate new technologies into teaching. The framework, which includes teachers' integrated **technological, pedagogical and content knowledge,** is named **TPACK** (for short). In this framework, the teacher needs to be a pedagogical and content expert, and technological expertise is a complementary addition to teachers' knowledge domains. This framework is useful for both pre-service and in-service professional development, but in terms of integrating technology, we need to encapsulate the different notions described above and in the literature. The technology integration framework outlined here takes the approach of considering the factors that influence teachers' decision making in the uptake of technology as well as how these factors interact with each other and affect technology-enhanced pedagogy (Figure 9.2).

Influential factors can be looked at from *context, teacher, resources* and *professional development* levels. These are the four interlocking factors that affect the teachers' use of technology. The direction of the arrows is explained as 'leading to'. For example, as illustrated, school factors interlock with the teacher and resources: a school can provide the teachers with a more open, innovative teaching context, and it can also support teachers by providing more resources. Teachers, as active members of schools, are affected by the organisational cultures and also shaped by the development of the organisation; meanwhile, professional development efforts must address teachers' beliefs in order to effect change in their teaching practices, which result in affecting the development, growth and change of the culture of the organisation. In practice, teachers must be presented with practical models

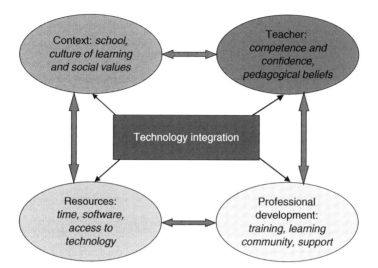

FIGURE 9.2 INTERLOCKING FACTORS CONTRIBUTING
TO TECHNOLOGY INTEGRATION LEVELS

and demonstrations for their professional development. Professional development, however, in the successful technology integration circle, cannot be treated solely as a channel whereby teachers collect and update teaching ideas. It should be viewed more as a learning community where teachers are supported in their work in planning, learning, solving problems and sharing. Professional development should also not be viewed as the duty of the local education authorities, but more of the schools as a community and of the teachers themselves. The interfaces of the four factors are complex and intertwined, but without any one of them, effective technology integration is impossible.

Several studies suggest that school support is one of the strongest motivators of technology use in teaching: schools therefore must have positive attitudes and policies regarding integrating technology into teaching across subject areas. If the schools are slow in embracing technology and have misconceptions about why they should make changes and what changes constitute, the school as an organisation would therefore appear to hold a resistant attitude. Also, schools with active and less active attitudes towards integrating technology will take different approaches in school practice. For example, a school that actively integrates technology can provide teachers with more support and put more effort into facilitating implementation than those schools that are less active. The support includes providing teachers with more and different levels of training (including technical and fundamental pedagogical considerations) and sufficient on-site technical support, allowing time to learn skills and techniques.

As teachers, we need to leave our 'comfort zone' and shift our values from knowledge transmission to skills development, from teachers to learners; otherwise, the desired implementation and integration of technology will never occur. Teachers need to believe that integrating technology into teaching may be a way to change teaching and learning in which teacher-oriented instruction will be finally replaced by a learner-centred one, and one in which class participation, collaboration, as well as student-initiated projects are encouraged. A teacher must experience the different stages of technology use before they can reach the stage of 'integration'. Cuban (2001) outlines levels of technology integration (pp. 53–54) based on the work of Sandholtz et al. (1997) as shown below in Table 9.3.

As argued earlier, teachers need to shift their beliefs and values, and at the same time, more professional development opportunities should be provided to make the shift to capable technology users, before expecting teachers to consider integration. Technology-related professional development, however, must not be restricted to pure technology but must instead focus on pedagogical considerations in the context where teachers teach. Teachers learn better from the related 'cases' through which they can see themselves, applied to what they have learnt in their classrooms. Therefore, based on what has been discussed above, successful teachers who integrate technology effectively into teaching should demonstrate the following characteristics:

- Student-centred beliefs about teaching and learning. Teaching and learning should be based on learners' needs and evolve with learners. Teaching should focus more on improving learners' communicative competence

Levels of technology integration	
Entry	Teachers are beginner users of computers.
Adoption	Teachers tend to take more traditional approaches to instruction but do provide some explanation on how to use computers.
Adaptation	Traditional approaches to instruction prevail, but some class time is allowed for students to use computers for homework and daily class work.
Appropriation	Teachers regularly integrate technology into the curriculum.
Invention	Teachers find new ways to connect students and use project-based and interdisciplinary approaches to instruction.

TABLE 9.3   LEVELS OF TECHNOLOGY INTEGRATION (CUBAN, 2001, PP. 53–54)
(Reproduced with kind permission from Larry Cuban (2001), *Oversold and Underused: Computers in the Classroom*. Cambridge, MA: Harvard University Press)

rather than purely improving linguistic competence. Teachers must be aware of their multiple roles in teaching and learning and learners should be encouraged to make contributions in class. Teachers must be aware that providing scaffolding is more important than lecturing.

- High technology integration competence and confidence. Teachers must be able to use and confident in their use of technology. Although they do not necessarily need to be able to develop courseware or write programmes, they must be engaged in active learning to update their technology integration skills, knowledge and related pedagogical ideas. In this way, teachers' confidence will be improved.

- Beliefs that trust in the effectiveness of TELL. Teachers need to understand and explore what technology can do to ensure and improve on successful language learning and teaching rather than focus on defining TELL effectiveness as improving student examination achievement. Teachers should be aware of how to use technology as a tool to improve input (linguistic/non-linguistic) for learners to exploit, to provide an individualised learning process and feedback, to enhance collaborative learning and to transform traditional teaching into contextualised teaching.

Summary

Bax (2003b) described CALL as 'normalised' when computers become 'an integral part of every lesson, like a pen or a book' (p. 23). Apart from appropriate hardware, software, easy access to technology, technology training for teachers and top-down policies, reaching normalisation needs help from some essential factors:

- access to resources and technological tools/applications;

- teacher training regarding CALL implementation/pedagogy and follow-up technical and pedagogical support;

- high technology competence and confidence for both teachers and learners;

- an appropriate teaching methodology where technology is integrated into the syllabus: teachers and students need to realise that technology is an integral part of learning rather than 'add-on' when there is time;

- an environment and culture where teachers feel comfortable to experiment with different ideas and which fosters essentials such as encouragement and a community where teachers can share their experience and learn together.

Student project

Brown, J. (2014) Teachers' perceptions and uses of online games and virtual worlds for English language learning. Unpublished M.Ed. dissertation, University of Exeter.

This dissertation examined teachers' perceptions and used of two areas of technological application for English language learning; online games (OGs) and virtual worlds (VWs). The perceived benefits of technology in education are highlighted in the literature, and its use has become a global trend that may help resolve a crisis regarding which direction to take in learning and teaching. While teachers are best placed to evaluate classroom technology, uptake has been disappointing despite massive government investment. The study sought to understand this situation and to suggest tentative solutions.

Brown researched teachers in a master's degree programme at a UK university. The research study was conducted in three steps: first, a group of students participated in an interview, which helped the researcher design a questionnaire. Then participants were asked to complete an online questionnaire regarding VWs and OGs. The final step involved a subset of volunteers exposed to VWs and OGs, followed up by a focus group interview.

The findings revealed that while IT was an important part of their lives, their uses of OGs and VWs was very limited. Despite holding positive theoretical perceptions, many indicated that they were unlikely to use OGs/VWs in class. They did not provide a clear rationale for these decisions, which was reflected in a lack of clear factors to encourage use. These findings reflect the dilemmas about the role of the teacher in a technological classroom. Research efforts need to be refocused to better understand teachers' beliefs as well as the language-learning potential in these environments. The issues raised are symptomatic of the wider debate about how the empowerment of technology should be represented in the learning objectives of future technology-driven generations.

Annotated further reading

1. Li, L. (2014) Understanding language teachers' practice with educational technology: a case from China. *System*, 46, 105–119.

   This article explores how eight secondary school teachers integrated educational technology into English language teaching in China and considers their views on the factors that influence technology use. Analysing data from classroom recordings and follow-up interviews revealed that teachers employed educational technology for different pedagogical purposes, including addressing professional needs in improving teaching, designing materials and conducting professional development. Teachers also claimed that they used technology to address learners' needs, such as improving engagement, enhancing language acquisition, facilitating understanding and establishing a context for language use. The study identified four important factors in influencing teachers' use of technology, including sociocultural contexts, teachers' beliefs, access to resources and technology competence and confidence. This study suggests that a critical reflective approach is useful for assisting teachers to understand their needs and pedagogical beliefs concerning technology use. Ongoing professional development is also valuable in promoting teachers' technology competence and confidence, thereby improving the use of technology in their teaching.

2. Li, L. (2011) Three important issues in using CALL. *21st Century English Teachers*. Available at http://elt.i21st.cn/article/9610_1.html

This article was written in an online newspaper for Chinese English language teachers (in English). It outlines three key important issues that teachers need to consider when integrating technology into their teaching: understanding affordances of technology, material evaluation and factors affecting technology uptake.

References

Abrams, Z. I. (2003) The effect of synchronous and asynchronous CMC on oral performance in German. *Modern Language Journal*, 87(2), 157–167.

AbuSeileek, A. F. & Rabab'ah, G. A. (2007) The effect of computer-based grammar instruction on the acquisition of verb tenses in an EFL context. *The JALT CALL Journal*, 3(1–2), 59–80.

AbuSeileek, A. & Abualsha'r, A. (2014) Using peer computer-mediated corrective feedback to support EFL learners' writing. *Language Learning & Technology*, 18(1), 76–95.

Ahmed, M. K. (1994) Speaking as cognitive regulation: a Vygotskyan perspective on dialogic communication, in J. P. Lantolf (ed.), *Vygotskyan Approach to Second Language Research* (pp. 157–172). Norwood, NJ: Ablex.

Akyel, A. & Erçetin, G. (2009) Hypermedia reading strategies employed by advanced learners of English. *System*, 37(1), 136–152.

Alastuey, M. C. B. (2010) Synchronous-voice computer-mediated communication: effects on pronunciation. *CALICO Journal*, 28(1), 1–20.

Aljaafreh, A. & Lantolf, J. P. (1994) Negative feedback as regulation and second language learning in the Zone of Proximal Development. *The Modern Language Journal*, 78(4), 465–483.

Alvarez, I. Guasch, T. and. & Espasa, A. (2009) University teacher roles and competencies in online learning environments: a theoretical analysis of teaching and learning practices. *European Journal of Teacher Education*, 32: (3), 321–336.

Alyousef, H. & Picard, M. (2011) Cooperative or collaborative literacy practices: mapping metadiscourse in a business students' wiki group project. *Australasian Journal of Educational Technology*, 27(3), 463–480.

Angouri, J. & Harwood, N. (2008) This is too formal for us…: a case study of variation in the written products of a multinational consortium. *Journal of Business and Technical Communication*, 22(1), 38–64.

Anthony, L. (2011) AntConc (Windows, Macintosh OSX, and Linux). Center for English Language Education in Science and Engineering, School of Science and Engineering.

Armstrong, K. & Retterer, O. (2008) Blogging as L2 writing: a case study. *AACE Journal*, 16(3), 233–251.

Armstrong, K. M. & Yetter-Vassot, C. (1994) Transforming teaching through technology. *Foreign Language Annuals*, 27(4), 475–486.

Arndt, V. (1993) Response to writing: using feedback to inform the writing process, in M. N. Brock and L. Walters (eds), *Teaching Composition Around the Pacific Rim: Politics and Pedagogy* (pp. 90–116). Clevedon: Multilingual Matters.

Arnó, E., Soler, A. & Rueda, C. (2006) The role of information technology in languages for specific purposes: some central issues, in E. Arnó, A. Soler and C. Rueda (eds), *Information Technology in Languages for Specific Purposes: Issues and Prospects* (pp. 3–18). New York: Springer.

Arnó-Macià, E. (2012) The role of technology in teaching languages for specific purposes courses. *Modern Language Journal*, 96(Focus Issue), 89–104.

Arnold, N., Ducate, L. & Kost, C. (2009) Collaborative writing in wikis: insights from culture projects in intermediate German classes, in L. Lomicka and G. Lord (eds), *The Next Generation: Social Networking and Online Collaboration in Language Learning* (pp. 115–144). San Marcos, TX: CALICO.

Aydin, Z. & Yildiz, S. (2014) Using wikis to promote collaborative EFL writing. *Language Learning & Technology*, 18(1), 160–180. Retrieved from http://llt.msu.edu/issues/february2014/aydinyildiz.pdf

Badger, R. & White, G. (2000) A process genre approach to teaching writing. *ELT Journal*, 54(2), 153–160.

Baek, Y., Jung, J. & Kim, B. (2008) What makes teachers use technology in the classroom? Exploring the factors affecting facilitation of technology with a Korean sample. *Computers and Education*, 50(1), 224–234.

Bai, H. & Ertmer, P. (2004) Teacher educators' beliefs and technology uses in relation to preservice teachers' beliefs and technology attitudes. Paper presented at the annual convention of the Association for Educational Communications and Technology, Chicago, IL. Available at http://www.aect.org/pdf/proccedings/2006/06_1.pdf (last accessed 7 March 2016).

Bangert-Drowns, R. L., Kulik, C. C., Kulik, J. A. & Morgan, M. T. (1991) The instructional effect of feedback in test-like events. *Review of Educational Research*, 61(2), 213–238.

Baralt, M., Pennestri, S. & Selvandin M. (2011) Using wordles to teach foreign language writing. *Language Learning & Technology*, 15(2), 12–22. Retrieved from http://llt.msu.edu/issues/june2011/actionresearch.pdf

Barcroft, J., Sunderman, G. & Schmitt, N. (2011) Lexis, in J. Simpson (ed.), *The Routledge Handbook of Applied Linguistics* (pp. 571–583). London: Routledge.

Barrett, H. (2004) Electronic portfolios, in A. Kovalchick and K. Dawson (eds), *Education and Technology: An Encyclopedia* (pp. 271–276). Santa Barbara, CA: ABC-CLIO.

Barrett, H. (2011) Balancing the two faces of e-portfolios, in S. Hirtz and K. Kelly (eds), *Education for a Digital World 2.0 Innovations in Education* (Volume 2) (pp. 291–310). British Columbia, Canada: Open School.

Bax, S. (2003a) The end of CLT: a context approach to language teaching. *ELT Journal*, 57(3), 278–287.

Bax, S. (2003b) CALL—Past, present and future. *System*, 31(1), 13–28.

Baylor, A. L. & Ritchie D. (2002) What factors facilitate teacher skill, teacher morale, and perceived student learning in technology-using classrooms? *Computers and Education*, 39(4), 395–414.

Beatty, K. (2003) *Teaching and Researching Computer-assisted Language Learning*. London: Pearson Education.

Beauvois, M. (1994) E-talk: attitudes and motivation in computer-assisted classroom discussion. *Computers and the Humanities*, 28(1), 177–190.

Beauvois, M. (1998) Conversations in slow motion: computer-mediated communication in the foreign language classroom. *The Canadian Modern Language Review*, 54(2), 198–217.

Beauvois, M. H. & Eledge, J. (1996) Personality types and megabytes: student attitudes towards computer mediated communication (CMC) in the language classroom. *CALICO Journal*, 13(2–3), 27–45.

Becker, H. J. (2000) Findings from the teaching, learning and computing survey: Is Larry Cuban right? *Education Policy Analysis Archives*, 8(51). Available at http://epaa.asu.edu/ojs/article/view/442 (last accessed 5 October 2016).

Becker, H. & Ravitz, J. (1999) The influence of computer and Internet use on teachers' pedagogical practices and perceptions. *Journal of Research on Computing in Education*, 31, 356–384.

Belcher, D. (2004) Trends in teaching English for specific purposes. *Annual Review of Applied Linguistics*, 24, 165–186.

Belcher, D. (2009) *English for Specific Purposes in Theory and Practice*. Michigan: University of Michigan Press.

Bell, L. (2001) Preparing tomorrow's teachers to use technology: perspectives of the leaders of twelve national education associations. *Contemporary Issues in Technology and Teacher Education* [Online Serial], 1(4). www.citejournal.org/vol1/iss4/currentissues/general/article1.htm (last accessed 5 March 2016).

Belz, J. A. & Kinginger, C. (2003) Discourse options and the development of pragmatic competence by classroom learners of German: the case of address forms. *Language Learning*, 53(4), 591–647.

Belz, J. A. & Thorne, S. L. (eds) (2006) *Internet-mediated Intercultural Foreign Language Education and the Intercultural Speaker*. Boston, MA: Heinle & Heinle.

Berge, Z. L. (1995) Facilitating computer conferencing: recommendations from the field. *Educational Technology*, 35, 22–30.

Biber, D., Johansson, S., Leech, G., Conrad S. & Finegan E. (1999) *Longman Grammar of Spoken and Written English*. Harlow, UK: Pearson Education.

Bickart, T. S., & Dodge, D. T. (2000) *Reading Right from the Start: What Parents Can Do in the First Five Years*. Washington, DC: Teaching Strategies.

Bikowski, D. & Kessler, G. (2002) Making the most of discussion boards in the ESL classroom. *TESOL Journal*, 11(3), 27–30.

Bird, S. A. & Williams, J. N. (2002) The effect of bimodal input on implicit and explicit Emory: an investigation into the benefits of within-language subtitling. *Applied Psycholinguistics*, 23(4), 509–533.

Bitner, N. & Bitner, J. (2002) Integrating technology into the classroom: eight keys to success. *Journal of Technology and Teacher Education*, 10(1), 95–100.

Blake, R. (2000) Computer mediated communication: a window on L2 Spanish interlanguage. *Language Learning and Technology*, 40(1), 120–136.

Blake, R. J. (2008) *Brave New Digital Classroom: Technology and Foreign Language Learning*. Washington, DC: Georgetown University Press.

Blake, R. J. (2013) *Brave New Digital Classrooms: Technology and Foreign-Language learning* (2nd edition). Washington, DC: Georgetown University Press.

Blankenship, M. (2011) How social media can and should impact higher education. *The Education Digest*, 76(7), 39–42.

Bloch, J. (2007) Abdullah's blogging: a generation 1.5 student enters the blogosphere. *Language Learning & Technology*, 112, 128–141.

Bloch, J. (2009) The design of an online concordancing program for teaching about reporting verbs. *Language Learning & Technology*, 13(1), 59–78.

Block, D. (2003) *The Social Turn in Second Language Acquisition*. Washington, DC: Georgetown University Press.

Boers, F., Eyckmans, J., Kappel, J., Stengers, H. & Demecheleer, M. (2006) Formulaic sequences and perceived oral proficiency: putting a Lexical Approach to the test. *Language Teaching Research*, 10(3), 245–261.

Bonnett, M. (1997) Computers in the classroom: some value issues, in A. McFarlane (ed.), *Information Technology and Authentic Learning* (pp. 145–159). London: Routledge.

Borja, R. R. (2005) Podcasting craze comes to K-12 schools. *Education Week*, 25(14), 8.

Bradin, C. (1999) CALL issues: instructional aspects of software evaluation, in J. Egbert and E. Hanson-Smith (eds), *CALL Environments: Research, Practice, and Critical Issues* (pp. 159–175). Alexandria, VA: Teachers of English to Speakers of Other Languages.

Bradley, L., Linstrom, B. & Rystedt, H. (2010) Rationalities of collaboration for language learning on a wiki. *ReCALL*, 22(2), 247–265.

Braine, G. (2004) Teaching second and foreign language writing on LANs, in S. Fotos and C. Browne (eds), *New Perspectives on CALL for Second Language Classrooms* (pp. 93–107). Mahwah, NJ: Lawrence Erlbaum Associates.

Breen, M. P. (1987) Contemporary paradigms in syllabus design, Part II. *Language Teaching*, 20(3), 157–174.

Brinton, D. M. (2001) The use of media in language teaching, in M. Celce-Murcia (ed.), *Teaching English as a Second or Foreign Language*, (pp. 459–475). Boston, MA: Heinle and Heinle.

British Educational Communications and Technology Agency (Becta) (2002) *Becta's Research Strategy 2002–2003*. Coventry: Becta.

British Educational Communications and Technology Agency (Becta) (2004) A Review of the Research Literature on Barriers to the Uptake of ICT by Teachers. Coventry: Becta. Available at www.becta.org.uk (last accessed 20 February 2006).

Brown, H. D. (2000) *Teaching by Principles* (2nd edition). Boston, MA: Heinle and Heinle Publishers.

Brown, H. D. (2007) *Principles of Language Learning and Teaching* (5th edition). New York: Pearson Education.

Brown, J. (2014) Teachers' perceptions and uses of online gaming and virtual worlds for English language learning. Unpublished MEd dissertation, University of Exeter.

Brown, S. & Adler, R. P. (2008) Minds on fire. Open education, the long trail, and learning 2.0. *Educause Review*, 43(1), 16–32. Retrieved from http://net.educause. edu/ir/library/pdf/ERM0811.pdf

Burniske, R. W. (2008) *Literacy in the Digital Age* (2nd edition). Thousand Oaks, CA: Corwin.

Burns, A., Gollin, S. & Joyce, H. (1997) Authentic spoken texts in the language classroom. *Prospect*, 12, 72–86.

Burston, J. (1996) CALL at the crossroads: myths, realities, promises and challenges. *Australian Review of Applied Linguistics*, 19(2), 27–36.

Bushweller, K. (2000) The smarter office: how school districts are automating administrative tasks. *American School Board Journal*, 187(3), 26–28.

Butler-Pascoe, M. E. (2009) English for specific purposes (ESP), innovation, and technology. *English Education and ESP*, 1–15.

Bygate, M. (1996) Effects of task repetition: appraising the developing language of learners, in J. Willis and D. Willis (eds), *Challenge and Change in Language Teaching* (pp. 136–146). Oxford: Heinemann.

Bygate, M. (2001) Speaking, in R. Carter and D. Nunan (eds), *The Cambridge Guide to Teaching English to Speakers of Other Languages* (pp. 14–20). Cambridge: Cambridge University Press.

Bygate, M. (2005) Oral second language abilities as expertise, in K. Johnson (ed.), *Expertise in Second Language Learning and Teaching* (pp. 104–127). Basingstoke: Palgrave Macmillan.

Bygate, M. & Samuda, V. (2005) Integrating planning through the use of task-repetition, in R. Ellis (ed.), *Planning and Task Performance in a Second Language* (pp. 37–74). Amsterdam: John Benjamins Publishing Company.

Byrne, D. (1986) *Teaching Oral English*. London: Longman.

Cabanatan, P. (2003) Integrating pedagogy and technology: the SEAMEO INNOTECH experience. Presentation to Experts Meeting on Teachers/Facilitators Training in Technology-Pedagogy Integration. Bangkok, Thailand. 18–20 June.

Campbell, G. (2005) There's something in the air: podcasting in education. *Educause Review*, 40(6), 32–47.

Can, G. & Cagiltay, K. (2006) Turkish prospective teachers' perceptions regarding the use of computer games with educational features. *Educational Technology & Society*, 9(1), 308–321.

Canale, M. & Swain, M. (1980) Theoretical bases of communicative approaches to second language teaching and testing. *Applied Linguistics*, 1(1), 1–47.

Carman, L. (2003) Pedagogy, connectivity, multimodality and interdisciplinarity. *Research Quarterly*, 38, 397–403.

Carr, N. (2010) *The Shallows: What the Internet is Doing to Our Brains*. New York: Norton.

Carter, D. (1983) Some propositions about ESP. *The ESP Journal*, 2, 131–137.

Carter, R. A. & McCarthy, M. J. (2006) *The Cambridge Grammar of English*. Cambridge: Cambridge University Press.

Casal, J. E. (2016) Criterion online writing evaluation. *Computer-Assisted Language Instruction Consortium*, 33(1), 146–155.

Chambers, A. (2007) Popularising corpus consultation by language learners and teachers, in E. H. Tenorio, L. Querada-Navarro and J. Santana (eds), *Corpora in the Foreign Language Classroom: Selected Papers from the Sixth International Conference on Teaching and Learning Corpora* (pp. 3–16). Amsterdam: Rodopi.

Chapelle, C. A. (1989) Using intelligent computer-assisted language learning. *Computers and the Humanities*, 23(1), 59–70.

Chapelle, C. A. (1998) Multimedia CALL: lessons to be learned from research on instructed SLA. *Language Learning and Technology*, 2, 22–34.

Chapelle, C. (2001) *Computer Applications in Second Language Acquisition: Foundations for Teaching, Testing, and Research*. Cambridge: Cambridge University Press.

Chapelle, C. A. (2003) *English Language Learning and Technology: Lectures on Applied Linguistics in the Age of Information and Communication Technology*. Amsterdam: John Benjamins Publishing Company.

Chapelle, C. A. (2007) Challenges in evaluation of innovation: observations from technology research. *Innovation in Language Learning and Teaching*, 1(1), 30–45.

Chapelle, C. A. & Hegelheimer, V. (2004) The language teacher in the 21st century, in S. Fotos and C. M. Browne (eds), *New Perspectives on CALL for Second Language Classrooms* (pp. 299–316). Mahwah, NJ: Lawrence Erlbaum.

Chapelle, C. A. & Jamieson, J. (2003) Three Challenges in English Language Assessment. Available at http://www.longmanusahome.com/images/stories/monographs/challenges_in_assessment.pdf

Chapelle, C. & Jamieson, J. (2008) *Tips for Teaching with CALL: Practical Approaches to Computer-Assisted Language Learning*. White Plains, NY: Pearson Education.

Chen, C.-M. & Chung, C.-J. (2008) Personalized mobile English vocabulary learning system based on item response theory and learning memory cycle. *Computers & Education*, 51(2), 624–645.

Chenoweth, N. A. & Murday, K. (2003) Measuring student learning in an online French course. *CALICO Journal*, 20(2), 285–314.

Chenoweth, N. A., Ushida, E. & Murday, K. (2006) Student learning in hybrid French and Spanish courses: an overview of Language Online. *CALICO Journal*, 24(1), 285–314.

Cheung, W. S. & Hew, K. F. (2009) A review of research methodologies used in studies on mobile handheld devices in K-12 and higher education settings. *Australasian Journal of Educational Technology*, 25(2), 153–183.

Chomsky, N. (1957) *Syntactic Structures*. The Hague/Paris: Mouton.

Chomsky, N. (1986) *Knowledge of Language: Its Nature, Origin, and Use*. New York: Praeger.

Christie, F. & Martin, J. R. (eds) (1997) *Genre in Institutions: Social Processes in the Workplace and School*. New York: Continuum.

Chun, D. M. (1994) Using computer networking to facilitate the acquisition of interactive competence. *System*, 22(1), 17–31.

Coe, R. M. (2002) The new rhetoric of genre: writing political briefs, in A. M. Johns (ed.), *Genre in the Classroom* (pp. 195–205). Mahwah, NJ: Erlbaum.

Coiro, J., Knnobel, M., Lankshear, C. & Leu, D. J. (eds) (2008) *Handbook of Research on New Literacies*. Mahwah, NJ: Lawrence Erlbaum.

Collis, B., & Moonen, J. (2002) Flexible learning in a digital world. *Open Learning*, 17(3), 217–230.

Comas-Quinn, A., Mardomingo, R. and Valentine, C. (2009) Mobile blogs in language learning: Making the most of information and situated learning opportunities. *ReCALL*, 21(1), 96–112.

Coniam, D. (2004) Using language engineering programs to raise awareness of future CALL potential. *Computer Assisted Language Learning*, 17, 149–175.

Coniam, D. & Wong, R. (2004) Internet relay chat as a tool in the autonomous development of ESL learners' English language ability: an exploratory study. *System*, 32(3), 321–335.

Conklin, K. & Schmitt, N. (2008) Formulaic sequences: are they processed more quickly than nonformulaic language by native and nonnative speakers? *Applied Linguistics*, 29(1), 72–89.

Constantine, P. (2007) Podcasts: another source for listening input. *The Internet TESL Journal*. Available at http://iteslj.org/Techniques/Constantine-PodcastListening.html (last accessed 22 February 2016).

Cook, V. (2001) *Second Language Learning and Language Teaching* (3rd edition). Oxford: Oxford University Press.

Cooper, M. M. & Selfe, C. L. (1990) Computer conferencing and learning: authority, resistance and internally persuasive discourse. *College English*, 52(8), 847–869.

Corl, M., Johnson, P., Rowell, M. & Fishman, E. (2008) Internet-based dissemination of educational video presentations: a primer in video podcasting. *American Journal of Roentgenology*, 191, 23–27.

Cox, M., Rhodes, V. and Hall, J. (1988) The use of computer assisted learning in primary schools: some factors affecting the uptake. *Computers and Education*, 12(1), 173–178.

Crook, C. (1994) *Computers and the Collaborative Experience of Learning*. London, New York: Routledge.

Crookall, D., Coleman, D. W. & Versluis, E. B. (1990) Computerized language learning simulations: form and content, in D. Crookall and R. L. Oxford (eds), *Simulation, Gaming, and Language Learning* (pp. 165–182). New York: Newbury House.

Csikszentmihalyi, M. (1990) *Flow: The Psychology of Optimal Experience*. New York: Harper, Perennial.

Cuban, L. (2001) *Oversold and Underused: Computers in the Classroom*. Cambridge, MA: Harvard University Press.

Cuban, L., Kirkpatrick, H. & Peck, C. (2001) High access and low use of technologies in high school classrooms: explaining an apparent paradox. *American Educational Research Journal*, 38(4), 813–834.

Cunningsworth, A. (1995) *Choosing Your Coursebook*. Oxford: Heinemann.

Danan, M. (2004) Captioning and subtitling: undervalued language learning strategies. *Meta*, 49(1), 67–77.

Davies, G. D. (1989) CALL and NCCALL in the United Kingdom: past, present, and future, in W. F. Smith (ed) *Modern Technology in Foreign Language Education: Applications and Projects* (pp. 161–180). Lincolnwood: National Textbook Co.

Davis, F. D., Bagozzi, R. P. & Warshaw, P. R. (1989) User acceptance of computer technology: a comparison of two theoretical models. *Management Science*, 35, 982–1003.

Davis, J. N. & Lyman-Hager, M. (1997) Computers and L2 reading: student performance, student attitudes. *Foreign Language Annals*, 30(1), 58–72.

Dawns, S. (2004) Educational blogging. *Educause Review*, 39(5), 14–26.

de Guerrero, M. C. M. & Villamil, O. S. (1994) Social-cognitive dimensions of interaction in L2 peer revision. *The Modern Language Journal*, 78(4), 484–496.

de Guerrero, M. C. M. & Villamil, O. S. (2000) Activating the ZPD: mutual scaffolding in L2 peer revision. *The Modern Language Journal*, 84, 51–68.

DeKeyser, R. M. (1998). Beyond focus on form: Cognitive perspectives on learning and practicing second language grammar, in C. Doughty & J. Williams (eds.) Focus on form in classroom second language acquisition (pp. 42–63). New York: Cambridge University Press.

DeKeyser, R. (2000) The robustness of critical period effects in second language acquisition. *Studies in Second Language Acquisition*, 22(4), 499–533.

Delcloque, P. (2000) History of CALL. www.history-of-call.org/ (last accessed 3 March 2015).

DeliCarpini, M. (2012) Building computer technology skills in TESOL teacher education. *Language Learning & Technology*, 16(2), 14–23.

Derwing, T., Rossiter, M., Munro, M. & Thomson, R. (2004) Second language fluency: judgments on different tasks. *Language Learning*, 54(4), 655–679.

Dickinson, M., Eom, S., Kang, Y., Lee, C. H. & Sachs, R. (2008) A balancing act: how can intelligent computer-generated feedback be provided in learner-to-learner interactions? *Computer Assisted Language Learning*, 21(4), 369–382.

Diniz, L. (2005) Comparative Review: Textstat 2.5, AntConc 3.0, and Compleat Lexical Tutor 4.0. *Language Learning & Technology*, 9(3), 22–27.

Dippold, D. (2009) Peer feedback through blogs: student and teacher perceptions in an advanced German class. *ReCALL*, 21, 18–36. doi:10.1017/S095834400900010X

Doherty, K. M. & Orlofsky, G. F. (2001) Student survey says: schools are probably not using educational technology as wisely or effectively as they could. *Educational Week*, 20(35), 45–48.

Donaghue, H. (2003) An instrument to elicit teachers' beliefs and assumptions. *ELT Journal*, 57(4), 344–351.

Donato, R. (1994) Collective scaffolding in second language learning, in J. P. Lantolf and G. Appel (eds), *Vygotskian Approaches to Second Language Research* (pp. 33–56). Norwood, NJ: Ablex Publishing Corporation.

Dooly, M. & O'Dowd, R. (eds) (2012) *Researching Online Foreign Language Interaction and Exchange*. New York: Peter Lang.

Dörnyei, Z. (2001) New themes and approaches in L2 motivation research. *Annual Review of Applied Linguistics*, 21, 43–59.

Dörnyei, Z. (2005) *The Psychology of the Language Learner: Individual Differences in Second Language Acquisition*. Mahwah, NJ: Lawrence Erlbaum.

Dörnyei, Z. (2009) *The Psychology of Second Language Acquisition*. Oxford: Oxford University Press.

Dörnyei, Z. & Ushioda, E. (2011) *Teaching and Researching Motivation* (2nd edition). Harlow: Longman.

Doughty, C. (1987) Relating second-language acquisition theory to CALL research and application', in W. F. Smith (ed.), *Modern Media in Foreign Language Education: Theory and Implementation* (pp. 133–167). Lincolnwood, IL: National Textbook Company.

Doughty, C. (2001) Cognitive underpinnings of focus on form, in P. Robinson (ed) *Cognition and Second Language Instruction* (pp. 206–257). Cambridge: Cambridge University Press.

Doughty, C. & Pica, T. (1986) Information gap tasks: do they facilitate second language acquisition? *TESOL Quarterly*, 20(2), 305–325.

Droop, M. & Verhoeven, L. (2003) Language proficiency and reading ability in first and second language learners. *Reading Research Quarterly*, 38, 78–103.

Dudeney, G., Hockly N. & Pegrum M. (2013) *Digital Literacies*. Harlow, UK: Pearson Education.

Dudley-Evans, T. & St. John, M. J. (1998) *Developments in English for Specific Purposes: A Multi-disciplinary Approach*. Cambridge: Cambridge University Press.

Duffy, T. M. & Cunningham, D. J. (1996) Constructivism: implications for the design and delivery of instruction, in D. H. Jonassen (ed.), *Handbook for Research for Educational Communications and Technology* (pp. 170–198). New York: Simon & Schuster Macmillan.

Dulay, H. & Burt, M. (1977) Remarks on creativity in language acquisition, in M. Burt, H. Dulay and M. Finocchiaro (eds), *Viewpoints on English as a Second Language*. New York: Regents.

Dunkel, P. (1991) Listening in the native and second/foreign language: toward an integration of research and practice. *TESOL Quarterly*, 25(3), 431–457.

Dwyer, D., Ringstaff, C. & Sandholtz, J. (1991) Changes in teachers' beliefs and practices in technology-rich classrooms. *Educational Leadership*, 48(8), 45–52.

Eftekhari, S. (2013) Student's experience with technology-supported error correction for speaking in promoting accuracy and fluency in preparing in the IELTS, Unpublished M.Ed. dissertation, University of Exeter.

Egbert, J. (2001) Choosing software for the English language classroom. *ESL Magazine*, January–February, 22.

Egbert, J. L. (2005) Conducting Research on CALL, in J. Egbert and G. Petrie (eds), *CALL Research Perspectives* (pp. 3–8). Mahwah, NJ: Lawrence Erlbaum.

Egbert, J., Chao, C. & Hanson-Smith, E. (1999) Computer-enhanced language learning environments, in J. Egbert and E. Hanson-Smith (eds), *CALL environments: Research Practice and Critical Issues* (pp. 1–13). Alexandria, VA: TESOL.

Egbert, J., Paulus, T. M. & Nakamichi, Y. (2002) The impact of CALL instruction on classroom computer use: a foundation for rethinking technology in teacher education. *Language Learning and Technology*, 6(3), 108–126.

Ehri, L. (2006) Alphabetics instruction helps students learn to read, in R. Joshi and P. Aaron (eds), *Handbook of Orthography and Literacy* (pp. 649–677). Mahwah, NJ: Lawrence Erlbaum.

Elia, A. (2006) Language learning in tandem via Skype. *The Reading Matrix*, 6(3), 269–280.

Ellis, N. C. (1994) A theory of instructed second language acquisition, in N.C. Ellis (ed.), *Implicit and Explicit Learning of Languages* (pp. 79–114). San Diego, CA: Academic.

Ellis, R. (1985) *Understanding Second Language Acquisition*. Oxford: Oxford University Press.

Ellis, R. (1990) *Instructed Second Language Acquisition*. Oxford: Blackwell.

Ellis, R. (1992) Comprehension and the acquisition of grammatical knowledge in a second language, in R. J. Courchãene (ed.), *Comprehension-based Second Language Teaching*. Ottawa, ON: University of Ottawa Press.

Ellis, R. (1999) Theoretical perspectives on interaction and language learning, in R. Ellis (ed.), *Learning a Second Language Through Interaction* (pp. 3–31). Amsterdam: John Benjamins Publishing Company.

Ellis, R. (2000) Task-based research and language pedagogy. *Language Teaching Research*, 49(3), 193–220.

Ellis, R. (2001) Investigating form-focused instruction, in R. Ellis (ed.), *Form-focused Instruction and Second Language Learning* (pp. 1–46). Malden, MA: Blackwell.

Ellis, R. (2003) *Task-based Language Learning and Teaching*. Oxford: Clarendon Press.

Ellis, R. (2005) *Instructed Second Language Acquisition: A Literature Review*. Wellington: Ministry of Education, NZ.

Ellis, R. (2006) Current issues in the teaching of grammar: an SLA perspective. *TESOL Quarterly*, 40(1), 83–107.

Ellis, R. (2008) *The Study of Second Language Acquisition* (2nd edition). Oxford: Oxford University Press.

Ellis, R., Basturkmen, H. & Loewen, S. (2002) Doing focus-on-form. *System*, 30(4), 419–432.

Ellis, R. & Barkhuizen, G. (2005) *Analyzing Learner Language*. Oxford: Oxford University Press.

Elola, I. & Oskoz, A. (2010) Collaborative writing: Fostering foreign language and writing conventions development. *Language Learning & Technology*, 14(3), 51–71. Retrieved from http://llt.msu.edu/issues/october2010/elolaoskoz.pdf

Erben, T., Ban, R. & Castaneda, M. (2009) *Teaching English Language Learners Through Technology*. New York: Routledge.

Ericsson, P. F. & Haswell, R. H. (2006) *Machine Scoring of Student Essays: Truth and Consequences*. Logan, UT: All USU Press Publications.

Evans, D. (n.d.) *Corpus Building and Investigation for the Humanities: An On-line Information Pack About Corpus Investigation Techniques for the Humanities. University of Nottingham. Unit 2: Compiling a Corpus.* Available at http://www.birmingham.ac.uk/Documents/college-artslaw/corpus/Intro/Unit2.pdf

Evans, S. (2012) Designing email tasks for the Business English classroom: implications from a study of Hong Kong's key industries. *English for Specific Purposes,* 31(3), 202–212.

Fabry, D. L. & Higgs, J. R. (1997) Barriers to the effective use of technology in education: current status. *Journal of Educational Computing Research,* 174, 385–395.

Farr, F. & Riordan, E. (2015) Tracing the reflective practice of student teachers in online modes. *ReCALL,* 27(1), 104–128.

Felix, U. (2005) Analysing recent CALL effectiveness research: Towards a common agenda. *Computer Assisted Language Learning,* 18(1–2), 1–32.

Fellner, T. & Apple, M. (2006) Developing writing fluency and lexial complexity with blogs. *The JALT CALL Journal,* 2(1), 15–26.

Ferris, D. (2003) *Responding to Student Writing.* Mahwah, NJ: Erlbaum.

Field, J. (2008) *Listening in the Language Classroom.* Cambridge: Cambridge University Press.

Firth, A. & Wagner, J. (1997) On discourse, communication, and (some) fundamental concepts in SLA research. *Modern Language Journal,* 81, 285– 300.

Firth, A. & Wagner, J. (2007) Second/foreign language learning as a social accomplishment: Elaborations on a reconceptualized SLA. *Modern Language Journal,* 91(1), 800–819.

Fleming, L., Motamedi, V. & May, L. (2007) Predicting preservice teacher competence in computer technology: Modeling and application in training environments. *Journal of Technology and Teacher Education,* 15(2), 207–231.

Flowerdew, J. (ed.) (2002) *Academic Discourse.* Harlow, UK: Longman.

Flowerdew, J. & Miller, L. (2005) *Second Language Listening: Theory and Practice.* Cambridge: Cambridge University Press.

Fotos, S. & Brown, C. (2004) Development of CALL and current options, in S. Fotos and C. M. Browne (eds), *New Perspectives on CALL for Second Language Classrooms* (pp. 3–14). Mahwah, NJ: Lawrence Erlbaum.

Freiermuth, M. (2002) Connecting with computer science students by building bridges. *Simulation & Gaming,* 3(3), 299–315.

Freedman, A. & Medway, P. (eds.). (1994) Genre and the New Rhetoric. London: Taylor & Francis.

Fries, C. C. (1945) *Teaching and Learning English as a Foreign Language.* Ann Arbor, MI: University of Michigan Press.

Friginal, E. (2013) Developing research report writing skills using corpora. *English for Specific Purposes,* 32(4), 208–220.

Fung, L. & Carter, R. (2007) Discourse markers and spoken English: native and learner use in pedagogical settings. *Applied Linguistics,* 28(3), 410–439.

Gardner, R. C. (1985) *Social Psychology and Second Language Learning: The Role of Attitudes and Motivation.* London: Edward Arnold.

Gardner, R. C. (2001) Integrative motivation and second language acquisition, in Z. Dornyei and R. Schmidt (eds), *Motivation and Second Language Acquisition* (pp. 1–20). Honolulu, HI: University of Hawaii Press.

Gardner, R. C. (2005) *Integrative Motivation and Second Language Acquisition.* London, ON: Canadian Association of Applied Linguistics/Canadian Linguistics Association Plenary Talk.

Garrett, N. (1987) A psycholinguist perspective on grammar and CALL, in W. F. Smith (ed.), *Modern Media in Foreign Language Education: Theory and Implementation* (pp. 169–196). Lincolnwood, IL: National Textbook Company.

Gass, S. M. (1997) *Input, Interaction and the Second Language Learner*. Mahwah, NJ: Lawrence Erlbaum Associates.

Gass, S. M. (2003) Input and interaction, in C. J. Doughty and M. H. Long (eds), *The Handbook of Second Language Acquisition* (pp. 224–255). Oxford: Blackwell.

Gass, S. M., Mackey, A. & Pica, T. (1998) The role of input and interaction in second language acquisition: introduction to special issue. *The Modern Language Journal*, 82(3), 299–307.

Gass, S. M. & Selinker, L. (1994) *Second Language Acquisition: An Introductory Course*. Hillsdale, NJ: Lawrence Erlbaum Associates.

Gass, S. M. & Selinker, L. (2001) *Second Language Acquisition: An Introductory Course* (2nd edition). Mahwah, NJ: Lawrence Erlbaum.

Gass, S. M. & Varonis, E. (1994) Input, interaction, and second language production. *Studies in Second Language Acquisition*, 16, 283–302.

Gedera, S. D. (2012) The dynamics of blog peer feedback in ESL classroom. *Teaching English with Technology*, 12(4), 16–30.

Gee, J. P. (1996) *Social Linguistics and Literacies*. London: Taylor and Francis.

Ghadirian, S. (2003) Providing controlled exposure to target vocabulary through the screening and arranging of texts. *Language Learning & Technology*, 6, 147–164. http://llt.msu.edu/vol6num1/ghadirian/default.html

Gibbs, G. & Simpson, C. (2004) Conditions under which assessment supports student learning. *Learning and Teaching in Higher Education*, 1, 3–31.

Gilabert, R. (2007) Effects of manipulating task complexity on self-repairs during L2 oral production. *IRAL*, 45, 215–240.

Gilmore, A. (2009) Using online corpora to develop students' writing skills. *ELT Journal*, 63(4), 363–372.

Godwin-Jones, R. (2000) Emerging technologies: literacies and technology tools/trends. *Language Learning & Technology*, 4(2), 11–18.

Godwin-Jones, R. (2003) Emerging technologies blogs and wikis: environments for online collaboration. *Language Learning and Technology*, 7(2), 12–16.

Godwin-Jones, R. (2005) Messaging, gaming, peer-to-peer sharing: language learning strategies & tools for the Millennial Generation. *Language Learning & Technology*, 9(1), 17–22. Retrieved from http://llt.msu.edu/vol9num1/emerging/default.html

Godwin-Jones, R. (2008) Emerging technologies web-writing 2.0: enabling, documenting, and assessing writing online. *Language Learning & Technology*, 12(2), 7–13.

Godwin-Jones, R. (2010a) Emerging technologies from memory palaces to spacing algorithms: Approaches to second language vocabulary learning. *Language Learning & Technology*, 14(2), 4–11. http://llt.msu.edu/vol14num2/emerging.pdf

Godwin-Jones, R. (2010b) Emerging technologies literacies and technologies revisited. *Language Learning & Technology*, 14(3), 2–9. http://llt.msu.edu/vol-14num3/emerging.pdf

Goh, C. C. M. (2007) *Teaching Speaking in the Language Classroom*. Singapore: SEAMEO Regional Language Centre.

González-Bueno, M. (1998) The effects of electronic mail on Spanish L2 discourse. *Language Learning and Technology*, 1(2), 50–65.

Goodyear, P., Salmon, G., Spector, J. M., Steeples, C. & Tickner, S. (2001) Competences for online teaching: a special report. *Educational Technology Research and Development*, 49(1), 65–72.

Grabe, W. (2009) *Reading in a Second Language: Moving from Theory to Practice.* New York: Cambridge University Press.

Grabe, W. (2014) Key Issues in L2 Reading Development. Proceedings of the 4th CELC Symposium for English Language Teachers – Selected Papers. 8–18.

Grabe, W. & Stoller, F. (2011) *Teaching and Researching Reading* (2nd edition). Harlow, UK: Pearson Longman.

Grabe, W. & Kaplan, R. B. (1996) *Theory and Practice of Writing: An Applied Linguistic Perspective.* New York: Longman.

Groot, P. J. M. (2000) Computer assisted second language vocabulary acquisition. *Language Learning & Technology*, 4(1), 60–81.

Grosse, C. U. (2002) Research priorities in languages for specific purposes. *Global Business Languages*, 7, Article 2. Available at http://docs.lib.purdue.edu/gbl/vol7/iss1/2

Grosse, C. U. & Voght, G. (1991) The evolution of languages for specific purposes in the United States. *Modern Language Journal*, 75(2), 181–195.

Gruber-Miller, J. & Benton, C. (2001) How do you say 'MOO' in Latin?: assessing student learning and motivation in beginning Latin. *CALICO Journal*, 18(2), 305–338.

Gu, Y. (2003) Vocabulary learning in a second language: person, task, context and strategies. *TESL-EJ*, 7(2). Available at www.tesl-ej.org/ej26/a4.html (last accessed 10 December 2013).

Gunderson, L., Murphy Odo, D. & D'Silva, R. (2011) Second language literacy, in E. Hinkel (ed.), *Handbook of Research in Second Language Teaching and Learning* (Vol. 2) (pp. 472–487). New York: Routledge.

Haas, C. (1996) *Writing Technology: Studies on the Materiality of Literacy.* Mahwah, NJ: Lawrence Erlbaum Associates.

Hadley, A. O. (1993) *Teaching Language in Context* (2nd edition). Boston, MA: Heinle and Heinle Publishers.

Hadley, M. & Sheingold, K. (1993) Commonalities and distinctive patterns in teachers' integration of computers. *American Journal of Education*, 101, 261–315.

Hagood, M. C. (2003) New media and online literacies. *Research Quarterly*, 38, 387–391.

Hall, G. (2011) *Exploring English Language Teaching Language in Action.* London: Routledge.

Hall, J. K., Hellermann, J. & Doehler, S. P. (eds) (2011) *L2 Interactional Competence and Development.* Clevedon, UK: Multilingual Matters.

Halliday, M. A. K. (1993) Towards a language-based theory of learning. *Linguistics and Education*, 5(2), 93–116.

Halliday, M. A. K. (1994) *An Introduction to Functional Grammar* (2nd edition). London: Edward Arnold.

Hampel, R. (2003) Theoretical perspectives and new practices in audio-graphic conferencing for language learning. *ReCALL*, 15(1), 21–36.

Hampel, R. & Hauck, M. (2004) Towards an effective use of audioconferencing in distance language courses. *Language Learning & Technology*, 8(1), 66–82.

Hamp-Lyons, L. (2011) English for academic purposes, in E. Hinkel (ed.), *Handbook of Research in Second Language Teaching and Learning* (Vol. 2) (pp. 89–105). New York and Oxford: Routledge.

Hannon, B. (2011) Understanding the relative contributions of lower-level word processes, higher level processes, and working memory to reading comprehension performance in proficient adult readers. *Reading Research Quarterly*, 47, 125–152.

Hanrahan, S. J. & Isaacs, G. (2001) Assessing self and peer assessment: The students' views. *Higher Education Research and Development*, 20, 53–70.

Hanson-Smith, E. (2006) Expert-novice teacher mentoring in language learning technology, in P. Hubbard and M. Levy (eds), *Teacher Education and CALL* (pp. 301–317). Amsterdam: John Benjamins Publishing Company.

Harasim, L. (2012) *Learning Theory and Online Technologies*. New York: Routledge.

Harris, H. & Park, S. (2008) Educational usages of podcasting. *British Journal of Educational Technology*, 39(3), 548–551.

Harrison, C., Comber, C., Fisher, T., Haw, K., Lewin, C., Lunzer, E., McFarlane, A., Mavers, D., Scrimshaw, P., Somekh, B. & Watling, R. (2003) The Impact of Information and Communication Technologies on Pupil Learning and Attainment: Full report March 2003. www.becta.org.uk/research/reports/impact2/index.cfm (last accessed 18 October 2013).

Hatime, C. & Zeynep, K. (2012) Effects of peer e-feedback on Turkish EFL students' writing performance. *The Journal of Educational Computing Research*, 46(1), 61–84.

Hattie, J. & Timperley, H. (2007) The power of feedback. *Review of Educational Research*, 77(1), 81–112.

Hayati, A. & Mohmedi, F. (2011) The effect of films with and without subtitles on listening comprehension of EFL learners. *British Journal of Educational Technology*, 42(1), 181–192.

He, A. W. & Young, R. (1998) Language proficiency interviews: A discourse approach, in R. Young and A. W. He (eds), *Talking and Testing: Discourse Approaches to the Assessment of Oral Proficiency* (pp. 1–24). Amsterdam, and Philadelphia, PA: John Benjamins Publishing Company.

Hedge, T. (2000) *Teaching and Learning in the Language Classroom*. Oxford: Oxford University Press.

Hegelheimer, V. & Chapelle, C. A. (2000) Methodological issues in research on learner-computer interactions in CALL. *Language Learning and Technology*, 4, 41–59.

Hegelheimer, V., Dursun, A. & Li, Z. (2016) Automated writing evaluation in language teaching: theory, development, and application. *CALICO Journal*, 33(1), i–v.

Hellekjær, G. O. (2007) Reading: from a forgotten to a basic skill. *Språk og språkundervisning*, 2, 23–29.

Herring, S. (ed.) (1996) *Computer Mediated Communication: Linguistic, Social and Cross-cultural Perspectives*. Amsterdam: John Benjamins Publishing Company.

Herring, S. C. (2007) A faceted classification scheme for computer-mediated discourse. *Language@Internet*, 4, article 1. Available at http://www.languageatinternet.de/articles/2007/761 (last accessed 17 January 2014).

Herron, C., Dubreil, S., Cole, S. P. & Corrie, C. (2002) A classroom investigation: can video improve intermediate-level foreign language students ability to learn about a foreign culture? *Modern Language Journal*, 86, 36–53.

Hewings, M. (2002) A History of ESP Through English for Specific Purposes. Available at http://www.esp-world.info/Articles_3/Hewings_paper.htm

Hieke, A. E. (1985) A componential approach to oral fluency evaluation. *The Modern Language Journal*, 69(2), 135–142.

Higgins, S. & Miller, J. (2000) ICT as support for development in literacy and numeracy teaching. *Professional Development Today*, 3(2), 49–56.

Hinkel, E. & Fotos, S. (2002) From theory to practice: a teacher's view, in E. Hinkel and S. Fotos (eds), *New Perspectives on Grammar Teaching in Second Language Classrooms* (pp. 1–12). Mahwah, NJ: Lawrence Earlbaum.

Hodges, B. H., Steffensen, S. V. & Martin, J. E. (2012) Caring, conversing, and realizing values: new directions in language studies. *Language Sciences*, 34, 499–506.

Hoey, M. (2005) *Lexical Priming. A New Theory of Words and Language.* London: Routledge.

Holland, V. M., Kaplan, J. D. & Sabol, M. A. (1999) Preliminary tests of language learning in a speech-interactive graphics microworld. *CALICO Journal*, 16(3), 339–359.

Holliday, L. (1995) NS syntactic modifications in NS-NNS negotiations as input data for second language acquisition of syntax. Unpublished doctoral dissertation. Philadelphia, PA: University of Pennsylvania.

Horst, M., Cobb, T. & Nicolae, I. (2005) Expanding academic vocabulary with an interactive on-line database. *Language Learning & Technology*, 9, 90–110.

Horwitz, E. K. (2001) Language anxiety and achievement. *Annual Review of Applied Linguistics*, 21, 112–126.

Hruskocy, C., Cennamo, K. S., Ertmer, P. A. & Johnson, T. (2000) Creating a community of technology users: students become technology experts for teachers and peers. *Journal of Technology and Teacher Education*, 8, 69–84.

Hsu, J. (1994). *Computer assisted language learning (CALL): The effect of ESL students' use of interactional modifications on listening comprehension.* Unpublished doctoral dissertation. Department of Curriculum and Instruction, College of Education, Iowa State University, Ames, IA.

Huang, H., Cher, C. & Lin, C. (2009) EFL learners' use of online reading strategies and comprehension of texts: an exploratory study. *Computers & Education*, 52(1), 13–26.

Huang, H. T. & Liou, H. C. (2007) Vocabulary learning in an automated graded reading program. *Language Learning & Technology*, 11(3), 64–82.

Hubbard, P. (1988) An integrated framework for CALL courseware evaluation. *CALICO Journal*, 6(2), 51–72. Available at http://calico.org/journalarticles.html

Hubbard, P. (2004) Learner training for effective use of CALL, in S. Fotos and C. Browne (eds), *New Perspectives on CALL for Second Language Classrooms* (pp. 45–68). Mahwah, NJ: Erlbaum.

Hubbard, P. (2006) Evaluating CALL software, in L. Ducate and N. Arnold (eds), *Calling on CALL: From Theory and Research to New Directions in Foreign Language Teaching.* San Marcos: CALICO.

Hubbard, P. & Siskin, C. B. (2004) Another look at tutorial CAL. *ReCALL*, 16(2), 448–461.

Hulstijn, J. H. (2001) Intentional and incidental second language vocabulary learning: a reappraisal of elaboration, rehearsal and automaticity, in P. Robinson (ed.), *Cognition and Second Language Instruction* (pp. 258–287) Cambridge: Cambridge University Press.

Hulstijn, J. H. (2003) Incidental learning and intentional learning, in J. Doughty and M. L. Long (eds), *Handbook of Second Language Research* (pp. 349–381). Oxford: Blackwell Publishing Ltd.

Hunt, A., & Beglar, D. (1998). Current research and practice in teaching vocabulary. *The Language Teacher.* Retrieved from www.jalt-publications.org/old_tlt/articles/1998/01/hunt

Hurt, T., Joseph, K. & Cook, C. (1977) Scales for the measurement of innovativeness. *Human Communication Research*, 4(1), 58–65.

Hyland, K. (2003). Genre-based pedagogies: a social response to process. *Journal of Second Language Writing*, 12, 17–29.

Hyland, K. & Hyland, F. (2006a) *Feedback in Second Language Writing: Contexts and Issues.* Cambridge: Cambridge University Press.

Hyland, K. & Hyland, F. (2006b) Feedback on second language students' writing. *Language Teaching*, 39(2), 83–101.

Hyland, K. & Tse, P. (2007) Is there an 'academic vocabulary'? *TESOL Quarterly*, 41(2), 235–253.

Hymes, D (1971) *On Communicative Competence.* Philadelphia, PA: University of Pennsylvania Press.

Hymes, D. (1972) On communicative competence, in J. B. Pride and J. Holmes (eds), *Sociolinguistics: Selected Readings* (pp. 269–293). Harmondsworth, UK: Penguin Books.

Hyon, S. (1996) Genre in three traditions: implications for ESL. *TESOL Quarterly*, 30(4), 693–722.

Jamieson, J., Chapelle, C. A. & Preiss, S (2005) Putting principles into practice. *ReCALL*, 16(2), 396–415.

Jenks, C. J. (2009) When is it appropriate to talk? Managing overlapping talk in multiparticipant voice-based chat rooms. *Computer Assisted Language Learning*, 22(1), 19–30.

Jenks, C. (2014) *Social Interaction in Second Language Chat Rooms.* Edinburgh: Edinburgh University Press.

Jepson, J. (2005) Conversations—and negotiated interaction—in text and voice chat rooms. *Language Learning & Technology*, 9(3), 79–98.

Jogan, K. M., Heredia, A. H. & Aguilera, G. M. (2001) Cross-cultural e-mail: Providing cultural input for the advanced foreign language student. *Foreign Language Annals*, 34(4), 341–346.

Johns, A. M., Bawarshi, A., Coe, R. M., Hyland, K., Paltridge, B., Reiff, M. J. & Tardy, C. (2006) Crossing the boundaries of genre studies: commentaries by experts. *Journal of Second Language Writing*, 15, 234–249.

Johnson, K. E. (2006) The sociocultural turn and its challenges for second language teacher education. *TESOL Quarterly*, 40(1), 235–257.

Johnson, K. E. (2009) *Second Language Teacher Education: A Sociocultural Perspective.* New York: Routledge.

Jones, J. F. (2001) CALL and the responsibilities of teachers and administrators. *ELT Journal*, 55(4), 360–367.

Jones, L. & Plass, J. (2002) Supporting listening comprehension and vocabulary acquisition in French with multimedia annotations. *The Modern Language Journal*, 86, 546–561.

Jung, U. O. H. (2005) CALL: past, present and future—a bibliometric approach. *ReCALL*, 17(1), 4–17.

Kalantzis, M. & Cope, B. (2012) *Literacies.* New York: Cambridge University Press.

Kasper, G. (2006) Beyond repair: Conversation analysis as an approach to SLA. *AILA Review*, 19, 83–99.

Kasper, G. & Rose, K. (2002) *Pragmatic Development in a Second Language.* Blackwell Publishing, Inc.

Keh, C. (1990) Feedback in the writing process: a model and methods for implementation. *ELT Journal*, 44(4), 294–304.

Kern, N. (2013) Technology-integrated English for specific purposes lessons: real-life language, tasks, and tools for professionals, in G. Motteram (ed.), *Innovations in Learning Technologies for English Language Teaching.* British Council.

Kern, R. (1995) Restructuring classroom interaction with networked computers: effects on quantity and quality of language production. *Modern Language Journal*, 79(4), 457–476.

Kern, R. (2006) Perspectives on technology in learning and teaching languages. *TESOL Quarterly*, 40(1), 183–210.

Kern, R. & Warshauer, M. (2000) Introduction: theory and practice in network-based language teaching, in M. Warschauer and R. Kern (eds), *Networked-based Language Teaching: Concepts and Practice* (pp. 1–19). Cambridge: Cambridge University Press.

Kessler, G. (2007) Formal and informal CALL preparation and teacher attitude toward technology. *Computer Assisted Language Learning*, 20(2), 173–188.

Kessler, G. (2009) Student-initiated attention to form in wiki-based collaborative writing. *Language Learning & Technology*, 13(1), 79–95. Available at http://llt.msu.edu/vol13num1/kessler.pdf

Kessler, G. & Bikowski, D. (2010) Developing collaborative autonomous learning abilities in computer mediated language learning: attention to meaning among students in wiki space. *Computer Assisted Language Learning*, 23(1), 41–58.

Kessler, G., Bikowski, D. & Boggs, J. (2012) Collaborative writing among second language learners in academic web-based projects. *Language Learning & Technology*, 16(1), 91–109.

Kim, D. & Gilman, D. A. (2008) Effects of text, audio, and graphic aids in multimedia instruction for vocabulary learning. *Educational Technology & Society*, 11(3), 114–126.

Kinginger, C. (2000) Learning the pragmatics of solidarity in the networked foreign language classroom, in J. K. Hall and L. S. Verplaetse (eds), *Second and Foreign Language Learning Through Classroom Interaction* (pp. 23–46). Mahwah, NJ: Erlbaum.

Kitade, K. (2000) L2 learners' discourse and SLA theories in CMC: collaborative interaction in Internet chat. *Computer Assisted Language Learning*, 13(2), 143–166.

Klopfer, E. (2008) *Augmented learning: Research and design of mobile educational games.* Cambridge, MA: MIT Press.

Kluger, A. N. & DeNisi, A. (1996) The effects of feedback interventions on performance: a historical review, a meta-analysis, and a preliminary feedback intervention theory. *Psychological Bulletin*, 119(2), 254–284.

Kollias, V., Mamalougos, N., Vamvakoussi, X., Lakkala, M. & Vosniadou, S. (2005) Teachers' attitudes to and beliefs about web-based collaborative learning environments in the context of an international implementation. *Computers & Education*, 45(3), 295–315.

Kolln, M. (2007) *Rhetorical Grammar: Grammatical Choice, Rhetorical Effects*. New York: Pearson.

Kormos, J. & Dénes, M. (2004) Exploring measures and perceptions of fluency in the speech of second language learners. *System*, 32(2), 145–164.

Kozma, R. & Anderson, R. (2002) Qualitative case studies of innovative pedagogical practices using ICT. *Journal of Computer Assisted Learning*, 18(4), 387–394.

Kramsch, C. (1986) From language proficiency to interactional competence. *Modern Language Journal*, 70(4), 366–372.

Kramsch, C., A'Ness, F. & Lam, E. (2000) Authenticity and authorship in the computer mediated acquisition of L2 literacy. *Language Learning and Technology*, 4(2), 78–104.

Krashen, S. D. (1981) *Second Language Acquisition and Second Language Learning*. Oxford: Pergamon.

Krashen, S. D. (1982) *Principles and Practice in Second Language Acquisition*. Oxford: Pergamon.

Krashen, S. D. (1985) *The Input Hypothesis: Issues and Implications*. New York: Longman.

Krashen, S. D. & Terrell, T. D. (1983) *The Natural Approach: Language Acquisition in the Classroom*. Oxford Pergamon.

Krashen, S. (2011) The Compelling (not just interesting) Input Hypothesis. The English Connection. A Publication of KOTESOL. 15(3). Retrieved from http://www.koreatesol.org/sites/default/files/pdf_publications/TECv15n3-11Autumn.pdf

Kuteeva, M. (2011) Wikis and academic writing: changing the writer-reader relationship. *English for Specific Purposes*, 30, 44–57.

Kung, S. C. (2004) Synchronous electronic discussions in an EFL reading class. *ELT Journal*, 58(2), 164–173.

Kwong, V. (2007) Reach out to your students using MySpace and Facebook. *Indiana Libraries*, 26(3), 53–57.

Lado, R. (1957) *Linguistics Across Cultures: Applied Linguistics for Language Teachers*. Ann Arbor, MI: The University of Michigan Press.

Lai, C. & Zhao, Y. (2006) Noticing and text-based chat. *Language Learning & Technology*, 10(3), 102–120.

Lam, Y. (2000) Technophilia v. technophobia: a preliminary look at why second language teachers do or do not use technology in their classrooms. *Canadian Modern Language Review*, 56, 389–420.

Lamy, M.-N. & Goodfellow, R. (1999) 'Reflective conversation' in the virtual language classroom. *Language Learning and Technology*, 2(2), 43–61.

Lankshear, C. & Knobel, M. (2011) *Literacies: Social, Cultural and Historical Perspectives*. New York: Peter Lang.

Lantolf, J. P. (2000) Introducing sociocultural theory, in J. P. Lantolf (ed.), *Sociocultural Theory and Second Language Learning* (pp. 1–26). Oxford: Oxford University Press.

Lantolf, J. P. (2001) *Sociocultural Theory and Second Language Learning*. Oxford: Oxford University Press.

Lantolf, J. & Thorne, L. (2006) *Sociocultural Theory and the Genesis of Second Language Development*. Oxford: Oxford University Press.

Larsen-Freeman, D. (1983) The importance of input in second language acquisition, in R. Andersen (ed.), *Pidginization and Creolization as Language Acquisition* (pp. 87–93). Rowley, MA: Newbury House.

Larsen-Freeman, D. (1991) Teaching grammar, in M. Celce-Murcia (ed.), *Teaching English as a Second or Foreign Language* (2nd edition) (pp. 279–296). New York: Newbury House.

Larsen-Freeman, D. (2001) Grammar, in R. Carter and D. Nunan (eds), *The Cambridge Guide to Teaching English to Speakers of Other Languages* (pp. 34–41). Cambridge: Cambridge University Press.

Laufer, B. & Hill, M. (2000) What lexical information do L2 learners select in a CALL dictionary and how does it affect word retention? *Language Learning and Technology*, 3(2), 58–76.

Laufer, B. & Ravenhorst-Kalovski, G. C. (2010) Lexical threshold revisited: lexical text coverage, learners' vocabulary size and reading comprehension. *Reading in a Foreign Language*, 22, 15–30.

Lawler, R. W. & Yazdani, M. (1987) *Artificial Intelligence and Education*. Norwood, NJ: Ablex Publishing.

Lazaraton, A. (2001) Teaching oral skills, in M. Celce-Murcia (ed.), *Teaching English as a Second or Foreign Language* (3rd edition) (pp. 103–115). Boston, MA: Heinle & Heinle, Thomson Learning Inc.

Leahy, C. (2004) Observations in the computer room: L2 output and learner behaviour. *ReCALL*, 16(1), 124–144.

Lee, K.-W. (2000) English teachers' barriers to the use of computer-assisted language learning. *Internet TESOL Journal*, 6(12). Available at http://iteslj.org/Articles/Lee-CALLbarriers.html

Lee, L. (2002) Synchronous online exchanges: a study of modification devices on non-native discourse interaction. *System*, 30, 275–288.

Lee, L. (2010) Fostering reflective writing and interactive exchange through blogging in an advanced language course. *ReCALL*, 22(2), 212–227.

Lee, B. & VanPatten (1995) *Making Communicative Language Teaching Happen*. New York: McGraw-Hill.

LeLoup, J. W. & Ponterio, R. (2000) Literacy: reading on the net. *Language Learning & Technology*, 4(2), 5–10.

Lenk, U. (1998) Discourse markers and global coherence in conversation. *Journal of Pragmatics*, 30(2), 245–257.

Leu, D. J., Kinzer, C. K., Coiro, J. L. & Cammack, D. W. (2004) Toward a theory of new literacies emerging from the Internet and other information and communication technologies', in R. B. Ruddell and N. J. Unrau (eds), *Theoretical Models and Processes of Reading*. Newark, DE: International Reading Association.

Leuf, B., & Cunningham, W. (2001). The Wiki way. Quick Collaboration on the Web: Addison-Wesley.

Levy, M. (1997) *Computer Assisted Language Learning: Context and Conceptualization*. Oxford: Clarendon Press.

Levy, M. (2000) *CALL Context and Conceptualization*. Oxford: Oxford University Press.

Levy, M. & Kennedy, C. (2004) A task-cycling pedagogy using audio-conferencing and stimulated reflection for foreign language learning. *Language Learning & Technology*, 8(2), 50–68. Retrieved from http://llt.msu.edu/vol8num2/pdf/levy.pdf

Levy, M. & Stockwell, G. (2006) *CALL Dimensions: Options and Issues in Computer Assisted Language Learning*. Mahwah, NJ: Lawrence Erlbaum.

Lewis, M. (1993) *The Lexical Approach*. Hove: LTP.

Li, L. (2004) Perceptions of the impact of ICT on motivation in learning English as a second language in a Chinese context. Unpublished M.Phil. dissertation. Cambridge: University of Cambridge.

Li, L. (2008) EFL teachers' beliefs about ICT integration in Chinese secondary schools. Unpublished doctoral thesis. Belfast: Queen's University.

Li, L. (2011) Three important issues in using CALL. *21st Century English Teachers*. Available at http://elt.i21st.cn/article/9610_1.html

Li, L. (2014) Understanding language teachers' practice with educational technology: a case from China. *System*, (46), 105–119.

Li, L. (2015) What's the use of technology? Insights from EFL classrooms in Chinese secondary schools, in C. Jenks and P. Seedhouse (eds), *International Perspectives on Classroom Interaction* (pp. 168–187). Palgrave Macmillan.

Li, L. & Walsh, S. (2011a) 'Seeing is believing': looking at EFL teachers' beliefs through classroom interaction. *Classroom Discourse*, 2(1), 39–57.

Li, L. & Walsh, S. (2011b) Technology uptake in Chinese EFL classes. *Language Teaching Research*, 15(1), 99–125.

Li, M. & Zhu, W. (2013) Patterns of computer-mediated interaction in small writing groups using wikis. *Computer Assisted Language Learning*, 26(1), 61–82.

Li, Z. & Hegelheimer, V. (2013) Mobile-assisted grammar exercises: effects on self-editing in L2 writing. *Language Learning & Technology*, 17(3), 135–156.

Lightbown, P. M. & Spada, N. (2006) *How Languages are Learned* (3rd edition). Oxford: Oxford University Press.

Lim, K. & Shen, H. (2006) Integration of computers into an EFL reading classroom. *ReCALL*, 18(2), 212–229.

Liou, H. C. (2000) The electronic bilingual dictionary as a reading aid to EFL learners: research findings and implications. *Computer Assisted Language Learning*, 13, 467–476.

Littlewood, W. (1981) *Communicative Language Teaching*. Cambridge: Cambridge University Press.

Liu, D. & Jiang, P. (2009) Using a Corpus-based lexicogrammatical approach to grammar instruction in EFL and ESL contexts. *The Modern Language Journal*, 93(1), 61–78.

Liu, J. & Hansen, J. (2002) *Peer Response in Second Language Writing Classroom*. Ann Arbor, MI: The University of Michigan Press.

Liu, J. & Sadler, R. W. (2003) The effect and affect of peer review in electronic versus traditional modes on L2 writing. *Journal of English for Academic Purposes*, 2, 193–227.

Liu, M., Moore, Z., Graham, L. & Lee, S. (2002) A look at the research on computer-based technology use in second language learning: a review of the literature from 1990–2000. *Journal of Research on Technology in Education*, 34, 250–273.

Liu, X., Bonk, C. J., Magjuka, R. J., Lee, S. & Su, B. (2005) Exploring four dimensions of online instructor roles: a program level case study. *Journal of Asynchronous*, 9(4), 29–48.

Loewen, S. & Reinders, H. (2011) *Key Concepts in Second Language Acquisition*. Basingstoke: Palgrave Macmillan.

Lomicka, L. (1998) To gloss or not to gloss: An investigation of reading comprehension online. *Language Learning & Technology*, 1, 41–50.

Long, M. (1983) Inside the 'Black Box', in H. Seliger and M. Long (eds), *Classroom Oriented Research in Second Language Acquisition* (pp. 3–38). Rowley: Newbury House.

Long, M. H. (1985) Input and second language acquisition theory, in S. M. Gass and C. G. Madden (eds), *Input in Second Language Acquisition* (pp. 377–393). Rowley, MA: Newbury House Publishers.

Long, M. H. (1988) Instructed interlanguage development, in L. M. Beebe (ed.), Issues in second language acquisition: Multiple perspectives (pp. 115–141). Cambridge, MA: Newbury House/Harper and Row.

Long, M. H. (1991) Focus on form: a design feature in language teaching methodology, in K. de Bot, R. Ginsberg and C. Kramsch (eds), *Foreign Language Research in Cross-Cultural Perspective* (pp. 39–52). Amsterdam: John Benjamins Publishing Company.

Long, M. H. (1996) The role of the linguistic environment in second language acquisition, in W. Ritchie and T. Bahtia (eds), *Handbook of Second Language Acquisition* (pp. 413–468). San Diego, CA: Academic Press.

Loschky, L. (1994) Comprehensible input and second language acquisition. *Studies in Second Language Acquisition*, 16(3), 303–323.

Lotherington, H. & Xu, Y. (2004) How to chat in English and melody: emerging digital language conventions. *ReCALL*, 16(2), 308–329.

Louhiala-Salminen, L. (2002) The fly's perspective: discourse in the daily routine of a business manager. *English for Specific Purposes*, 21(3), 211–231.

Loveless, A., Devoogd, G. L. & Bohlin, R. M. (2001) Something old, something new … is pedagogy affected by ICT? in A. Loveless and V. Ellis (eds), *ICT, Pedagogy and the Curriculum: Subject to Change* (pp. 63–83). London and New York: Routledge Falmer.

Luckin, R. (2010) *Re-designing Learning Contexts*. Routledge: London.

Lund, A. (2008) Wikis: a collective approach to language production. *ReCALL*, 20(1), 35–54.

Lunde, K. (1990) Using electronic mail as a medium for foreign language study and instruction. *CALICO Journal*, 7(3), 68–78.

Lynch, T. (2007) Learning from the transcripts of an oral communication task. *ELT Journal*, 61(4), 311–320.

Lynch, T. (2009) *Teaching Second Language Listening*. Oxford: Oxford University Press.

Lynch, T. & Maclean, J. (2001) A case of exercising: effects of immediate task repetition on learners' performance, in M. Bygate, P. Skehan and M. Swain (eds), *Researching Pedagogic Tasks: Second Language Learning, Teaching and Testing* (pp. 141–162). Harlow, UK: Pearson.

Lyster, R. (1998a) Recasts, repetition, and ambiguity in L2 classroom discourse. *Studies in Second Language Acquisition*, 20, 51–81.

Lyster, R. (1998b) Negotiation of form, recasts, and explicit correction in relation to error types and learner repair in immersion classrooms. *Language Learning*, 48, 183–281.

Lyster, R. & Ranta, L. (1997) Corrective feedback and learner uptake: Negotiation of form in communicative classrooms. *Studies in Second Language Acquisition*, 19(1), 37–66.

Macaro, E., Handley, Z. & Walter, C. (2012) A systematic review of CALL in English as a second language: focus on primary and secondary education. *Language Teaching*, 45(1), 1–43.

MacGilchrist, B., Myers, K. and Reed, J. (1997) *The Intelligent School*. London: Paul Chapman.

Mackey, A. & Philp, J. (1998) Conversational interaction and second language development: recasts, responses, and red herrings? *The Modern Language Journal*, 82(3), 338–356.

Mackay, M. (2003). Researching new forms of literacy. *Research Quarterly*, 38, 403–407.

Mak, B. & Coniam, D. (2008) Using Wikis to enhance and develop writing skills among secondary school students in Hong Kong. *System*, 36(3), 437–455.

Mangelsdorf, K. & Schlumberger, A. (1992) ESL student response stances in a peer-review task. *Journal of Second Language Writing*, 1(3), 235–254.

Marcinkiewicz, H. R. (1993–1994) Computers and teachers: factors influencing computer use in the classroom. *Journal of Research on Computing in Education*, 26(2), 220–237.

Markee, N. (2004) Zones of interactional transition in ESL classes. *Modern Language Journal*, 88(4), 583–596.

Markee, N. (2008) Toward a learning behavior tracking methodology for CA-for-SLA. *Applied Linguistics*, 29(3), 404–427.

Markham, P. (1999) Captioned videotapes and second-language listening word recognition. *Foreign Language Annals*, 32(3), 321–328.

Markham, P. L. (2001) The influence of culture-specific background knowledge and captions on second language comprehension. *Journal of Educational Technology Systems*, 29(4), 331–343.

Martinez, R. & Schmitt, N. (2010) Invited commentary: vocabulary. *Language Learning & Technology*, 14(2), 26–29.

McCarthy, M. J. (2010) Spoken fluency revisited. *English Profile Journal*, 1(1), e4.

McCarthy, M. J., O'Keefe, A. & Walsh, S. (2010) *Vocabulary Matrix*. Andover, UK: Heinle Cengage.

McDonough, J. & Shaw, C. (2003) *Materials and Methods in ELT*. Oxford: Blackwell.

McGrath, I. (2002) *Materials Evaluation and Design for Language Teaching*. Edinburgh: Edinburgh University Press.

McKinnon, M. (online) Teaching technologies: teaching English using video. Onestopenglish website. Available at http://www.onestopenglish.com/methodology/methodology/teaching-technologies/teaching-technologies-teaching-english-using-video/146527.article

McLaughlin, B. & Heredia, R. (1996) Information-processing approaches to research on second language acquisition and use, in W. C. Ritchie and T. K. Bhatia (eds), *Handbook of Second Language Acquisition* (pp. 213–228). San Diego, CA: Academic Press.

McMeniman, M. & Evans, R. (1998) CALL through the eyes of teachers and learners of Asian languages: panacea or business as usual? *ON-CALL*, 12(1), 2–9.

Melendy, G. (2008) Motivating writers: the power of choice. *The Asian EFL Journal*, 10(3), 187–198.

Memari Hanjani, A. & Li, L. (2014) Exploring L2 writers' collaborative revision interactions and their writing performance. *System*, (44), 101–114.

Merler, S. (2000) Understanding multimedia dialogues in a foreign language. *Journal of Computer Assisted Learning*, 16(2), 148–159.

Meskill, C. and Anthony, N. (2005) Foreign language learning with CMC: Forms of online instructional discourse in a hybrid Russian Class. *System*, 33(1), 89–105.

Meskill, C. & Ranglova, K. (2000) Curriculum innovation in TEFL: a study of technologies supporting socio-collaborative language learning in Bulgaria, in M. Warschauer and R. Kern (eds), *Network-Based Language Teaching: Concepts and Practice*. Cambridge: Cambridge University Press.

Meskill, C., Anthony, N., Hilliker-Vanstrander, S., Tseng, C. & You, J. (2006). CALL: A survey of K-12 ESOL teacher uses and preferences. *TESOL Quarterly*, 40(2), 439–451.

Meunier, L. (1998) Personality and motivational factors in computer-mediated foreign language communication, in J. A. Muyskens (ed.), *New Ways of Learning and Teaching: Focus on Technology and FL Education* (pp. 145–197). Boston, MA: Heinle & Heinle.

Mishra, P. & Koehler, M. J. (2006) Technological pedagogical content knowledge: a new framework for teacher knowledge. *Teachers College Record*, 108(6), 1017–1054.

Mitchell, R. & Myles, F (1998) *Second Language Learning Theories*. London: Edward Arnold.

Mokhtari, K., Kymes, A. & Edwards, P. (2008) Assessing the new literacies of online reading comprehension: an informative interview with W. Ian O'Byrne, Lisa Zawilinski, J. Greg McVerry & Donald J. Leu at the University of Connecticut. *The Reading Teacher*, 62(4), 354–357.

Montero Perez, M., Peters, E., Clarebout, G. & Desmet, P. (2014) Effects of captioning on video comprehension and incidental vocabulary learning. *Language Learning & Technology*, 18(1), 118–141. Available at http://llt.msu.edu/issues/february2014/monteroperezetal.pdf

Montgomery, J. L., & Baker, W. (2007) Teacher-written feedback: Student perceptions, teacher self-assessment, and actual teacher performance. *Journal of Second Language Writing*, 16(2), 82–99.

Moseley, D., Higgins, S., Bramald, R., Hardman, F., Millier, J., Mroz, M., Newton, D., Tse, H., Thompson, I., Williamson, J., Halligan, J., Bramald, S., Newton, L., Tymms, P., Henderson, B. & Stout, J. (1999) Ways forward with ICT: effective pedagogy using information and communications technology in literacy and numeracy in primary schools. Newcastle: Newcastle University.

Mueller, J. (2010) What is authentic assessment? Available at http://jonathan.mueller.faculty.noctrl.edu/toolbox/whatisit.htm

Müller, S. (2004) Well you know that type of person: functions of well in the speech of American and German students. *Journal of Pragmatics*, 33, 193–208.

Müller-Hartmann, A. (2000) The role of tasks in promoting intercultural learning in electronic learning networks. *Language Learning & Technology*, 4(2), 129–147.

Müller-Hartmann, A. (2012) The classroom-based action research paradigm in telecollaboration, in M. Dooly and R. O'Dowd (eds), *Research Methods for Online Interaction and Exchange* (pp. 56–192). Bern, Switzerland: Peter Lang.

Mumtaz, S. (2000) Factors affecting teachers' use of information and communications technology: a review of the literature. *Journal of Information Technology for Teacher Education*, 93, 319–341.

Nadzrah A. B. & Kemboja, I. (2009) Using blogs to encourage ESL students to write constructively in English. *AJTLHE*, 1(5), 45–57.

Nagata, N. (1993) Intelligent computer feedback for second language instruction. *The Modern Language Journal*, 77(3), 330–339.

Nagata, N. (1997) An experimental comparison of deductive and inductive feedback generated by a simple parse. *System*, 25(4), 515–534.

Nagata, N. (1998) Input vs. output practice in educational software for second language acquisition. *Language Learning and Technology*, 1(2), 23–40.

Nagata, N. (2002) BANZAI: an application of natural language processing to web-based language learning. *CALICO Journal*, 19, 583–599.

Nakata, T. (2008) English vocabulary learning with word lists, word cards and computers: implications from cognitive psychology research for optimal spaced learning. *RECALL*, 20(1), 3–5.

Nakata, T. (2012) Web-based lexical resources, in C. Chappelle (ed.), *Encyclopedia of Applied Linguistics* (pp. 6166–6177). Oxford: Wiley-Blackwell.

Narciss, S. (2008) Feedback strategies for interactive learning tasks, in J. M. Spector, M. D. Merrill, J. J. G. Van Merriënboer and M. P. Driscoll (eds), *Handbook of Research on Educational Communications and Technology* (3rd edition) (pp. 125–143). Mahwah, NJ: Erlbaum.

Nation, I. S. P. (2001) *Learning Vocabulary in Another Language*. Cambridge: Cambridge University Press.

Nation, I. S. P. (2006) How large a vocabulary is needed for reading and listening? *Canadian Modern Language Review*, 63(1), 59–82.

Nation, P. & Kyongho, H. (1995) Where would general service vocabulary stop and special purposes vocabulary begin? *System*, 23, 35–41.

Nelson, M. (2003) Worldly experience. *The Guardian*, 20 March 2003. Available at www.theguardian.com/education/2003/mar/20/tefl2

New Media Consortiu (2007) The Horizon Report. Available at www.nmc.org/pdf/2007_Horizon_Report.pdf (last accessed 3 March 2016).

Ngu, B. H. & Rethinasamy, S. (2006) Evaluating a CALL software on the learning of English prepositions. *Computers & Education*, 47, 41–55.

Niederhauser, D. S. & Stoddart, T. (1994) Teachers' perspectives on computer-assisted instruction: transmission versus construction of knowledge. Paper presented at the Annual Meeting of the American Educational Research Association, New Orleans, LA.

Níkleva, D. G. & López, M. (2012) Competencia digital y herramientas de autor en la didáctica de las lenguas. *Tejuelo*, 13, 123–140.

Nikolova, O. R. (2002) Effect of students' participation in authoring of multimedia materials on student acquisition of vocabulary. *Language Learning and Technology*, 6(1), 100–122.

Noytim, U. (2010) Weblogs enhancing EFL students' English language learning. *Procedia Social & Behavioral Sciences*, 2(1), 127–132.

Nunan, D. (1987) Communicative language teaching: the learner's view, in B. Das, (ed) *Communicating and Learning in the Classroom Community*, 176–190. Singapore: RELC.

Nunan, D. (1989) *Designing Tasks for the Communicative Classroom*. Cambridge: Cambridge University Press.

Nunan, D. (1993) Task-based syllabus design: selecting, grading and sequencing tasks, in G. Crookes and S. Gass (eds), *Tasks in a Pedagogical Context: Integrating Theory and Practice* (pp. 55–68). Clevedon, UK: Multilingual Matters.

O'Dowd, R. (2006a) The use of videoconferencing and E-mail as mediators of inter-cultural student ethnography, in J. A. Belz and S. L. Thorne (eds), *Computer-mediated Intercultural Foreign Language Education* (pp. 86–120). Boston, MA: Heinle & Heinle.

O'Dowd, R. (2006b) *Telecollaboration and the Development of Intercultural Communicative Competence*. Munich: Langenscheidt-Longman.

O'Dowd, R. (2007) *Online Intercultural Exchange: An Introduction for Foreign Language Teaching*. Clevedon, UK: Multilingual Matters.

O'Hara, S. & Pritchard, R. (2008) Hypermedia authoring as a vehicle for vocabulary development in middle school English as a second language classrooms. *Clearing House: A Journal of Educational Strategies, Issues and Ideas*, 82(2), 60–65.

Ohta, A. (1995) Applying sociocultural theory to an analysis of learner discourse: learner-learner collaborative interaction in the zone of proximal development. *Issues in Applied Linguistics*, 6(2), 93–121.

Ohta, A. (2000) Rethinking interaction in SLA: Developmentally appropriate assistance in the zone of proximal development and the acquisition of L2 grammar, in J. Lantolf (ed.), *Sociocultural Theory and Second Language Acquisition* (pp. 51–78). Oxford: Oxford University Press.

O'Keeffe, A., McCarthy, M. & Carter, R. (2007) *From Corpus to Classroom: Language Use and Language Teaching*. Cambridge: Cambridge University Press.

Omaggio, A. C. (1986) *Teaching Language in Context: Proficiency-Oriented Instruction*. Boston, MA: Heinle and Heinle.

Onrubia, J. & Engel, A. (2012) The role of teacher assistance on the effects of a macro-script in collaborative writing tasks. *IJCSCL*, 7(1), 161–186.

Ortega, L. (2009) *Understanding Second Language Acquisition*. London: Hodder Education.

Oskoz, A. & Elola, I. (2011a) Academic writing in the foreign language classroom: wikis and chats at work, in M. Pennington and P. Burton (eds), *The College Writing Toolkit: Tried and Tested Ideas for Teaching College Writing* (pp. 345–356). London: Equinox.

Oskoz, A. & Elola, I. (2011b) Meeting at the Wiki: the new arena for collaborative writing in foreign language courses, in M. J. W. Lee and C. MacLoughlin (eds), *Web 2.0-Based E-Learning: Applying Social Informatics for Tertiary Teaching* (pp. 209–227). Hershey, PA: IGI Global.

Oskoz, A. & Elola, I. (2014) Promoting FL collaborative writing through the use of Web 2.0 tools, in M. Lloret and L. Ortega (eds), *Technology and Tasks: Exploring Technology-Mediated TBLT* (pp. 115–147). Philadelphia, PA: John Benjamins Publishing Company.

Osuna, M. & Meskill, C. (1998) Using the World Wide Web to integrate Spanish language and culture: a pilot. *Language Learning and Technology Journal*, 1(2).

Ottenbreit-Leftwicha, A. T., Glazewskib, K. D., Newbyc, T. & Ertmerc, P. (2010) Teacher value beliefs associated with using technology: Addressing professional and student needs. *Computers and Education*, 55(3), 1321–1335.

Park, H.-R. & Kim, D. (2011) Reading-strategy use by English as a second language learners in online reading tasks. *Computers & Education*, 57, 2156–2166.

Park, J., Yang, J. S. & Hsieh, Y. C. (2014) University level second language readers' online reading and comprehension strategies. *Language Learning & Technology*, 18(3), 148–172. http://llt.msu.edu/issues/october2014/parketyanghsieh.pdf

Parry, D. (2011) Mobile perspectives on teaching: mobile literacy. *Educause Review*, 46(2), 14–18. Available at http://net.educause.edu/ir/library/pdf/ERM1120.pdf (last accessed 4 March 2016).

Pegrum, M. (2009) *From Blogs to Bombs: The Future of Digital Technologies in Education*. Crawley, WA: UWA Publishing.

Pegrum, M. (2011) Modified, multiplied, and (re-)mixed: social media and digital literacies, in M. Thomas (ed.), *Digital Education: Opportunities for Social Collaboration* (pp. 9–35). New York: Palgrave Macmillan.

Pegrum, M. (2014) *Mobile Learning: Languages, Literacies and Cultures.* Basingstoke: Palgrave Macmillan.

Pelgrum, W. (2001) Obstacles to the integration of ICT in education: results from a worldwide educational assessment. *Computers and Education*, 37, 163–178.

Pellettieri, J. (2000) Negotiation in cyberspace: the role of chatting in the development of grammatical competence, in M. Warschauer and R. Kern (eds), *Network-based Language Teaching: Concepts and Practice* (pp. 59–86). Cambridge: Cambridge University Press.

Perez Basanta, C. & Rodriguez Martin, M. E. (2006) Data-driven learning-DDL-as a new tool for teaching conversation: exploring a small-scale corpus of film scripts, in E. Hidalgo, L. Quereda and J. Santana (eds), *Corpora in the Foreign Language Classroom* (pp. 141–158). Amsterdam: Rodopi.

Pérez Sanz, A. (2011) Escuela 2.0. Educación para el mundo digital. Madrid: Instituto de la Juventud, Ministerio de Sanidad, Política Social e Igualdad (92), 63–86.

Perfetti, C. & Adlof, S. (2012) Reading comprehension: a conceptual framework for word meaning to text meaning, in J. Sabatini, E. Albro & and T. O'Reilly (eds), *Measuring up: Advances in how to assess reading abilities* (pp. 3–20). Lanham, MD: Rowman & Littlefield Education.

Peterson, M. (1997) Language teaching and networking. *System*, 25(1), 29–37.

Phillips, M. (1985) Logical possibilities and classroom scenarios for the development of CALL, in C. Brumfit, M. Phillips and P. Skehan (eds), *Computers in English language teaching* (pp. 25–46). New York: Pergamon.

Pica, T. (1995) Teaching language and teaching language learners: the expanding roles and expectations of language teachers in communicative, content-based classrooms. Paper presented at Georgetown Roundtable. Washington, DC: Georgetown University.

Pica, T., Holliday, L., Lewis, N. and Morgenthaler, L. (1989) Comprehensible input as an outcome of linguistic demands on the learner. *Studies in Second Language Acquisition*, 11(1), 63–90.

Plass, J., & Jones, L. (2005) Multimedia learning in second language acquisition, in R. Mayer (ed), *The Cambridge Handbook of Multimedia Learning* (pp. 467–488). New York: Cambridge University Press.

Platt, E. & Brooks, F. B. (1994) The 'acquisition-rich environment' revisited. *Modern Language Journal*, 78, 479–511.

Polio, C. & Gass, S. (1998) The role of interaction in native speaker comprehension of nonnative speaker speech. *Modern Language Journal*, 82, 308–319.

PricewaterhouseCoopers (2001) *Teacher Workload Study: Final Report.* London: DfES.

Proctor, C. P., Dalton, B. & Grisham, D. L. (2007) Scaffolding English language learners and struggling readers in a universal literacy environment with embedded strategy instruction and vocabulary support. *Journal of Literacy Research*, 39(1), 71–93.

Qian, D. (2002) Investigating the relationship between vocabulary knowledge and academic reading performance: an assessment perspective. *Language Learning*, 52, 513–536.

Raimes, A. (1985) What unskilled ESL students do as they write: a classroom study of composing. *TESOL Quarterly*, 19(2), 229–258.

Raimes, A. (1991) Out of the woods: emerging traditions in the teaching of writing. *TESOL Quarterly*, 25(3), 407–430.

Rama, P. S., Black, R. W., Van Es, E. & Warschauer, M. (2012) Affordances for second language learning in World of Warcraft. *ReCALL*, 24(3), 322–338.

Ramírez Verdugo, M. D. & Alonso Belmonte, I. (2007) Using digital stories to improve listening comprehension with Spanish young learners of English. *Language Learning & Technology*, 11(1), 87–101. Available at http://llt.msu.edu/vol11num1/ramirez

Ranalli, J. (2008) Learning English with The Sims: Exploiting authentic computer simulation games for L2 learning. *Computer Assisted Language Learning*, 21(5), 441–455.

Reinders, H. (ed.) (2012) *Digital Games in Language Learning and Teaching*. Basingstoke: Palgrave Macmillan.

Reinders, H. & Hubbard, P. (2013) CALL and learner autonomy: affordances and constraints, in M., Thomas, H. Reinders and M. Warschauer (eds), *Contemporary Computer-Assisted Language Learning*. New York: Continuum.

Reppen, R. (2001) Review of MonoConc pro and Wordsmith tools. *Language Learning & Technology*, 5(3), 32–36. Available at http://llt.msu.edu/vol5num3/pdf/review4.pdf

Rheingold, H. (2009) Attention literacy. SFGate. http://blog.sfgate.com/rheingold/2009/04/20/attention-literacy/

Richards, C. (2000) Hypermedia, internet communication, and the challenge of redefining literacy in the electronic age. *Language Learning & Technology*, 4(2), 59–77. Retrieved from http://llt.msu.edu/vol4num2/richards/default.html

Richards, J. C. (1990) *The Language Teaching Matrix*. New York: Cambridge University Press.

Richards, J. & Rodgers, T. (1982) Method: approach, design, procedure. *TESOL Quarterly*, 16(2), 153–168.

Robb, T. & Susser, B. (2000) The life and death of software. *CALICO Journal*, 18(1), 41–52.

Robbins, S. (2007) A futurist's view of Second Life education: a developing taxonomy of digital spaces, in D. Livingstone & J. Kemp (eds), *Proceedings of the Second Life Education Workshop* (pp. 27–33). Chicago, IL.

Robinson, P. (1995) Attention, memory, and the 'noticing' hypothesis. *Language Learning*, 45, 281–331.

Robinson, P. (2001) Task complexity, cognitive resources, and syllabus design: a triadic framework for examining task influences on SLA, in P. Robinson (ed.), *Cognition and Second Language Instruction*. Cambridge: Cambridge University Press.

Robinson, M. & Mackey, M. (2006) Assets in the classroom: comfort and competence with media among teachers present and future, in J. Marsh & and E. Millard (eds), *Popular Literacies, Childhood and Schooling* (pp. 200–220). London: Routledge.

Roblyer, M. D. (2006) *Integrating Educational Technology into Teaching* (4th edition.) Upper Saddle River, NJ: Pearson Merrill Prentice Hall.

Rosell-Aguilar, F. (2005) Task design for audiographic conferencing: promoting beginner oral interaction in distance language learning. *Computer Assisted Language Learning*, 18(5), 417–442.

Rosenberg, M. J. (2001) *E-learning: Strategies for Delivering Knowledge in the Digital Age*. McGraw Hill.

Rossiter, M. J. (2009) Perceptions of L2 fluency by native and non-native speakers of English. *Canadian Modern Language Review*, 65(3), 395–412.

Rost, M. (2002) *Teaching and Researching Listening*. London: Longman.

Rusanganwa, J. (2013) Multimedia as a means to enhance teaching technical vocabulary to physics undergraduates in Rwanda. *English for Specific Purposes*, 32, 36–44.

Sacks, H., Schegloff, E. A. & Jefferson, G. (1974) A simplest systematics for the organization of turn-taking for conversation. *Language*, 50(4, Part 1), 696–735.

Sandars, J. & Morrison, C. (2007) What is the net generation? The challenge for future medical education. *Med Teach*, 29, 85–88.

Sanders, R. (ed.) (1995) *Thirty Years of Computer Assisted Language Instruction: Festschrift for John R. Russell*. CALICO Monograph Series 3.

Sanders, R. F. (2005) Redesigning introductory Spanish: increased enrollment, online management, cost reduction, and effects on student learning. *Foreign Language Annals*, 38(4), 523–532.

Sandholtz, J., Ringstaff, C. & Dwyer, D. (1997) *Teaching with Technology: Creating Student-Centered Classrooms*. New York: Teachers College Press.

Salaberry, M. R. (2000) L2 morphosyntactic development in text-based computer-mediated communication. *Computer Assisted Language Learning*, 13, 5–27.

Sanaoui, R. & Lapkin, S. (1992) A case study of an FSL senior secondary course integrating computer networking. *The Canadian Modern Language Review*, 43(3), 524–552.

Satar, H. M. & Özdener, N. (2008) The effects of synchronous CMC on speaking proficiency and anxiety: text versus voice chat. *The Modern Language Journal*, 92, 595–613.

Saunders, W. M. & O'Brien, G. (2006) Oral language, in F. Genesee, K. Lindholm-Leary, W. M. Saunders & and D. Christian (eds), *Educating English Language Learners: A Synthesis of Research Evidence* (pp. 14–45). Cambridge: Cambridge University Press.

Sauro, S. & Smith, B. (2010) Investigating L2 performance in text chat. *Applied Linguistics*, 31(4), 554–577.

Schieffelin, B. B. & Ochs, E. (1986) Language socialization. *Annual Review of Anthropology*, 15, 163–191.

Schiffrin, D. (1987) *Discourse Markers*. Cambridge: Cambridge University Press.

Schmidt, R. (1990) The role of consciousness in second language learning. *Applied Linguistics*, 11(2), 129–158.

Schmidt, R. (1995) Consciousness and foreign language learning: a tutorial on the role of attention and awareness, in R. Schmidt (ed.), *Attention and Awareness in Foreign Language Teaching and Learning* (Technical Report No. 9) (pp. 1–64). Honolulu, HI: University of Hawaii at Manoa.

Schmidt, R. W. (2001) Attention, in P. Robinson (ed.), *Cognition and Second Language Instruction* (pp. 3–32). New York: Cambridge University Press.

Schmitt, N. (2008) Instructed second language vocabulary learning. *Language Teaching Research*, 12(3), 329–363.

Schoelles, M. & Hamburger, H. (1996) Cognitive tools for language pedagogy. *International Journal of Computer Assisted Language Learning*, 9, 213–234.

Schocker-von Ditfurth, M. & Legutke, M. K. (2002) Vision of what is possible in teacher education—or lost in complexity? *ELT Journal*, 56(2), 162–171.

Schwienhorst, K. (2007). *Learner Autonomy and CALL Environments*. Oxon: Routledge.

Scida, E. E. & Saury, R. E. (2006) Hybrid courses and their impact on student and classroom performance: a case study at the University of Virginia. *CALICO Journal*, 23(3), 517–531.

Scott, M. (2008) *WordSmith Tools. Version 5*. Liverpool: Lexical Analysis Software.

Selwyn, N. (1999) Why the Computer is not Dominating Schools: a failure of policy or a failure of practice? *Cambridge Journal of Education*, 29, 77–91.

Selwyn, N. (2009) Faceworking: exploring students' education-related use of Facebook. *Learning, Media & Technology*, 34(2), 157–174.

Sert, O. (2009) Developing interactional competence by using TV series, in 'English as an Additional Language' classrooms. *Enletawa Journal*, 2, 23–50.

Sharples, M., Milrad, M., Arnedillo-Sánchez, I. and Vavoula, G. (2009) Mobile learning: Small devices, big issues, in N. Balacheff, S. Ludvigsen, T. de Jong, A. Lazonder, S. Barnes and L. Montandon (eds) *Technology Enhanced Learning: Principles and Products*. Springer, Berlin, Germany.

Sharwood Smith, M. (1993) Input enhancement in instructed SLA: theoretical bases. *Studies in Second Language Acquisition*, 15, 165–179.

Shekary, M. & Tahririan, M. H. (2006) Negotiation of meaning and noticing in text-based online chat. *The Modern Language Journal*, 90(4), 557–573.

Shermis, M. D. and Burstein, J. (2013) (eds) *Handbook of Automated Essay Evaluation: Current Applications and New Directions*. New York: Routledge.

Shiotsu, T. (2010) *Components of L2 Reading*. Cambridge: Cambridge University Press.

Shulman, L. S. (1987) Knowledge and teaching: foundations of the new reform. *Harvard Educational Review*, 57(1), 1–22.

Silverman, R. & Hines, S. (2009) The effects of multimedia enhanced instruction on the vocabulary of English-language learners and non-English-language learners in pre-kindergarten through second grade. *Journal of Educational Psychology*, 101(2), 305–314.

Simensen, A. M. (2007) *Teaching a Foreign Language – Principles and Procedures* (2 ed.). Oslo: Fagbokforlaget.

Simpson, J. (2005) Conversational floors in synchronous text-based CMC discourse. *Discourse Studies*, 7(3), 337–361.

Skehan, P. (1996) Second language acquisition research and task-based instruction, in J. Willis and D. Willis (eds), *Challenge and Change in Language Teaching* (pp. 17–30). Oxford: Heinemann.

Skehan, P. (1998) *A Cognitive Approach to Language Learning*. Oxford: Oxford University Press.

Skehan, P. & Foster, P. (1999) The influence of task structure and processing conditions on narrative retellings. *Language Learning*, 49(1), 93–120.

Slavin, R. E. (2003) *Educational Psychology: Theory and Practice* (7th edition). Boston, MA: Pearson Education.

Sleeman, D. & Brown, J. S. (1982) *Intelligent Tutoring Systems*. London: Academic.

Smith, B. (2004) Computer-mediated negotiated interaction and lexical acquisition. *Studies in Second Language Acquisition*, 26, 365–398.

Smith, B. (2012) Eye tracking as a measure of noticing: a study of explicit recasts in SCMC. *Language Learning and Technology*, 16(3), 53–81.

Smoak, R. (2003) What is English for specific purposes? *English Teaching Forum*, 41(2), 22–27.

Snoeyink, R. & Ertmer, P. (2001) Thrust into technology: how western teachers respond. *Journal of Educational Technology Systems*, 30(1), 85–111.

Sommers, N. (1982) Responding to student writing. *College Composition and Communication*, 33(2), 148–156.

Son, J. B. (2005) Exploring and evaluating language learning Web sites, in J. B. Son and S. O'Neill (eds), *Enhancing Learning and Teaching: Pedagogy, Technology and Language* (pp. 215–227). Flaxton, Australia: Post Pressed.

Stakhnevich, J. (2002) Reading on the web: implications for ESL professionals. *The Reading Matrix*, 2(2). Available at www.readingmatrix.com/articles/stakhnevich/ (last accessed 4 January 2017).

Stanley, G. (2006) Podcasting: audio on the internet comes of age. *TESL-EJ*, 9(4). Available at www.tesl-ej.org/ej36/int.pdf (last accessed 3 March 2016).

Stepp-Greany, J. (2002) Student perceptions on language learning in a technological environment: implications for the new Millennium. *Language Learning and Technology*, 6(1), 165–180.

Stephens, M. (2007) All about podcasting. *Library Media Connection*, 25(5), 54–57.

Stern, H. H. (1983) *Fundamental Concepts of Language Teaching*. Oxford: Oxford University Press.

Stewart, M. A. & Pertusa, I. (2004) Gains to foreign language while viewing target language closed caption films. *Foreign Language Annals*, 37(3), 438–443.

St. John, E. & Cash, D. (1995) Language learning via e-mail: demonstrable success with German, in M. Warschauer (ed.), *Virtual Connections: Online Activities and Projects for Networking Language Learners* (pp. 191–197). Honolulu, HI: University of Hawaii, Second Language Teaching and Curriculum Center.

Stockwell, G. (2013) Technology and motivation in English-language teaching and learning, in E. Ushioda (ed.), *International Perspectives on Motivation: Language Learning and Professional Challenges* (pp. 156–175). Basingstoke: Palgrave Macmillan.

Storch, N. (2002) Patterns of interaction in ESL pair work. *Language Learning*, 52(1), 119–158.

Storch, N. (2005) Collaborative writing: product, process, and students' reflections. *Journal of Second Language Writing*, 14, 153–173.

Storch, N. (2011) Collaborative writing in L2 contexts: processes, outcomes, and future directions. *Annual Review of Applied Linguistics*, 31, 275–288.

Storch, N. (2013) *Collaborative Writing in L2 Classrooms*. Bristol: Multilingual Matters.

Strijbos, J., Narciss, S. & Dunnebier, K. (2010) Peer feedback content and sender's competence level in academic writing tasks: are they critical for feedback perceptions and efficiency? *Learning and Instruction*, 20, 291–303.

Sturm, M., Kennell, T., McBride, R. & Kelly, M. (2009) The pedagogical implications of Web 2.0, in M. Thomas (ed.), *Handbook of Research on Web 2.0 and Second Language Learning* (pp. 367–384). Hershey, PA: Information Science Reference.

Sugar, W. (2002) Applying human-centered design to technology integration. *Journal of Computing in Teacher Education*, 19(1), 12–17.

Sun, Y. C. (2009) Voice blog: an exploratory study of language learning. *Language Learning & Technology*, 13(2), 88–103.

Sun, Y. C. & Chang, Y. J. (2012) Blogging to learn: becoming EFL academic writers through collaborative dialogues. *Language Learning and Technology*, 16(1), 43–61.

Susser, B. (1994) Process approaches in ESL/BFL writing instruction. *Journal of Second Language Writing*, 3, 1–47.

Susser, B. (2001) A defense of checklists for courseware evaluation. *ReCALL*, 13(2), 261–276.

Swain, M. (1983) Understanding Input through Output. Paper presented at the Tenth University of Michigan Conference on Applied Linguistics.

Swain, M. (1985) Communicative competence: some roles of comprehensible input and comprehensible output in development, in S. Gass and C. Madden (eds), *Input in Second Language Acquisition* (pp. 235–253). Rowley, MA: Newbury House.

Swain, M. (1993) The output hypothesis: just speaking and writing aren't enough. *Canadian Modern Language Review*, 50, 158–164.

Swain, M. (1995) Three functions of output in second language learning, in G. Cook and B. Seidhofer (eds), *For H. G. Widdowson: Principles and Practice in the Study of Language* (pp. 125–144). Oxford: Oxford University Press.

Swain, M. & Lapkin, S. (1995) Problems in output and the cognitive processes they generate: a step towards second language learning. *Applied Linguistics*, 16, 371–391.

Swales, J. (1990) *Genre Analysis: English in Academic and Research Settings*. Cambridge: Cambridge University Press.

Swan, M. & Walter, C. (1984) *The Cambridge English Course 1 (teacher's book)*. Cambridge: Cambridge University Press.

Sydorenko, T. (2010) Modality of input and vocabulary acquisition. *Language Learning & Technology*, 14(2), 50–73.

Sykes, J. M., Oskoz, A. & Thorne, S. L. (2008) Web 2.0, synthetic immersive environments, and mobile resources for language education. *CALICO Journal*, 25(3), 528–546.

Tecedor Cabrero, M. (2013) Developing interactional competence through video-based computer-mediated conversations: beginning learners of Spanish. Unpublished PhD thesis, University of Iowa. Available at http://ir.uiowa.edu/etd/4918

Tamela D., Scolari, J. & Bedient, D. (2000) Too few computers and too many kids: What can I do? (Part one). *Learning and Leading with Technology*, 27(5), 28–31.

Tan, J. P. & McWilliam, E. (2009) From literacy to multiliteracies: diverse learners and pedagogical practice. *Pedagogies: An International Journal*, 4(3), 213–225.

Tapscott, D. & Williams, A. D. (2006) *Wikinomics: How Mass Collaboration Change Everything*. New York: Portfolio.

Taylor, R. (1980) *The Computer in the School: Tutor, Tool, Tutee*. New York: Teachers College Press.

Thanawan S. & Punchalee W. (2012) Effects of using Facebook as a medium for discussions of English grammar and writing of low-intermediate EFL students. *Electronic Journal of Foreign Language Teaching*, 9(2), 194–214. Available at http://eflt.nus.edu.sg/v9n22012/suthiwartnarueput.pdf

Thao, V. T. (2003) The contribution of multimedia tools to EFL settings unfamiliar with technology. *Asian EFL Journal*, 5(3), 1–14.

Thomas, M. & Reinders, H. (eds) (2010) *Task-based Language Learning and Teaching with Technology*. London & New York: Continuum.

Thorne, S. L. (2003) Artifacts and cultures-of-use in intercultural communication. *Language Learning & Technology*, 7(2), 38–67.

Thorne, S. L. (2008) Transcultural communication in open internet environments and massively multiplayer online games, in S. Sieloff Magnan (ed.), *Mediating Discourse Online* (pp. 305–327). Amsterdam: John Benjamins Publishing Company.

Thorne, S. L., Black, R. W. & Sykes, J. M. (2009) Second language use, socialization, and learning in Internet interest communities and online gaming. *Modern Language Journal*, 93, 802–821.

Tileston, D. W. (2000) *10 Best Teaching Practices: Brain Research, Learning Styles and Standards Define Teaching Competencies*. Thousand Oaks, CA: Corwin Press.

Tomlinson, B. (2003) *Developing Materials for Language Teaching*. London: Continuum.

Torlakovic, E. & Deugo, D. (2004) Application of a CALL system in the acquisition of adverbs in English. *Computer Assisted Language Learning*, 17(2), 203–235.

Toyoda, E. & Harrison, R. (2002) Categorization of text chat communication between learners and native speakers of Japanese. *Language Learning and Technology*, 6(1), 82–99.

Tozcu, A. & Coady, J. (2004) Successful learning of frequent vocabulary through CALL also benefits reading comprehension and speed. *Computer Assisted Language Learning*, 17(5), 473–495.

Traxler, J. (2007) Defining, discussing and evaluating mobile learning: the moving finger writes and having writ... *The International Review in Open and Distance Learning*, 8, 1–13.

Tribble, C. (2002) Corpora and corpus analysis: new windows on academic writing, in J. Flowerdew (ed.), *Academic Discourse* (pp. 131–149). Harlow, UK: Longman.

Tschirner, E. (2001) Language acquisition in the classroom: the role of digital video. *Computer Assisted Language Learning*, 14(3/4), 305–319.

Tsou, W., Wang, W. & Li, H.-Y. (2002) How computers facilitate English foreign language learners acquire English abstract words. *Computers & Education*, 39(4), 415–428.

Tsukamoto, M., Nuspliger, B. & Senzaki, Y. (2009) Using Skype to connect a classroom to the world: providing students an authentic language experience within the classroom. CamTESOL Conference on English Language Teaching: Selected Papers, Volume 5, 162–168. Available at http://etec.hawaii.edu/otec/classes/645/skype_2009_camtesol.pdf

Tsutsui, M. (2004) Multimedia as a means to enhance feedback. *Computer Assisted Language Learning*, 17(3), 377–402.

Underwood, J. (1984) *Linguistics, Computers, and the Language Teacher: A Communicative Approach*. Rowley, MA: Newbury House.

Urquhart, A. H. & Weir, C. J. (1998) *Reading in a second language: Process, product and practice*. London and New York: Longman.

Van den Branden, K. (1997) Effects of negotiation on language learners' output. *Language Learning*, 47, 589–636.

Vandergrift, L. (2011) Second language listening: presage, process and pedagogy, in E. Hinkel (ed.), *Handbook of Research in Second Language Teaching and Learning*, (Volume II) (pp. 455–471). New York: Routledge.

Van Lier, L. (1996) *Interaction in the Language Curriculum*. London: Longman.

Vannestål, M. E. & Lindquist, H. (2007) Learning English grammar with a corpus: experimenting with concordancing in a university grammar course. *RECALL*, 19, 329–350.

Van Zeeland, H. & Schmitt, N. (2013) Incidental vocabulary acquisition through L2 listening: a dimensions approach. *System*, 41, 609–624.

Vargas, J. P. Z. & Modernas, G. S. (2014) Considering the use of hot potatoes in reading comprehension, autonomy in TEFL and learning styles. *Revista de Lenguas Modernas*, 20, 309–321.

Virkus, S. (2008) Use of Web 2.0 technologies in LIS education: experiences at Tallin University, Estonia. *Program: Electronic Library and Information Systems*, 42(3), 262–274.

von der Emde, S. & Schneider, J. (2003) Experiential learning and collaborative reading: literacy in the space of virtual encounters, in P. Patrikis (ed.), *Reading Between the Lines: Perspectives on Foreign Language Literacy* (pp. 118–143). New Haven, CT: Yale University Press.

Vygotsky, L. S. (1978) *Mind in Society: The Development of Higher Psychological Processes*. Cambridge, MA: Harvard University Press.

Walker, A. & White, G. (2013) *Technology Enhanced Language Learning*. Oxford: Oxford University Press.

Walsh, S. & Li, L. (2013) Conversations as space for learning. *International Journal of Applied Linguistics*, 23(2), 247–266.

Wang, L. & Coleman, J. A. (2009) A survey of Internet-mediated intercultural foreign language education in China. *ReCALL*, 21(1), 113–129.

Wang, Y. (2004) Distance language learning: Interactivity and fourth generation Internet-based videoconferencing. *CALICO Journal*, 21(2), 373–395.

Wang, S. & Smith, S. (2013) Reading and grammar learning through mobile phones. *Language Learning & Technology*, 17(3), 117–134.

Wang, S. & Vásquez, C. (2012) Web 2.0 and second language learning: what does the research tell us? *CALICO Journal*, 29(3), 412–430.

Wang, Y. Y. & Acero, A. (2006) Rapid development of spoken language understanding grammars. *Speech Communication*, 48(3–4), 390–416.

Ware, P. D. (2003) From involvement to engagement in online communication: Promoting intercultural competence in foreign language education. Berkeley, CA: University of California.

Ware, P. D. (2005) 'Missed' communication in online communication: tensions in a German-American telecollaboration. *Language Learning & Technology*, 9(2), 64–89. Available at http://llt.msu.edu/vol9num2/ware/

Waring, R. & Takaki, M. (2003) At what rate do learners learn and retain new vocabulary from reading a graded reader? *Reading a Foreign Language*, 15, 130–163.

Warner, C. N. (2004) It's just a game, right? Types of play in foreign language CMC. *Language Learning & Technology*, 8(2), 69–87.

Warschauer, M. (1996a) Computer-assisted language learning: an introduction, in S. Fotos (ed.), *Multimedia Language Teaching* (pp. 3–20). Tokyo: Logos.

Warschauer, M. (1996b) Motivational aspects of using computers for writing and communication, in M. Warschauer (ed.), *Telecollaboration in Foreign Language Learning: Proceedings of the Hawaii Symposium*, 12 (pp. 29–46). Honolulu, HI: University of Hawaii, Second Language Teaching and Curriculum Center. www.lll.hawaii.edu/nflrc/NetWorks/NW1/

Warschauer, M. (1996c) Comparing face-to-face and electronic discussion in the second language classroom. *CALICO*, 13(2), 7–26.

Warschauer, M. (2000a) The death of cyberspace and the rebirth of CALL. *English Teachers' Journal*, 53, 61–67.

Warschauer, M. (2000b) The changing global economy and the future of English teaching. *TESOL Quarterly*, 34(3), 511–535.

Warschauer, M. (2003) *Technology and Social Inclusion: Rethinking the Digital Divide*. Cambridge: Cambridge University Press.

Warschauer, M. (2004). Technological change and the future of CALL, in S. Fotos and C. Brown (eds), *New Perspectives on CALL for Second and Foreign Language Classrooms* (pp. 15–25). Mahwah, NJ: Lawrence Erlbaum Associates.

Warschauer, M. & Grimes, D. (2008) Audience, authorship, and artifact: the emergent semiotics of Web 2.0. *Annual Review of Applied Linguistics*, 27, 1–23.

Warschauer, M. & Healey, D. (1998) Computers and language learning: an overview. *Language Teaching*, 31, 57–71.

Webb, S. & Rodgers, M. P. H. (2009a) The vocabulary demands of television programs. *Language Learning*, 59, 335–366.

Webb, S. & Rodgers, M. P. H. (2009b) The lexical coverage of movies. *Applied Linguistics*, 30, 407–427.

Weissberg, R. (2006) Scaffolded feedback: theoretical conversations with advanced L2 writers, in K. Hyland & and F. Hyland (eds), *Feedback in Second Language Writing: Contexts and Issues* (pp. 81–104). Cambridge: Cambridge University Press.

Wells, G. (2000) Dialogic inquiry in education. Building on the legacy of Vygotsky, in C. Lee and P. Smagorinsky (eds), *Vygostkian Perspectives on Literacy Research. Constructing Meaning Through Collaborative Inquiry* (pp. 51–85). Cambridge: Cambridge University Press.

Wenger, E. (1998) *Communities of Practice: Learning, Meaning, and Identity*. Cambridge, MA: Harvard University Press.

Westerfield, K. (2010) *An Overview of Needs Assessment in English for Specific Purposes. Best Practices in ESP E-teacher Course*. Eugene, OR: University of Oregon.

Wheeler, S., Yeomans, P. & Wheeler, D. (2008) The good, the bad and the wiki: evaluating student-generated content for collaborative learning. *British Journal of Educational Technology*, 39(6), 987–995.

Wichadee, S. & Nopakun, P. (2012) The effects of peer feedback on students' writing ability. *European Journal of Social Sciences*, 33(3), 393–400.

Wiechmann, D. & Fuhs, S. (2006) Corpus Linguistic Resources – Concordancing Software. *Corpus Linguistics and Linguistic Theory*, 2(1), 109–130.

Wilkins, D. (1972) *Linguistics in Language Teaching*. London: Edward Arnold.

Williams, H. S. & Williams, P. N. (2000) Integrating reading and computers: an approach to improve ESL students reading skills. *Reading Improvement*, 37(3), 98–100.

Willis, J. (1981) *Teaching English through English*. London: Longman.

Willis, J. (1996) *A Framework for Task-based Learning*. Harlow, UK: Longman.

Willis, J. (2005) Introduction: aims and explorations into tasks and task-based teaching, in C. Edwards & and J. Willis (eds), *Teachers Exploring Tasks in English Language Teaching* (pp. 1–12). Basingstoke: Palgrave Macmillan.

Windschitl, M. & Sahl, K. (2002) Tracing teachers' use of technology in a laptop computer school: the interplay of teacher beliefs, social dynamics and institutional culture. *American Educational Research Journal*, 39(1), 165–205.

Winke, P., Gass, S. & Sydorenko, T. (2010) The effect of captioning videos used for foreign language listening activities. *Language Learning & Technology*, 14(1), 65–86.

Winke, P. & MacGregor, D. (2001). *Review on Hot Potatoes*. *Language Learning & Technology*, 5(2), 28–33.

Winne, P. H. & Butler, D. L. (1994) Student cognition in learning from teaching, in T. Husen and T. Postlewaite (eds), *International Encyclopedia of Education: Student Cognition in Learning from Teaching* (2nd edition) (pp. 5738–5745). Oxford: Pergamon.

Wipf, J. (1984) Strategies for teaching second language listening comprehension. *Foreign Language Annals*, 17, 345–348.

Wolff, D. (1997) Computers as cognitive tools in the language classroom, in A.-K. Korsvold and B. Rüschoff (eds), *New Technologies in Language Learning and Teaching* (pp. 17–26). Education Committee: Council for Cultural Co-operation. Strasbourg: Council of Europe Publishing.

Wolff, D. (1999) Review of 'Levy, M., CALL: context and conceptualization'. *System*, 27, 119–132.

Wolff, D. (2003) Web-based teaching and learning: a research perspective. Paper presented at EuroCALL 2003, Limerick, Ireland.

Wood, D. (2001) In search of fluency: what is it and how can we teach it? *The Canadian Modern Language Review*, 57(4), 573–589.

Wood, D. (2004) An empirical investigation into the facilitating role of automatized lexical phrases in second language fluency development. *Journal of Language and Learning*, 2(1), 27–50.

Wood, J. (2001) Can software support children's vocabulary development? *Language Learning and Technology*, 5(1), 166–201.

Woodill, G. (2011). *The Mobile Learning Edge: Tools and Technologies for Developing Your Teams*. New York: McGraw-Hill Professional.

Woodward-Kron, R. (2008) More than just jargon—The nature and role of specialist language in learning disciplinary knowledge. *Journal of English for Academic Purposes*, 7, 234–249.

Wozney, L., Venkatesh, V. & Abrami, P. (2006) Implementing computer technologies: teachers' perceptions and practices. *Journal of Technology and Teacher Education*, 14(1), 173–207.

Wright, T. (2010) Second language teacher education: review of recent research on practice. *Language Teaching*, 43(3), 259–296.

Xiao, Y., Sharpling, G. & Liu, H. (2011) Washback of national matriculation English test on students' learning in the Chinese secondary school context. *Asian EFL Journal*, 33(3), 103–129.

Xue, G. & Nation, I. S. P. (1984) A university word list. *Language Learning and Communication*, 3, 215–229.

Yamada, M. (2009) The role of social presence in learner-centered communicative language learning using synchronous computer-mediated communication: experimental study. *Computers & Education*, 52(4), 820–833.

Yamada, M. & Akahori, K. (2007) Social presence in synchronous CMC-based language learning: How does it affect the productive performance and consciousness of learning objectives? *Computer Assisted Language Learning*, 20(1), 37–65.

Yang, J. C. & Akahori, K. (1999) An evaluation of Japanese CALL systems on the WWW comparing a freely input approach with multiple selection. *Computer Assisted Language Learning*, 12(1), 59–79.

Yang, S. C. & Huang, Y. (2008) A study of high school English teachers' behavior, concerns and beliefs in integrating information technology into English instruction. *Computers in Human Behavior*, 24(3), 1085–1103.

Yang, Y. C. & Chang, L. (2008) No improvement—reflections and suggestions on the use of Skype to enhance college student's oral English proficiency. *British Journal of Educational Technology*, 39, 721–725.

Yang, Y.-T. C. & Chan, C.-Y. (2008) Comprehensive evaluation criteria for English learning websites using expert validity surveys. *Computers & Education*, 51(1), 403–422.

Yanguas, Í. (2010) Oral computer-mediated interaction between L2 learners: it's about time. *Language Learning & Technology*, 14(3), 72–93.

Yong, M. F. (2010) Collaborative writing features. *RELC Journal*, 41(1), 18–30.

Yoon, C. (2011) Concordancing in L2 writing class: an overview of research and issues. *Journal of English for Academic Purposes*, 10, 130–139.

Yoon, H. (2008) More than a linguistic reference: the influence of corpus technology on L2 academic writing. *Language Learning & Technology*, 12(2), 31–48.

Yoshii, M. & Flaitz, J. (2002) Second language incidental vocabulary retention: the effect of text and picture annotation types. *CALICO Journal*, 20(1), 33–58.

Young, R. F. (2008) *Language and Interaction: An Advanced Resource Book*. London and New York: Routledge.

Young, R. F. (2013) Learning to talk the talk and walk the walk: interactional competence in academic spoken English. *Ibérica*, 25, 15–38.

Yuan, F. & Ellis, R. (2003) The effects of pre-task planning and on-line planning on fluency, complexity and accuracy in L2 monologic oral production. *Applied Linguistics*, 24(1), 1–27.

Yuksel, D. & Tanriverdi, B. (2009) Effects of watching captioned movie clip on vocabulary development of EFL learners. *The Turkish On-Line Journal of Educational Technology*, 8, 48–54.

Zahar, R., Cobb, T. & Spada, N. (2001) Acquiring vocabulary through reading: effects of frequency and contextual richness. *Canadian Modern Language Review*, 57(4), 541–572.

Zamel, V. (1982) Writing: the process of discovering meaning. *TESOL Quarterly*, 16(2), 195–209.

Zamel, V. (1983) The composing processes of advanced ESL students: six case studies. *TESOL Quarterly*, 17(2), 165–187.

Zamel, V. (1985) Responding to student writing. *TESOL Quarterly*, 19(1), 7–101.

Zamel, V. (1987) Recent research on writing pedagogy. *TESOL Quarterly*, 21(4), 697–715.

Zanón, N. T. (2006) Using subtitles to enhance foreign language learning. *Porta Linguarum*, 6, 41–52.

Zhang, T., Gao, T., Ring, G. & Zhang, W. (2007) Using online discussion forums to assist a traditional English class. *International Journal on E-learning*, 6(4), 623–643.

Zhao, Y. (2003) Recent development in technology and language: a literature review and meta-analysis. *CALICO Journal*, 21(1), 7–27.

Zhao, Y., Pugh, K., Sheldon, S. & Byers, J. (2002) Conditions for classroom technology innovations. *Teachers College Record*, 104, 482–515.

Zhong, Y. X. & Shen, H. Z. (2002) Where is the technology-induced pedagogy? Snapshots from two multimedia EFL classrooms. *British Journal of Educational Technology*, 33(1), 39–52.

Zhou, J. Y. & Wang, X. F. (2007) Chunking—An effective approach to vocabulary teaching and learning in college classrooms. *CELEA Journal*, 30(3), 79–84.

Index

Printed in Great Britain
by Amazon